MOTHER POWER

Discover the difference that women
have made all over the world

by Jacqueline Hornor Plumez, Ph.D.

SOURCEBOOKS, INC.®
NAPERVILLE, ILLINOIS

Published by Sourcebooks, Inc.

P.O. Box 4410, Naperville, Illinois 60567-4410

(630) 961-3900

FAX: (630) 961-2168

www.sourcebooks.com

Library of Congress Cataloging-in-Publication Data

Plumez, Jacqueline Hornor.
      Mother power / by Jacqueline Hornor Plumez.
              p. cm.
      ISBN 1-57071-823-7 (pbk.)
      1. Mothers—Biography. 2. Women political activists—Biography. 3.
Women social reformers—Biography. 4. Women in community
organization—Biography. 5. Women volunteers in social
service—Biography. I. Title.
HQ759 .P57 2002
305.42'092'2—dc21
                                                                   2001008113

Printed and bound in the United States of America

VP   10   9   8   7   6   5   4   3   2   1

For my son, Jean Paul Plumez III, who introduced me to all the intense pleasures and pains of motherhood. He lived joyfully and died bravely.

TABLE OF CONTENTS

ACKNOWLEDGMENTS

My family is small but supportive. My daughter, Nicole, inspires me with her kind heart and good mind. My husband, Jean, encourages my efforts, and was especially understanding during the last few months when I was stressed, working around the clock to finish this book. My daughter-in-law, Joy, is truly a joy to me and so is her family. I miss my parents, Helen and Tom Hornor, who were such fine role models, and my in-laws, Nenette and Jean Plumez.

Luckily, I also have a family of friends who provided support when I needed it so badly. I couldn't have gotten through the last few years without their help and kindness.

I have never worked with an editor who offered better insight and trustworthy assistance than Hillel Black. My agent, Loretta Barrett, introduced me to Hillel and shows that not all maternal women have children. Thanks also to Loretta's assistants: Alison Brooks who was so helpful and Nick Mullendore who made a crucial phone call.

The following friends helped with this book when I was discouraged. Guy Kettelhack was crucial in helping to turn my ideas into a coherent proposal. When I was stuck on the Bringing It Home sections, Rita Freedman offered practical suggestions that got me unstuck. My book club read the manuscript and gave me a much-needed rave review when I needed a boost.

Finally, over sixty people gave me their thoughts and insights in conversations and in-depth interviews. Many were busy, successful strangers who agreed to share their life stories or insights with me. I could not have written *Mother Power* without their input. Their names are listed individually in the Sources section at the end of the book.

Thank you all.

FINDING HEROES

"Why don't we think of women as heroes? Maybe it's because no one ever shows them to us. We have to take the time to find them, celebrate them, and make sure these heroes are seen, so we can find the inspiration to achieve whatever we dream."

—Nike ad

Motherhood brings with it enormous, often untapped, power. Maternal women have a depth of love and emotion, a fierce protective instinct, a sense of right and wrong, and a persistence that, when used outside the home, can change the world.

You may know this already, but I learned it only recently. Until a few years ago I would have said that Mother Power was an oxymoron. The word "mother" evoked an image of my own mom: a kind, giving, and nurturing woman. But powerful? Never. My father, like almost all the other fathers I knew growing up, was the one with the power.

The word "mother" also evoked feelings about my children. Before I had children, I thought I knew what love was. I was amazed to discover that motherhood brought a visceral sense of love and commitment greater than I had ever felt before. While I realized these maternal feelings made me a loving mother, I never associated them with power. I thought my power derived from the fact that I was a well-trained professional who earned a good income.

I was wrong. All maternal women have an innate set of skills and abilities, different from traditional male qualities, but equally powerful.

Maternal feelings, not the presence or absence of children, are the key to Mother Power. Many women who have never given birth use maternal instincts in powerful ways. Conversely, just because a woman is a mother, doesn't mean that she has Mother Power. Unfortunately, all mothers are not maternal. Equally unfortunate, many maternal women like my mother never realize the potential power they have.

I was using my maternal skills to be successful in my career, but didn't realize it. I only began to discover Mother Power—which is by no means an oxymoron—when I was on vacation in Argentina in 1998.

Discovering Mother Power

When I went to Argentina, I really needed a vacation. My work as a psychologist can be emotionally draining, but nothing compares to being the mother of a very sick child. My son, Jean Paul, a tall, bright, funny, twenty-six-year-old string bean, had been battling cancer for several years. He had gone into remission, but we knew the cancer could return at any time. If it returned, the prognosis was very bad. I wanted to run as far away as I could from that possibility.

When I travel, I always bring along books about the sights and history of the place I am visiting. During the long flight to Buenos Aires, I read about the natural beauty of the country, the tango, and the cosmopolitan mix of people. I also launched into the chilling recent history of Argentina: back in the 1970s a group of generals, "the junta," overthrew the government and began a reign of terror. Anyone who even questioned the junta was kidnapped, tortured, and killed—students handing out protest literature, journalists who criticized junta tactics, lawyers or clergy who tried to free prisoners, even innocent bystanders who just happened to be near any protest. Plainclothes police would come to their houses at night and drag them away. The victims were called "the disappeared." During the junta's reign (1976–1983), thirty thousand people "disappeared."

2

The only group brave and effective enough to consistently protest against the junta was the mothers of the disappeared. Every week, starting in 1977 and continuing to this day, they march in the Plaza de Mayo, in front of the Presidential Palace, carrying pictures of their sons and daughters who vanished in the terrifying days of the junta's reign.

The Mothers of the Plaza de Mayo generated both national and international pressure instrumental in forcing the junta out of office. While democracy returned to Argentina, the Mothers kept up their weekly protests, because the generals responsible for the disappearances were given amnesty and never punished.

In a flash I remembered seeing newspaper photos of the Mothers, marching with pictures of their missing children, stirring the conscience of the world with their silent vigils. I wanted to see those brave women for myself.

I was not disappointed. Even though some of the Mothers had become so frail that they could hardly complete their half-hour march in the sun, I realized that I was watching the strongest women I had ever seen. I became fascinated by their bravery and tenacity, and read everything I could find about them. Here's what I learned:

The women who became the Mothers of the Plaza de Mayo met by chance as they frantically went from police stations to hospitals to prisons and government offices begging for any information about their children. A number of them decided to petition the Cardinal at the main cathedral. They felt he would understand their plight and feel a moral obligation to help. He rebuffed them. Even the church hierarchy would not oppose the junta.

With no one left to turn to, fourteen mothers decided to risk their lives by protesting in front of the Presidential Palace, demanding information about their children. Their protest began with a few desperate women, but quickly their numbers increased, as did their mutual support system.

At first the secret police ignored them, because they were "only a group of mothers." But as their group grew rapidly over the weeks, the police approached and asked a few for identity papers. This was terrifying because it meant they were being marked for kidnapping. Instead of letting their members be intimidated one by one, all three hundred Mothers demanded that the police take their identity papers too. If one or two Mothers were hauled into police cars, all the Mothers would surround the police cars and police stations in noisy protest until their friends were released.

The police used fire hoses and dogs against the Mothers. They vandalized their houses and made some of the leaders disappear. But the number of protesting Mothers continued to grow nonetheless.

While the junta had stifled the free press in Argentina, the foreign press quickly picked up the story. Images of the Mothers marching with pictures of their missing children were published around the world, destroying the junta's credibility.

International sympathy and support flowed in to protect the Mothers and weaken the military stranglehold on Argentina. The junta was put in an untenable position: they couldn't ban the Mothers' demonstrations or harm too many of them with the world watching. But they also couldn't pretend that everything was normal in their country while the Mothers demonstrated.

Many of these women lacked a formal education. Many were homemakers who had never been outside their neighborhoods. Even so, they began traveling around the world, meeting with officials and the press, to gain support for their cause. In France, sympathetic mothers including Francoise Mitterand, the wife of the president, and Catherine Deneuve began weekly protests in front of the Argentine embassy. In Spain, where streets have been named after the Mothers, the courts began investigating what happened to six hundred Spanish nationals who "disappeared" in Argentina and Chile.

When I was in Buenos Aires in 1998, Argentine newspapers were carrying stories that infuriated the public: the Spanish court inquiries, which were still continuing after all this time, had just discovered that junta members and other military officers had Swiss bank accounts full of money earned by selling the babies and property of the disappeared. Those Swiss bank accounts were the final straw. The amnesty given to the generals was revoked. Finally, they would be punished. The Mothers had won.

Why did a group of old Argentine women have such an effect on me? Quite simply, they were the strongest people and the most effective role models I had ever encountered. Watching them march, I knew that whatever problems life sent me, even my son's cancer, could not compare to what they went through—risking their lives trying to save their children who were being tortured and killed by their own government.

I was in awe of their bravery and tenacity. Even when they gave up hope for their own children, when the junta fell and most people simply wanted to go back to being "normal," the Mothers doggedly continued to be the conscience of their country.

I felt proud to stand and watch these women—proud because their strength came from a resource that I shared: being a loving mother. But since society doesn't really respect mothers (a stay-at-home mom is "just a mother"), I needed pride in that department.

All women play many roles. Mine include psychologist, writer, wife, daughter, and friend. After giving birth, however, my most defining role became mother. It colored the way I saw and did everything. Although I loved being maternal, I felt I had to keep the depth of these feelings secret from everyone except my family—because I saw being maternal as being too soft.

In Argentina I began to see that soft maternal love has a flip side. I realized that good mothers also have the capacity to be brave and strong.

I came home and read everything I could find about the Mothers. I wanted to know how a group of mothers could succeed in their protests when journalists, lawyers, and other more conventionally powerful groups were silenced or destroyed. As I thought about it, I realized that only a group of mothers could have succeeded. Why? Several reasons: first, since they were "just" a group of mothers, the junta initially ignored them, assuming they could be no threat. Second, the world press discovered that pictures and stories of protesting, grieving mothers pack a huge emotional wallop. The brave, self-sacrificing Mothers had instant credibility—and provided stark contrast to the cruel, selfish junta. However, my most important realization was about a mother's passionate tenacity. A good mother, more than anyone else, will risk everything and stop at nothing to protect her child.

I remembered how a group of mothers from California formed Mothers Against Drunk Driving (MADD), which changed drunk-driving laws across the country. I recalled that the mother of a murdered child from New Jersey had insisted that children be better protected from sex offenders and made Megan's Law the law of the land. Looking around my county, I realized how many soup kitchens were founded by mothers who not only cared that their own families were fed, but that other families had enough to eat also.

In fact, so-called Mommy Issues cause the famous gender gap in politics, because mothers tend to feel maternal toward society as a whole. They want government money spent to ensure that everyone has access to a good education, health care, jobs, and social security. They want safe streets and housing not just for themselves, but for everyone—and they have a growing recognition that they have the power to create the needed changes to make it so.

As I became aware of this power, I saw how what I call Mother Power is being used more and more these days. In the United States and all around the world I discovered women using Mother Power to bring down corrupt governments, stop wars, change laws, and better society. Mothers have started grassroots organizations that have forced corporations and government to clean up toxic waste, forced scientists to investigate environmental causes of cancer, and forced gangs of criminals out of their neighborhoods.

Perhaps the most widespread use of Mother Power involves employed moms who buck society's workaholic pressures. Even in today's era of equal opportunity, if there are two full-time working parents, it tends to be the mother who takes time off to applaud the school play or care for a sick child. Likewise, it is far more likely that a mom, rather than a dad, will quit a successful career to raise the kids, work part-time, or start her own business.

While many still see such maternal caring as wimpy ("she isn't serious about her career"), increasingly, as employers have learned that mother-talent is valuable, they have devised creative ways to retain moms. Corporations have been forced to create flextime and part-time options, plus a host of other family friendly employee benefits.

If anything shows how serious mothers are about their careers *and* their families, it is the statistics that show how many women are starting their own businesses, usually to be in control of the time they can spend at home. Women now own one-third of all U.S. businesses and employ one-fourth of all workers—as many people as all the Fortune 500 companies combined!

Perhaps the most exciting thing I discovered about Mother Power, is that any mother can use it. Mother Power is truly democratic. Women who use it to accomplish their goals often have no other source of power: no wealth, position, or credentials. In the United States and all around the world, there are as many blue-collar women and homemakers using Mother Power as there are women with graduate degrees and high-level jobs. The key to success: for a woman to take her maternal convictions seriously and publicly stand up for what she believes.

Why is Mother Power so potent? There are many reasons, but, most important, mothers have great credibility. Because we trust our own mothers, we trust other mothers to be honest and caring. And these days, when there is so little honest caring and conscience in our political and business leaders, we are all hungry for someone who will stand up and apply maternal integrity to a problem. In our cynical world where it is hard to believe anyone, sometimes mothers are the only people we can trust.

Everyone knows that a good mother's job description includes teaching us right from wrong, being the peacemaker, guiding us out of trouble, plus nurturing and protecting us. So, when mothers bring these maternal strengths to bear on problems outside the home, we understand they are simply extending their natural roles.

Add "Mother" for Instant Credibility

Here's the proof that motherhood has power: if I said, "As a psychologist, I think the media should stop directing blatantly sexual messages to children," I might have some credibility. But if I said, "As a psychologist and a mother, I think the media should stop directing blatantly sexual messages to children," wouldn't I have more clout?

Doesn't the phrase "and a mother" give more impact to the following statements? "As a police officer and a mother, I think we need stronger gun control legislation," "As a senator and a mother, I think the government should encourage the development of alternate energy sources," "As a physician and a mother, I am concerned that chemical additives in food are making us ill." Add "and a mother" to almost any argument, and you get a credibility boost.

When a mother displays her grief, the impact is even stronger. The grieving mother is iconic. Think of Michelangelo's *Pieta*—the famous statue of the grieving Virgin Mary holding her dead son. Muslim, Hindu, and Jewish viewers feel the emotion as much as Christians do.

That's why grieving women with no credential other than motherhood are using Mother Power to change laws all over America—and the world. That's how MADD was able to overcome the powerful liquor lobby and change laws in every state. That's how Maureen Kanka was able to create a movement that she spread from state to state until Megan's Law was made federal law.

Of course, mothers don't have to be grieving to accomplish their goals. Recently, for example, a file clerk in Georgia took a lawsuit all the way to the Supreme Court, trying to protect her daughter from sexual harassment in school. Thanks to her effort, girls in the United States no longer have to tolerate schoolyard sexual bullies.

But, a mother's crusade doesn't always work. When Tipper Gore tried to clean up music lyrics and television, the entertainment industry organized against her. The media ridiculed her. But, if enough other mothers had banded together in an organized effort, she could have accomplished her goals.

Similarly, the Million Mom March for gun control was not as effective as expected. To accomplish their goals those moms don't need to become as well-funded as the gun lobby, but they do need to become as well-organized and tenacious.

Unfortunately, not all mothers are good parents, capable of using Mother Power in a positive way. Since there are over half a million American children in foster care, usually because of abuse and neglect, it is clear that motherhood is no royal road to sainthood.

But, the truth is that motherhood changes most women, usually for the better. Through the simple act of having a child, we discover depths of love we never knew existed, discover a desire and ability to protect and nurture that we may never have felt before. Feeling responsible for another life, we can't just pick up and leave when we want.

New research published by the American Psychological Association finds that mothers do not exhibit the classic "fight or flight" reaction to danger. Instead, our reaction is to "tend and befriend": tend to the children, nurturing and protecting them, and befriending other people, thus establishing social networks that are protective for ourselves and our children. Clearly the tend and befriend instinct gives mothers strong skills in nurturing, comforting, and connecting with others, which are key components of Mother Power.

However, if our children are in danger, we will stand our ground and fight. That's what makes good mothers fearless protectors of the young. Like mother lions, women will fight fiercely to protect their children. (I remember being shocked by a flood of fury that made me want to attack someone who was being mean to Jean Paul on a playground.) Like mother hens that if trapped in a fire will herd chicks under their wings and stand their ground through the flames, mothers will give their lives to protect their children. This is just part of the instinctive power source mothers can tap into.

Society isn't comfortable yet with the fierce strength of mothers. In fact, there is still a lot of pressure on moms to act sweet and helpless. So, when life gets rough, many women have been taught to supress their anger or stifle their resourcefulness. Likewise, when we see something wrong in our lives or society, many of us despair, thinking we could never correct the problem. Psychologists know that these are the main reasons why women are two to three times as likely to suffer from depression as men.

I saw this in my own home. My mother always wanted to work in a hospital. With her kind, caring, maternal style, she would have been very good at comforting the sick. She also loved going to art exhibits and plays, and would have enjoyed nurturing the growth of a local art museum or theater. My father convinced her that her health was too delicate (she was prone to "sick headaches") to engage in such activities. Now, I firmly believe that her health as well as her self-esteem would have improved if she had been able to use her maternal skills.

I was worried about slipping into a deep depression if my son couldn't be cured. I knew I couldn't do this, because my daughter, my husband, and my patients needed me. Researching women who have used Mother Power to cope with tragedy made me believe that if they could be strong, I could too.

If women understand Mother Power, instead of getting depressed, they can change their lives—and even society—for the better. They can tap into a full range of maternal strengths—everything from the way they care, to their ability to be verbal and relate to others—to accomplish their goals. Even qualities considered maternal weaknesses, for example, our "overly" emotional or "overly" protective reactions, can be used to achieve positive goals.

Weaknesses as Strengths

Mothers are often accused of being overly protective, and overly protective parents can smother their children's spirit. That fierce sense of protectiveness, though, inspires Russian mothers to make the cold, dangerous journey into the war zones of Chechnya to bring their soldier sons home from the war. In the United States, that sense of protectiveness makes mothers the backbone of the gun control movement.

It was mothers who, as lawyer and plaintiffs, engineered the first groundbreaking lawsuit against gun manufacturers (Hamilton vs. Accu-tek). If anything will prevail against the financial power of the NRA, it will be the growing volunteer army of mothers who want to make the streets safe for their kids.

Women, long considered the weaker sex, have stayed home and prayed for peace, while men went off to war. In the last few decades, those prayers have turned into action, as groups of mothers from opposing sides staged public demonstrations for peace around the world. For example, Israeli mothers are trying to end old hatreds. And in Northern Ireland, Protestant and Catholic mothers risked getting killed by extremists when they marched for peace together, becoming the voice of reason. The two mothers who started this movement won a Nobel Prize for their efforts.

Over the ages, mothers have been dismissed as too emotional. So, when women finally broke through the barriers and became news reporters, they tried to be as dispassionate as men. Recently, however, newswomen have become more comfortable about being themselves, and, ironically, have been gaining power in the process—not because they are pretty, but because they bring maternal, emotional concern to their projects. As Katie Couric of *The Today Show* said about her reporting style, "There is something about a maternal, comforting presence that is helpful." She describes many achieving mothers today when she says her fellow newswomen have "compassion mixed with *chutzpah*."

Mothers are infamous for nagging, and while no one likes to be nagged, mothers have used that skill to better the world. Anne Anderson, the real-life heroine of the book and movie *A Civil Action*, nagged her reluctant lawyer into bringing a lawsuit to clean up the toxic waste in her town. Now mothers all over the country are nagging corporations and legislators, forcing them to clean up the pollution that sickened their children.

We mothers are rarely the strong, silent type. We talk about our problems, but can be teased or criticized for doing so. So, it was extraordinarily courageous when Betty Ford went public with her addiction problems. She had agreed to combat her addictions for the sake of her family, after her daughter convened a family intervention meeting. Then, in a great gift to the public, she chose to reveal her problems. Her openness about her addictions—and her earlier openness about her breast cancer—is credited with bringing those problems out of the closet and saving millions of lives.

All a mother's weaknesses and strengths, in fact everything we are, everything we do, and everything we need, can be used in a positive way through Mother Power to make the world a better place. And the scale of our efforts is growing all the time.

Mothers have always been the glue of the community, making sure that neighbors who fell on hard times received a home cooked meal. Thank God, we still do that. These days, while some mothers are making a casserole for the family down the street, other mothers are starting non-profit operations that feed and clothe hundreds of people at a time. Whether it is the mother who helps one neighbor or the mother who helps a hundred homeless families, it all makes the world a better place.

Likewise, mothers have always been known for being creative and honest, but such credit was often given in limited, somewhat condescending ways. Moms were assumed to be creative enough to whip up a pot of soup from meager ingredients and honest enough not to cheat the grocer where we bought them. Now women in the arts are bringing their maternal creativity out of the home and finding that it feeds their larger creative spirit. For example, New York State Poet Laureate, Sharon Olds, achieved success after she stopped "trying to imitate Emerson," and wrote about her own experiences as a mother. She and some fiction writers have recently made the everyday feelings of motherhood a respected literary subject. And our reputation for honesty is getting us elected to high office all around the world.

When bad things happen to good mothers, Mother Power can keep women from becoming helpless victims. Through Mother Power, instead of turning anger inward and getting depressed, women are turning anger into action—and getting even. In a prototypical case, nurse/homemaker Carolyn McCarthy, whose husband was killed and son injured by a deranged gunman, was so infuriated when her Congressman voted against the ban on assault weapons that she challenged him for office. Even though she had no political experience, she won in a campaign fueled by Mother Power.

Mothers are not too proud to ask for help (and directions) from friends, politicians, and the media. If they don't get the help they need, these days, they are just doing it themselves. So, why did it take us so long to recognize the extraordinary power that we have and to use our Mother Power effectively?

The Odds We've Bucked

Until recently, by law and by society's expectations, mothers have been kept out of the limelight. While men were expected to go out to work and lead the world, mothers were supposed to wield power indirectly, through their sons and husbands. You know that saying, "The hand that rocks the cradle, rules the world?" Everyone knows it is merely a sop, but few mothers knew any other route to power.

Until very recently, women—especially married women—were second-class citizens even in Western countries. For example, France (whose national symbol, Marianne, is a woman) only gave women the right to vote in 1944. And while Americans let women vote in 1920, the government legislated our second-class status until only recently. As Cokie Roberts points out in her book, *We Are Our Mothers' Daughters*, until the 1960s Federal law dictated that female government workers be paid 25 percent less than males. Likewise, there were state laws that gave husbands control of their wives' earnings, prohibited married women from inheriting directly, and forbade women from going into business for themselves without permission of the court. It wasn't until her mother, a congresswoman from Louisiana, helped pass a law in 1972, that women and mothers had an equal right to credit as husbands and fathers did.

Finally, while the women's movement encouraged us to be strong and equal to men, being equal usually required acting like men.

Women who were maternal, especially women who stayed home and raised their children, were made to feel inferior. They might be envied for their free time and for not having to work, but they lacked the clout of women who earned an income.

All this and more gave mothers this strong message: you don't have any power, so keep quiet and stay home. Even today, as I am sitting here writing this book in a rented office, the paper towels in the office bathroom are printed with the phrase, "Love is a mother's apple pie." My husband gets no such subliminal messages to make him feel guilty that he is spending his time working instead of cooking.

So, while women found their voice in the 1960s and '70s, most mothers, especially homemakers, stayed relatively quiet. Many felt put down and resentful of, or intimidated by, their peers with jobs. In our increasingly materialistic world, mothers who stayed home and didn't earn money felt second-class. Even today, well-educated, liberated women who have left high-powered jobs to raise their kids often tell me the family money—and the power it wields—belongs to their husbands "because he earns the income."

Even though the majority of mothers are now employed, for a long time they kept themselves from effectively voicing their concerns in and out of the home. They were not only exhausted by unequally shared domestic duties, but, more importantly, they hadn't learned that they had the right to speak up. After all, it wasn't until the early '80s that women began to vote as often as men. When they did start voting in large numbers, the famous gender gap emerged, and they began to come out in large numbers and vote for candidates who supported Mommy Issues.

Once mothers realized that they had the right to speak up, and that they had something to say, they also began to understand that actions speak louder than words. And maternal action was called for, because paternal caring for kids, corporations, and country has waned. In part, mothers are flexing their muscles now because so many fathers have abdicated their public and private paternal duties.

The Need for Maternal Action

These days we hear too few stories of politicians and government leaders sacrificing for the public good. Instead, we are flooded with stories about politicians voting against important bills because special interest groups paid them off. With too many politicians caring about military spending instead of education, corporate campaign contributions instead of a decent minimum wage, and no one in power keeping drugs and guns off the streets, much less out of the school yards, who is going to see about these Mommy Issues if not mothers themselves?

Our political patriarchs aren't the only ones letting us down. It's happening in business, in the media, and in our very own homes. Corporations used to be paternalistic. Until the 1980s, the unwritten rule for employees was, take care of business and business will take care of you. Recently, in the antithesis of paternalism, CEOs who fire thousands of workers are rewarded with multi-million dollar bonuses. No one in business even questions why those millions aren't better spent keeping workers on the job—or retraining those who were fired. Few business leaders seem to care about the lives and families destroyed with every lost job. Few care about the increased hours everyone is expected to work at downsized companies, and the resulting stress on employees.

In a graphic and telling metaphor, men who work excessive hours and make excessive incomes on Wall Street are called Big Swinging Dicks. In this macho culture, long hours away from the family can be a badge of honor. Often the only people who see anything wrong with this behavior are wives who would rather their big swinging husbands spend less time at work and more time with the kids.

Then there is the media and entertainment industry, which, perhaps more than any other force in society, is abdicating its paternal role.

These days, the majority of television, movies, and song lyrics seem to involve some form of sex or violence.

Mary Pipher, a psychologist and mother, wrote a bestseller, *Reviving Ophelia*, which laid the blame for the rampant eating disorders and drug/alcohol abuse among young girls on the overly sexualized media messages that are bombarding our daughters and sons. She noted that even teen magazines present unhealthy images with anorexic models and articles that rarely feature girls achieving anything but beauty and popularity.

The huge, broad-based moral vacuum in our society is sucking mothers out of the home and into the fight for better government, better laws, and a cleaner environment. Whether they use their Mother Power in paid or unpaid pursuits, they often find great meaning in life through their efforts.

You Don't Have to Have Children to be Maternal

Is there any difference between Mother Power and Woman Power? Yes. Mother Power has nothing to do with feminine wiles, seduction, or beauty. Also, while Woman Power may or may not be completely selfish, Mother Power never is. A woman using Mother Power may get something out of it for herself, but there is always an unselfish or altruistic component to her efforts.

Can any mother use Mother Power? No. Not every woman with children is maternal. On the other hand, some women make important maternal contributions to society even though they are childless. For example, Oprah Winfrey, whose afternoon talk show is full of solid, caring information and non-denominational spiritual values, is in marked contrast to the sleaze TV competition. Oprah's approach is maternal and caring, even though she has no children.

Similarly, Joan Ganz Cooney, who created *Sesame Street* and the *Children's Television Workshop*, acted like a good surrogate mother to the

17

world's children, yet had no children of her own. Another example is Mother Teresa, who was a quiet, sickly young nun from Albania when she decided to care for the poor in Calcutta. While she is best known for her work with dying street people in India, she built a huge, multinational organization that houses the homeless, educates abandoned children, and cares for the sick all around the world. People who knew the young Mother Teresa, remember her as being a quite ordinary person with fragile health. She became an energetic dynamo only as she began to tap into her maternal caring and strength.

Women who decide to use Mother Power are often transformed. They may or may not become famous. They may make small contributions to their hometowns or they may change their state, nation, or the world. The only thing for sure is that they will change themselves for the better.

Women trying to cope with tragedy find courage and strength by tapping into their Mother Power. The Mothers of the Plaza de Mayo could easily have been consumed by depression or bitterness, but instead became examples of strength in the face of overwhelming tragedy and injustice.

Once you begin looking, you will see many other examples of how mothers turn fear and grief into useful purpose. Women with sick children raise money to fund research or pay for treatment for those who could not otherwise afford it; they start support groups to help others, or become public spokespeople to raise awareness of the illness. It doesn't matter which outlet mothers choose. What matters is that, through Mother Power, they go from feeling like helpless, tragic victims to people who are trying to change the situation—if not for their own children, then for someone else's. This constructive channel for pain, allows women to be strong instead of succumb to depression.

Those coping with tragedy are not the only ones who find that Mother Power transforms their lives. Just as network newswomen have found that by being more maternal they are becoming successful, the same is true in other professions. A large study found patients prefer female doctors. Why? Patients felt they could talk to women doctors because they were less autocratic and more inclusive—in other words, more maternal.

I now realize that I am a successful psychologist because I am maternal—not in spite of it. The maternal caring I feel for my patients cures every bit as much as all the therapeutic skills I learned in graduate school. In fact, often to help a patient all I have to do is what my mother did for me: listen with care and concern and then reinforce what is good and strong about the person.

In business, just as women no longer feel that they have to wear bow ties and stiff business suits, they are allowing their natural maternal qualities to show. These qualities were recently recognized in a study of almost twenty-five hundred managers in four hundred organizations in nineteen states. It found that women are perceived by their coworkers—both male and female—as better managers than their male counterparts. The author of the study says that women managers effectively use softer skills such as communication, feedback, and empowering other employees. They are also skilled in "such areas as decisiveness, planning, and setting standards." Male managers, he found, "still rely on a more autocratic style, emphasizing individual accomplishment, and competition."

Mother Power can allow both homemakers and employed moms to feel more balanced. Carl Jung, a famous early psychologist, explained that all men and women need a balance between what he labeled as our nurturing, artistic feminine side and our hard-driving, achieving masculine side. He found that executives and other hard-driving people eventually feel burnt out unless they counterbalance their drive for power with nurturing and artistic pursuits. On the other hand, those who spend too much time being nurturing and soft, will eventually feel burnt out if they do not engage in pursuits that make them feel strong and powerful. Both nurturers and hard-drivers can use Mother Power to achieve Jungian balance.

No one gets through life without suffering, but through Mother Power we can find a way to rise above the pain. We live in a broken world, but with Mother Power, we can begin to fix it. And if we let the men in our lives know how much we need their Father Power, we can join forces to really make the world a better place.

For the last few years, I have been researching Mother Power. This research was not just academic—it was visceral, because it was filling a deep, unmet need for something I had wanted all my life: maternal heroes. The more I looked, the more I found, and the more excited I became about discovering women who can be both kind and strong, caring and creative, assertive and feminine. They make me proud to be both a woman and a mother.

I no longer feel that I have to split my maternal self from my professional self—not that I ever really could or did. It's a comfort, knowing my maternal side is a great strength, both in and out of the home. After all, good mothers may be soft and loving, but they are never pushovers. They can be tough when they have to be. Most important for me, I saw how, through Mother Power, they can turn sadness and grief into constructive energy.

Not long after I returned from Argentina, Jean Paul relapsed. For the last three years of his life, I researched cancer cures, trying to help him survive—and I researched Mother Power, trying to help me do the same.

I have always been a strong person, but when I realized that my son might die, I didn't know if I could continue to be the source of strength that he and the rest of the family needed. Later, when I realized his death was inevitable, I didn't know how I could continue living without him.

He was such a joy to me, such a funny, smart, loving person. How could I survive the loss, much less continue to be a supportive mother to my much-loved daughter, a loving wife to my husband, and a good therapist for my patients? I was in desperate need of role models. Luckily, I found plenty.

The women in this book taught me how to wrestle with life's crises. Many learned how to live through grief and tragedy, and their strength inspired me. If they could do it, then I figured I could too. Most have developed other equally important keys to life: how to fulfill personal ambitions without neglecting personal responsibilities; how to be strong and independent but also loving; how to stay kind and giving in a harsh and troubled world; and how to find meaning in life.

So, now when life makes me feel overwhelmed, sad, or stymied, I think of other women who used Mother Power to transcend those feelings. When I get discouraged and think there is no way I can explain Mother Power on paper, I feel compelled to try, because I want to share what it has done, and what it can do.

When you read the following chapters about women who are such impressive examples of Mother Power, I hope you are as inspired as I have been. By reading about the many ways that women are using Mother Power to change themselves and the world, I hope you will discover your own sense of maternal strength and pride—and a greater commitment to making the world a better place.

Take the time to find your own Mother Power. Get comfortable with it. Use it. And pass along the word to others.

PART 1:

What Mothers Are

chapter one

FEARLESSLY PROTECTIVE: YOU'RE MORE POWERFUL THAN YOU THINK

"Even in an animal as lowly as the rat, such an 'unselfish' drive as the maternal drive (to protect her pups) can be stronger than the so-called 'self-preservation" drives of hunger and thirst."
—**Clifford T. Morgan,** *Introduction to Psychology*

What motivates mother animals to literally walk through fire if their babies are in danger? The protective maternal drive is caused by a combination of hormones secreted during pregnancy and nursing. If one of those hormones, prolactin, is injected into a virgin female rat, she will begin caring for young rats much the same way their mother would. However strong, the maternal instinct fades in rats and most other animals as babies grow up.

In humans, the maternal instinct is no less strong, but more complex. Adoptive mothers usually feel every bit as protective as those who produce prolactin through childbearing. Also, as every mother knows, the protective instinct lasts a lifetime.

This chapter explores how mothers have tapped into that protective instinct and transformed themselves from shy homemakers into heroes who risked their lives to save their children. It includes the story of how one woman joined the Mothers of the Plaza de Mayo and found courage and convictions she never knew she had. Equally inspiring are the heroic exploits of Russian mothers who made dangerous journeys into the war zones of Chechnya to bring their sons back to safety. Finally, there are stories of American mothers who used non-violent ways to fight gangs and gangsters—and won.

A Mother Finds the Plaza de Mayo

In 1998, watching the Mothers of the Plaza de Mayo demonstrating in Argentina, I wondered if I could ever be as brave as they were. Would I risk torture, death, and prison to save my child? Could I continue to be strong if I learned that my child had died? I kept wondering long after I flew home, so I later returned to ask some Mothers how they summoned such courage.

Two years after my first visit to Argentina, I arrived at the Mothers' headquarters, a small, walk-up building in downtown Buenos Aires, bought for them by sympathetic Dutch mothers. The leader of the group, Hebe Bonafini, was walking back and forth through the modest offices carrying her grandson. She proudly introduced the infant, and showed me her office filled with international peace prizes. I smiled as I compared this gray-haired grandma clucking over a baby to the typical Hollywood hero.

Since Hebe was busy baby-sitting, my main interview was with Ebel Petroni, secretary of the Mothers of the Plaza de Mayo. Ebel is a pretty, petite blonde with chocolate brown eyes that welled with tears during the interview. She says that, like most of the other Mothers, she was a completely apolitical homemaker before July 13, 1977—the night her son disappeared.

That night was like any other until twenty heavily armed men broke into her suburban home and began hitting and kicking her two sons. They wrestled the older one, a twenty-one-year-old engineering student into an unmarked van and drove off. Claiming there had been a robbery in the neighborhood, the men said they wanted to question her son. Ebel begged them to take her instead.

She had no idea who these men were or where they were taking her boy. "I was desperate, but I thought I would find him at a police station. I never thought that I would never see him again, that he would vanish into thin air."

The next morning her husband had to go to work, so she went to the local police station. The officers claimed to know nothing about her son. She went to other police stations, with a growing sense of panic as everyone claimed to know nothing. "I went everywhere, and I tried to ask everyone we knew who was close to the government," she says, but she could not find anyone who would tell her anything about her child.

"I knew there were some people who had 'disappeared,' but I didn't have any notion of who they were or why they were taken," she recalled. "My son had always been concerned about social problems. He asked me once, 'Mom, what is your reason for living?' And when I told him that I was living for my family, my kids, and my home, he told me that was wrong. He said that people also had to be concerned about what was happening to others. But I never thought he was in danger. At most I thought he might be detained because he had different political ideas—that was all."

As Ebel searched for information about her son, she kept running into other mothers doing the same. "We were all desperate. We saw the look of suffering on each other's faces and we began to ask each other what was going on. We started realizing it was useless to keep going to the prisons and police offices trying to find our children, because the authorities would always answer that they knew nothing.

"The Mother's movement wasn't planned, it just happened as life showed us what to do and what steps to take when we started realizing that we were not going to recover our children as fast as we thought.

We realized this was not just some casual political problem—it was a strong and terrible political problem."

When I asked how she kept from becoming depressed she said, "Once I realized my son was not coming back soon, I, like all the Mothers, realized I had two choices: I could stay at home and cry, or I could go out and struggle. And you know it is quite amazing that none of the Mothers in our association ever felt the need to consult a psychologist." The fact that they were taking action with other women relieved their stress. As Ebel says, "Our psychologist was the struggle."

On the other hand, she says that the fathers who went to work and had to act normal suffered terribly. "Many became so depressed they could not work. Many died of heart attacks, cancer, and other illnesses. But those of us who are lucky enough to still have our husbands by our sides had men who were dedicated to a different kind of struggle. They had to go out and work and maintain the family while we were out on the streets searching and demonstrating."

Ebel says that during the days of the junta, the police often attacked the Mothers. Some were taken to jail and some disappeared forever. When I asked how she kept from being overcome by fear, she said, "When your child is taken away, you struggle for him and his life, and your life ceases to have any importance." She could not allow herself "to look at fear, because if you start thinking about it, you become too fearful to go on." By keeping herself active with the other Mothers, she was able to ignore the fear because everyone felt they had to be brave for each other and their children.

It was very hard for her younger son to cope with the disappearance of his brother, but "he had to go on living. And I think it was reassuring for him to know that if anything happened to him, his mother would fight for him in the same way." Today he is a dentist living in Argentina with a wife and two children. Ebel never found out what happened to her "disappeared" son.

When the junta fell in 1983, and democracy returned to Argentina, a deal was made with the military. In exchange for their staying out of politics, the officers responsible for the thirty thousand disappearances were granted amnesty. Most citizens feared that "The Dirty War" (left-wing and right-wing terrorists battling each other) would resume without amnesty and there was tremendous pressure on the Mothers to drop their demands for justice. But how can a mother do that when she knows her child is still missing and unaccounted for—and that the people who kidnapped him were never punished?

As the civilian government became more secure in its control over the military, it offered to help relatives find out what happened to each "disappeared." The government is also building a monument to the disappeared and will pay reparations to their families. The Mothers adamantly refuse such help. They revile anyone who accepts government money and refuse to officially acknowledge that their children are dead.

Ebel and the other Mothers know full well that their children were killed. However, they are keeping them alive, at least in memory, by becoming as idealistic as their children were and caring about other people in need. She and the other Mothers have broadened their struggle. They now demonstrate to demand more jobs (the unemployment rate in Argentina was 18 percent when I was there), and they travel around the world supporting a wide variety of causes and groups that ask for their help. For example, Ebel and other Mothers wrapped their white bandanas around their heads, and acted as human shields for civilians caught in the crossfire in Serbia. Her husband supports her activities, travels with her, and watches when she marches.

In the early eighties, the Mothers of the Plaza de Mayo had thousands of followers. Now there are less than three hundred active members in all of Argentina. Some are simply too old and tired to continue the struggle. Many have gone back to their quiet lives, accepting government reparations and information about the death of their children. Others have become active in organizations that try to find grandchildren, babies of the disappeared who were secretly sold or adopted by friends of the junta.

Today the Mothers have a mixed reputation in Argentina. Some think they are saints. Others call them crazy or dismiss them as radicals. When I asked the South American bureau chief of an international news organization where she thought the truth lay, she said the Mothers should always be revered as human rights activists.

Whatever anyone else thinks, Ebel is at peace with herself and her situation. She knows her group was instrumental in overthrowing the Argentine dictators. She also knows that the Mothers' current struggle against poverty, war, and oppression will not be as successful. "We are not powerful enough to completely change Argentina or the world. There is terrible unemployment, and people are suffering. But we are part of the struggle to make things better. For all our lives we will be part of this. This way our children are still with us in our hearts and in our struggle."

The Soldiers' Mothers Committee

One secret to the Mothers' strength and fearlessness was the support they gave each other: whatever risks they took, they took as a group. Today, in Russia, another group of fearlessly protective mothers is discovering that they are more powerful than they ever knew. They venture into enemy territory trying to save their sons, ill-equipped soldiers fighting in Chechnya. While the Soldiers' Mothers Committee provides group support, in order to save their sons, individual mothers often travel into war zones all by themselves.

In November, 1999, as winter closed in on Chechnya, most of the country was a war zone, and Russian bombers were obliterating Grozny, the capital. Crowds of refugees were kept behind barbed wire fences, with only a small trickle allowed to cross the border into Russia. Some had waited there for weeks trying to get out of the country. They were incredulous as they watched a small group of middle-aged Russian women come in.

Those women, members of the Soldiers' Mothers Committee, knew why the refugees were desperate to get out. But whatever dangers Chechen civilians—and travelers like themselves—might face, they knew their sons, sent to Chechnya with the Russian army, were in greater danger. Those mothers were determined to find their sons and bring them out to safety.

Hundreds of mothers before and after this small group have made similar dangerous journeys through the war zones of Chechnya. Some went in small groups of two and three. Others went alone. Many had received notice that their sons were missing in action. Others, learning that their boys were prisoners of war, wanted to beg or bribe to get them released. Some knew their sons were wounded in hospitals or stationed with ill-equipped battalions, and were determined to force commanding officers to allow their sons to come home.

Regardless of her son's circumstance, each mother knew that other women on similar missions had been killed or held for ransom. They knew they might never find their sons, or that they might find them dead. They also knew that they might be their children's only hope for survival.

In 1999, conditions in the Russian army were scandalous. Defense experts estimated that nine out of ten soldiers were improperly trained for combat. Thousands of young men were conscripted (or offered sign-up bonuses that usually never materialized) and sent to the front lines without adequate supplies. In the winter, troops lucky enough to have tents to sleep in often had nothing to make fires for cooking or warmth. Food, blankets, clothing, and medical supplies were scarce. Gifts sent by families to enlisted men were often taken by the officers.

Thousands of soldiers languished in filthy Chechen prisoner camps or makeshift Russian field hospitals. Heartbreaking stories filtered back home of dead Russian soldiers left lying in Chechen streets—or dragged away to remain unidentified in mortuaries.

Russian families that suddenly stopped getting mail from their soldier sons rarely found support from the Ministry of Defense. One woman reported calling there every day for five months, only to be told each time, "We don't have any information." Finally, she contacted the Soldiers' Mothers Committee. They were able to tell her that her son was alive—but in Chechnya. (The Committee maintains an unofficial network of army contacts in Chechnya and elsewhere, so they can provide such information to fearful relatives.)

Who are these brave and resourceful mothers? The Soldiers' Mothers Committee was founded by a few women with draft-age sons back in 1989, after an estimated fifteen thousand Russian soldiers died in the ten-year occupation of Afghanistan. The Committee's initial purpose was to study the law, looking for loopholes to keep their boys out of the army. Within the first year, three hundred other mothers joined. By the next year, they had formed an effective lobbying effort that forced a partial demobilization of some of the more notoriously cruel and inadequate army units. Shortly thereafter, when the Russians pulled out of Afghanistan, the Committee set up a rehabilitation center for injured soldiers and began human rights training for conscripts and their parents.

Even when Russia is at peace, the army is a dangerous place for young men, with beatings, abuse, and hazing so severe that many commit suicide. War only increases the problems. When troops were sent to Chechnya in 1994, the Committee received up to two hundred letters a day from families describing abusive situations. During the first six months of the war, ten thousand more complaints were received in person. So much support poured in from so many frightened families that Committee volunteers opened fifty regional offices around the country.

Wealthy Russians could arrange a student deferment for their sons or pay a $2,000–$5,000 bribe to avoid service. This represents a fortune for most Russian families, where the base pay for conscripts, for example, was only $40 a month in 1999. So, less fortunate families flocked to the Committee for help.

The Committee sponsored public demonstrations against the war. They held press conferences reporting cases of torture and severe physical violence in the Army. They lobbied for improved living conditions and alternative service for conscientious objectors. They provided barracks for fugitive soldiers.

In January, 1995, the first group of mothers made the dangerous journey to Chechnya to bring back captured Russians from prisoner of war camps. After two months, they returned with one hundred released soldiers. The flow of mothers into the war zone never stopped after that.

Committee pressure and publicity helped force the Russian army to withdraw from Chechnya in 1996, but even this withdrawal was life threatening. The Russian news agency, Tass, reported that retreating Russian troops were freezing in the snow. Tass said the Committee, not the Army, led relief efforts sending trucks loaded with warm clothing, heating appliances, and food.

In 1999, several Russian apartment houses were bombed. Chechen rebels were blamed, causing a shift in popular opinion. Suddenly there was support for a return of the Russian army to Chechnya. So, once again, the Committee became the source of information for worried parents trying to keep their sons out of the army or trying to find a soldier's whereabouts. As reports of the dangers in Chechnya mounted, mothers again began going across the border to find their sons and bring them home.

Examples of the different possible outcomes can be seen in these three mothers who went with a Committee member several months after the war resumed: one managed to get her son released from the army because he was ill, one had no success, and the third came home desolate, carrying fragments of her son's body from a destroyed army barracks. The mothers told the press, "The conditions the soldiers are living in are terrible. Many of them haven't been paid for several months."

Around the same time, Chechen gangsters (who hold soldiers and sometimes mothers for ransom) released a captured army officer, who described the conditions in which he was held, "I was kept in a damp basement, with a floor space of one square meter (about a yard). They beat me. My daily ration was a piece of bread."

Whenever reports like these are published in the Russian press, lines of anxious mothers waiting at Committee offices swell, with each mother wanting to know how to keep her son from getting drafted, or, if necessary, how to go into Chechnya, dodge the bullets, avoid the gangsters, and bring him home. Committee volunteers vow that even when the Chechen war is over, they will stay active until conditions in the army are improved.

Gang Busters

In the United States we don't have to battle dictators or the army. We have a different, but no less deadly, threat to our children: crime and drugs. Increasingly, mothers are on the front line of the battle to rid neighborhoods of these problems.

Have you ever seen the Disney movie *North Avenue Irregulars*? Here's how Amazon.com describes it, "Typical of Disney's 1970s output, this squeaky-clean comic adventure about a group of church volunteers and soccer moms who take on local gangsters is packed with slapstick humor, sight gags, and nonlethal car crashes."

The good news is that kids love the video. The bad news is that Disney took the true story of twelve brave mothers who helped the Treasury Department convict mobsters, and made the women look like bumbling idiots. Here's why those moms deserve greater respect:

New Rochelle, New York, has beautiful suburban neighborhoods, where the mothers lived. It also had an extensive illegal gambling operation that had operated openly for thirty years. Every time there was an election, politicians would promise to clean up the gambling. After each election, things would go back to normal because of inertia and payoffs. A gangland murder provoked a state investigation that turned up tales of beatings and other killings. Still, gambling establishments operated openly. It seemed that no one in New Rochelle was willing to shut down "Heavy Eddie," "Big Chin Dino," or other local bookies.

Finally, a local Presbyterian minister and several upscale homemakers decided the situation had gone on long enough. They were outraged that their children had seen police officers placing bets at illegal establishments. They didn't want to raise kids in a town with blatant corruption. So, they formed the Citizen's Against Organized Crime Committee, and made contact with the Treasury Department because many gangsters had been jailed on tax evasion instead of their more violent acts. Then they began documenting criminal activities.

Some mothers placed bets while wired with tape recorders. Others, driving their station wagons with walkie-talkies, followed gangsters collecting gambling proceeds, and discovered their highly secret headquarters. The Treasury Department raided the headquarters and used the mothers' evidence to convict the gangsters. New Rochelle stopped being a haven for organized crime. Unfortunately, the heroic mothers never got the respect they deserved.

How times have changed. These days, police departments around the country are realizing that concerned mothers can be a key element in crime control. A case in point is Santa Ana, California, where the crime rate has fallen by 50 percent in the last ten years because of community-oriented policing that works with many brave moms.

In 1990, President George Bush came to Santa Ana to honor Rosa Perez, a thirty-eight-year-old homemaker and mother of three who helped the police make more than one hundred drug-related arrests. The president called her a "hero in the war on drugs," but local drug dealers called her "The Finger," because she wasn't afraid to point them out to the police.

Perez, a Mexican immigrant, lived in a ground-floor apartment on South Baker Street, a rough section of Santa Ana. From her windows, she could see drug dealers openly selling their wares on the street. She knew the neighborhood was too dangerous for her three children, but her husband was only a field hand on nearby farms, so they couldn't afford to move from their one bedroom apartment in this poor area of town. Since she had to stay, she decided to take the risk of helping the police make things better.

By the time Bush honored her, Rosa had reported four hundred crimes and saved the life of a police officer being attacked by a drug addict. Dealers vandalized her car and threatened her life many times. She refused to back down. "This is my home," she explained.

Rosa couldn't understand why a president would honor her. "I'm a nobody," she said. Not so, explained a Santa Ana police spokesman, "She's a mother standing up to all these dealers. You can't find a better hero."

Ten years later, there are many Rosas in Santa Ana's rough neighborhoods. The police have made special efforts to work with them, organize them into tenant and neighborhood associations, and bring in various kinds of government assistance to help their neighborhoods thrive after criminals are swept out. Lieutenant Michael Foote, commander of the area of Santa Ana that used to have extensive gang and drug activity, reports that all of South Baker Street has been cleaned up thanks to good police work, expanded social services, and new tenant/neighborhood associations that help the police keep crime down.

Part of Baker Street has small homes. "There is a new pride in ownership there," he told me. "Houses are being painted and repaired. Junk in the yards is gone." Even more dramatic is the change in the area with high density, low-income apartments on South Baker. Tenants associations, run by active mothers, have helped cut crime there by 75–90 percent.

How is that possible? Lieutenant Foote offers the example of one of the roughest neighborhoods in Santa Ana, the New Horizons area. "Ten years ago, no one would have given you a plug nickel for the prospects of that neighborhood organizing, let alone doing anything about gang activity there," he said. "It was the home of the violent Golden West street gang, which had about eighty hard-core members. They were heavily involved in narcotics trafficking, auto theft, armed robbery, and extortion. At one point they manned a checkpoint with automatic weapons, stopping people and collecting "taxes" from anyone who wanted to come into the neighborhood.

"Some gang members took over a house. Shots were fired in the street. There were drive-by shootings. Gang members hung out in front of the house molesting women walking by. Every time we as police would step in, no one was willing to testify."

Then, two women living near the gang house decided to do something about the problem. "Beatrice Calderon is a grandmother with a grandchild living with her," says Lieutenant Foote." She had seen what happened to the neighborhood and decided to stand up." The other brave neighbor was "Rosie Ramirez, a forty-year-old with four children. She had grown up in a gang, and she didn't want that for her children." The final straw for Rosie, explained Foote, was "when her fourteen-year-old daughter began running with the gang and becoming a truant."

Rosie and Beatrice organized a committee of twenty-five neighbors. They began documenting illegal gang activity and calling the police to report crimes. In 1997, Foote says, "We had mothers meeting us several miles away from the neighborhood, loading officers and surveillance equipment into the trunks of their cars, driving us into their garages, and then sneaking us into their houses to do video surveillance of narcotics and gang activities."

The gang retaliated. "Rosie had the windows of her car shot out. She, her daughter, and her son were threatened—but it didn't deter her. That woman has more intestinal fortitude than most," says the lieutenant. As a result of the joint police-mom operations, the gang house was shut down, a ringleader arrested, and others moved away. Now the block is quiet and kids play on the street in the evenings.

Mothers conducted most of the anti-gang activity. Why? Many of the women are single mothers, and the fathers aren't around. In families where there is a dad, he often works two or three jobs to pay the bills and can't afford the time.

Mothers at the nearby Immaculate Heart of Mary Catholic Church were organizing against crime, too. They held marches through the neighborhood carrying icons, statues, and pictures of saints, declaring the neighborhood's opposition to gangs. The local priest and police marched with them. The police were invited to come to the church every other Sunday to take crime reports, but they also stay to help residents (many of whom do not speak English) fill out forms, pay bills, and get in touch with community services. Two new community outreach centers have opened, staffed by volunteer mothers who tutor and mentor neighborhood children.

Ten years ago, street corner drug sales were common. Now they are gone. "There are still narcotics," says Lieutenant Foote, "but we are at a point where most drug dealers won't deliver to many areas with neighborhood associations." The police and community have formed a strong alliance to keep them out. Lieutenant Foote explains, "Mothers are patrolling and there is a high level of the female population involved in making communities safe."

Bringing It Home

The subtitle of this chapter proclaims, "You are more powerful than you think you are." Yet many women will read this chapter and think, "I could never be that brave." That's what all the mothers profiled in this chapter would have thought before life challenged them and they, without even knowing it, tapped into Mother Power to rise to the occasion.

To prove that you have similar strength, think what you would do if you and your child were walking down a street alone, and a vicious dog attacked your child. Or, think what you would do if you could not swim, but your child fell into the deep end of an unguarded pool. Instinct would propel you to risk your life to protect your child.

You may have never felt brave in your whole life, but you have a protective instinct that can make you act stronger than you ever thought possible. Like all mothers, you can use this power—with all its potential to transform—in every area of life. It is, after all, the very power that enabled all the otherwise ordinary women in this chapter to become heroes.

Here are some questions to help you find your power:

> • Who or what needs your protection? How can you begin to help? You don't have to risk your life like the women in this chapter to be brave and effective. In fact, I hope you won't do anything that could endanger yourself or your children.
>
> *continued*

• Did you ever feel fearless? If not, think of a time in your life when you felt the bravest. Look through photo albums and find pictures of yourself at that period of your life. See if you can recapture that feeling of power.

• Do you have a hero or heroine you admire for being brave and courageous? Your role model can be anyone: real or fictional, with children or without. What would you do if you were like this person? What are the first steps you can take to begin the process of finding power like this person.

chapter two

PEACEMAKERS: THE MATERNAL ART OF SETTLING DISPUTES

"During the first few minutes of the movie Saving Private Ryan, *when all those young men were being blown up, a thought flashed through my mind: 'If women ran the world, this wouldn't happen.' Fathers can send their sons into war thinking about stuff like honor and valor, but mothers wouldn't do that. They'd solve the issues in other ways."*

—Melany Gray, litigator and mother

"Perhaps the most consistently documented psychological gender difference is aggressive behavior, with males being more aggressive than females," says *Half the Human Experience* by Janet Shibley Hyde. Need practical proof? Think how often you have seen girls wrestling and punching each other, a favorite activity for boys. Consider how many young men versus women join our all-volunteer army. Finally, think about how mothers and fathers handle childhood squabbles. Moms tend to say things like, "You two stop fighting and be nice to each other," as opposed to phrases like the one Al Roker chose to be the title of his book on fatherhood, *Don't make me stop this car!*

It's not that mothers can't be aggressive. They are currently fighting beside their men in various wars around the world. But, given the choice, most mothers prefer peace because they want to keep their children safe.

While there are all too few women at peace tables negotiating, mothers are leading grassroots peace movements all over the world. In fact, the executive director of the Center for Women's Global Leadership at Rutgers University said the role of women in peacemaking "is one of the issues that's reached critical mass." The trend is especially strong in war-torn Africa. There, groups of women are refusing to let their children join army and guerilla units. They are also forming peace agreements between mothers in warring clans.

Just the mere presence of mothers can create a more peaceful atmosphere, as the security chief at Minnesota's huge Mall of America discovered. He hired mothers to patrol the premises, wearing jackets labeled "Mighty Moms," hoping this would reduce fights and other troublesome behavior among unchaperoned adolescents. In 1995, before the patrols started, there were three hundred serious incidents reported at the Mall. By 1999, Mother Power had created peace: there wasn't a single one.

In this chapter, we'll look at mothers whose peacekeeping activities extend way beyond shopping malls. First are the Irish mothers who won a Nobel Peace Prize by showing the world that Mother Power can breach the gulf between bitter enemies. Next are four Israeli mothers who forced their government to stop the war with Lebanon. The third section features an American mother who brokers peace agreements everyday. She is one of the growing number of divorce mediators, bringing much-needed peace to families all over the country.

The Beginning of Peace in Northern Ireland

By 1976, Northern Ireland was split into armed camps, the pro-British Protestants against the pro-independence Catholics. The warring factions killed people regularly. Hatred and suspicion grew day by day.

Then, in August that year, in a Catholic neighborhood, an IRA car being chased by British soldiers plowed into a young mother walking with her four children. The mother, Anne Corrigan Maguire, was severely injured and three of her children, including an infant in a baby carriage, were killed. Shocked neighbors made a makeshift memorial for the children and began circulating petitions for peace.

Petitioners knocked on Betty William's door, and she readily signed. Afterward, on impulse, she phoned the local newspaper, asking a reporter to print her phone number so anyone who wanted to talk about ending the violence could call her. Betty had no peacemaking credentials. She was just a mother who knew that if something wasn't done her children could be the next ones killed.

Meanwhile, at the hospital, Anne's husband and her sister, Mairead Corrigan, made emotional pleas for peace to television reporters. Mairead, who had no children but felt maternal toward her nieces and nephews, called Betty Williams who, by that time, was planning a peace demonstration.

The media began interviewing Betty and Mairead. When the two women met veteran journalist, Ciaran McKeown, he told them that the time was right for a real peace movement. If they would be the public leaders of such a movement, he would be their secret coach. He helped them create a name for the movement, Peace People, a mission statement that was free of blame and judgment, and taught them how to deal with the media.

Betty and Mairead cared passionately about bringing peace to Northern Ireland, but they were painfully aware that they lacked knowledge of political issues. McKeown advised them to just say "I don't know," if the media asked questions they couldn't answer. He convinced them that the public was sick of experts who were partisan or told half-truths. Instead, he said the public was yearning for people just like them: honest, caring women who would encourage peaceful protest.

Betty Williams remembers, "I gave voice to something that the women of Ireland were feeling at the time. They were sick of losing their husbands, sons, and daughters. They were in enormous pain. I think probably when I yelled for peace—because that's what I really did, you know—the women responded in kind.

"At our first rally, Protestant and Catholic women who had never before met each other came together, got off their buses and converged at a certain spot in Belfast. They were rolling off the buses into each other's arms. It was an incredible, powerful force of good that was there."

Other local community peace activists held rallies all around the country. Mairead Corrigan, who traveled to many of those rallies remembers how exciting it was to be part of Peace People in those early days. "It was a great experience for most people," she said. People would come in saying, 'Well, I'm only an ordinary housewife,' and would end up speaking at assemblies on things like emergency laws. It's really been a tremendous development for people. People who were afraid to speak at an assembly, now you can't shut them up!"

But the peace process was not smooth. Zealots, who wanted to keep old hatreds alive, tried to disrupt the rallies. Hecklers throwing bottles and bricks occasionally assaulted marchers. As leaders of the marches, Betty and Mairead were both attacked and injured. The rallies continued none the less. By December, hundreds of thousands of people had marched for peace. The whole world took notice.

One year later, in October, 1977 Betty and Mairead were given the Nobel Prize for Peace. Ironically, instead of strengthening Peace People, the prize caused jealousy and dissention that weakened it. Some people were angry that the two women were honored instead of the Peace People group as a whole. Others were upset that the original petitioners or Ciaran McKeown, who quit his job to join Peace People, had not received the Prize. The fact that Betty Williams kept her prize money instead of donating it to the group angered many more. All this dissention weakened, but did not stop the peace movement.

Betty Williams moved to the United States and dropped out of public view. In the mid-1990s she began speaking out against worldwide hunger and the arms race.

Anne Corrigan Maguire never emotionally recovered from the accident that killed her children, but started the peace movement. After having several more children, she committed suicide in 1980. Mairead Corrigan moved into the Maguire household to care for her nieces and nephews, and married their father the following year.

Mairead Corrigan and Ciaran McKeown continue to work with Peace People, which is still doing community work, but not on the same scale. While full peace has still not come to Northern Ireland, they know the movement they started was vital to their country. As the Peace People web page says, "The level of violence dropped like a stone, going down 70 percent and staying there. Hope grew....The nonviolent vision that inspired the original impetus is no longer the strangely alien concept it seemed at first: and Northern Ireland stands at the threshold of a new beginning after thirty years of nightmare."

Four Mothers Who Flexed Their Muscles

Like the Northern Irish Protestants and Catholics, Israel and its Arab neighbors seem mired in conflict. However, in Israel as in Ireland, mothers showed that peace is possible.

When the war between Israel and Lebanon began in 1982 there were large antiwar rallies in Israel protesting the invasion and occupation of a Lebanese "security zone." The Israeli government indicated it was ready to pull out in 1985, but never followed through. As the occupation dragged on, active protests diminished, but a growing silent majority felt the occupation was harmful to Israel, Lebanon, and prospects for peace. Not only were between twenty-five and thirty-five

Israeli soldiers killed in the security zone each year, but many people in northern Israel, the area supposedly protected by the occupation, felt the military presence inflamed the problem.

Then in 1997, fifteen years after the war began and twelve years after the pull out was promised, two Israeli helicopters collided on their way to Lebanon, killing seventy-three soldiers. One Israeli mother, Rachel Ben Dor, decided enough was enough.

The helicopters crashed in front of the school where Mrs. Ben Dor's children had been students. Her son was in the Israeli army, and she didn't want him sacrificed to a war that she felt was wrong.

"On the night of the helicopter disaster, I became forcefully aware of the terrible price we were paying in the Lebanese quagmire," she says. "I made up my mind that something must be done to stop the endless bloodletting." She gathered three friends to help decide what to do. The four mothers had raised their children together. Now their sons were in the army.

As the mothers brainstormed, they knew they were up against powerful pro-war forces. Rachel said, "Many former commanders of the Lebanese war play leading roles as Knesset members or ministers, and continue defending their creation, attempting to frighten or silence anyone who dares to claim there is a problem. After the helicopter crash, I was boiling mad when the minister of defense said that voices not raised in support slacken the hands of the fighting men." But what could just four mothers do?

Their first step was to write supportive letters to all pro-peace Knesset members. Then they wrote about why the occupation was wrong and how Israel could better be defended from within its own borders. This article was printed in a newspaper on Passover Eve under the title "Four Mothers," a reference to a well-known Passover song. "We decided to adopt this as our group's name," Rachel Ben Dor remembers, "But we did not imagine that our detractors would use it

46

as an opportunity to bypass the problem and focus on our being women and mothers."

Israeli television shows invited the mothers to appear with generals to debate the war. The generals were condescending and rolled their eyes when the mothers spoke. They and other pro-war people called the mothers hysterical and said they were traitors to their country.

The military also accused the Mothers of not supporting their sons in the army. In reply, the Mothers simply explained that they supported their sons—but not the war. As one of the founding Four Mothers said, "What my son does, he should do in the best way possible. He knows that I will not be able to look into a mirror knowing that I have done nothing to protect him. He is over there and I am over here, doing what I can. I do not want to live with the feeling that I am letting things roll along."

The New York Times wrote, "The women took a classic Israeli stereotype—the silent, suffering soldier's mother—stood it on its head and dared to challenge the military."

Their challenge succeeded. "Every time we received publicity, a lot more people joined our ranks, encouraging us to confront the government's entrenched position that 'there isn't anyone to talk to,' 'there is no solution,' and other clichés," recalled Rachel Ben Dor.

Men and women, young and old, with or without children, joined with the Four Mothers to push for peace. They stood with signs at road junctions, held demonstrations, and circulated petitions. They held popular memorials for every soldier who died. They met with Israeli public officials and foreign ambassadors.

Two years after their protests began, the three leading candidates for prime minister all promised to bring the army back from Lebanon. Ehud Barak, the winner, had not only made the promise, but put a date on it. When he lived up to that promise, he also held a ceremony to honor the Four Mothers.

Rachel Ben Dor described the scene: "There we were inside the Defense Ministry that we used to picket, kissing and hugging with the prime minister and the army chief. And all the generals were standing there, thinking I don't know what. It was so amazing."

Ending the War between the Roses

So far, all the examples of Mother Power in this and the previous chapter have involved women protecting their own children in one form or another. But there is a whole other side to Mother Power. It involves women who take the skills they have developed while being a good mother and use them to make the world a better place, addressing issues that do not affect their own children or family. The first example follows: a woman mediates divorces using the same kind of patience and reasoning she (and probably you) use when handling disputes between her kids.

Remember the 1989 movie *The War of the Roses*, a black comedy in which Michael Douglas and Kathleen Turner play a couple whose divorce becomes a war? Divorce mediators try to broker lasting peace agreements that avoid or end such destructive battles.

In the early 1980s a group of family law attorneys, mostly mothers, began to meet in San Diego to try to find a better way to handle divorce. They didn't like the adversarial process where couples, fighting through attorneys, were often angrier at the end of a divorce than when it began. They knew that in bitter divorces, children are usually the victims. So they, like other groups of lawyers around the country, decided to try mediation instead.

Mediation is a process that helps warring parties create their own solutions for a lasting peace by encouraging each to think not only about what they want, but also what the other can accept. Mediation has been around since human beings began living in tribes and villages. It has been used internationally to create the reunification of Vietnam and Berlin, in each case helping two very different cultures find ways to merge and cooperate with each other. Parents who successfully resolve sibling rivalry clashes or family disputes like who is going to do the chores, often use mediation techniques without even knowing it.

Mary Mudd Quinn, a prominent mediator who has met with the San Diego group for eighteen years, is a family therapist, not a lawyer. Bill Hargreaves, an attorney friend who had been practicing family law for ten years, recruited her to mediation. "Bill began sending me cases where he thought the couple could work out a divorce peacefully instead of litigating," she says. "He would advise them of their legal rights and then give them my name, because he didn't trust his own ability to make the shift from litigator where you see a case from one point of view, to mediator where you look at both parties' goals and help them come to agreement." However, after sharing several cases, Bill and Mary started working as a team.

She explains the mediation process: "We sit down with the couple and let each of them say how the situation seems to them. Next we try to get each to state their goals. Then—and this is the real switch in the brain when mediating disputes—we say, 'Can you think of a solution that you can accept and your partner might go for?'"

Mediators come up with lots of ideas themselves. Everyone brain-storms to find creative solutions. But Quinn says the main reason mediation works is that people devise their own solutions: "Divorce is usually the most painful thing the couple has ever done, but at least with mediation, there is a sense that we are in control of our own destiny. And living with the final agreement, there is a peacefulness that won't be achieved if a judge sits there and tells you how it's going to be."

The public tends to think that mediation is just for people who can still get along. However, Mary Mudd Quinn says that she often works with couples that are so angry they can hardly stand to be in the same room together. Even so, "as they work through the process," she says, "they change. It's common at the conclusion for people to say things like, 'We did a good job. If we had been able to do things like this when we were married, our marriage might have worked.'

"At the end of mediation, they can usually look at each other and thank each other for the good times they had in the marriage and for the care they spent in parenting. They know they will be able to go to family weddings, baptisms, and enjoy grandchildren without fighting." This is an enormous satisfaction for Quinn as well as the couple.

"The majority of mediations are done for couples with children," she says. "They choose mediation because they have read about horror-story divorces, or have seen the destruction with friends and neighbors when divorce goes badly. They are driven to do something better for their children. They don't want to destroy their children's lives. When we can keep them focused on that common interest, that is extremely helpful."

Another common motivation, says Quinn, is the desire to keep finances in tact. Quinn and Hargreaves typically see a couple for ten hours and the average total cost, including filing divorce papers, is $5,000. That is approximately what each person would have to pay just to retain a divorce lawyer. The typical divorce in San Diego without mediation, says Quinn, runs $20,000 if there are no major complications. So, while Mary Mudd Quinn earns a good living (she charges $150 an hour in addition to her partner's fee) she is still saving the couple time and money. More importantly, the couple usually ends the process with good feelings about each other.

Mary Mudd Quinn cites a couple who divorced after being married eight years. "The wife made very little money. Even though he made a lot more than she did, they had very little in home equity or savings, and both cars had car payments. The wife desperately wanted to keep their small house, not just because she loved it, but also because she felt she might never have another chance to buy one.

"They worked out a solution where she kept the house and he kept the small amount of savings and IRAs. He gave her support for a year or so, because she earned so little. But they were both strapped and afraid because there was so little money.

"Two years later, after the support payments ended, he called and asked to come back in to see us. His ex-wife had no idea why he wanted her at the meeting. He explained that the company he worked for had gone public, and with stock options he had become a millionaire. He said, 'I have had a windfall and I would like to pay off her mortgage, the entire $170,000. That isn't a lot for me now, but I know it will mean a lot for her.' He called us because he wanted to do it legally.

"She was blown away, saying, 'This will completely change my life!' That would never have happened had they not mediated their divorce. If they had litigated, they would have had lousy feelings about each other. But because of mediation, it felt good for him to do that for her."

Quinn says that while she uses much of what she learned in graduate school to be a successful mediator, "The whole concept of mediation is based on those basic principles of being a parent—being empathetic, giving advice, directing people, soothing them. I tell them I cannot control them, but I can be honest and tell them what I hope for them."

In fact, the necessary skills are so parental, that Mary Quinn has a forty-eight-year-old friend, who, after being a homemaker and raising five children, took a short training course in mediation and now works for a lawyer doing community mediation in San Diego. "When there is a complaint about a barking dog and stuff like that," Mary explains, "the civil court sends the case to the attorney, who turns it over to my friend. She goes out and sets up a community meeting and mediates."

The municipal court in San Diego set up a pilot program in 1997 where 70 percent of all civil cases—those not involving criminal or family court—were sent first for mediation. Mary Mudd Quinn was one of the first to volunteer to work with this program. About half of the cases were solved with four hours of mediation instead of days in court.

Mary gives typical examples of such cases: a partner claiming to have been defrauded out of a business; members of a community organization suing another faction for control claiming mismanagement; personal injury cases; people claiming discrimination at work. The pilot program was so successful that the courts are now paying mediators for their work.

Mary and a female attorney friend were happy to do the pilot program as community service. "We learned a lot and honed our mediation skills with different cases," Mary says. "And we love to see cases we know are going to be a mess if they get to court get settled peacefully with mediation."

Not every mediation case ends happily. There may be no happy solution when people have diametrically opposed goals. Mediation is also not appropriate when one party is far more aggressive and intimidating than the other is. Such cases may have to go to court to be litigated. But for most cases, Mary believes mediation helps people go through a painful process in the best and most peaceful way possible.

Furthermore, Mary knows that, by teaching her clients how to mediate their disputes, she has given them tools they can use their whole lives whenever problems and conflicts occur. That gives her a great deal of personal, professional, and parental satisfaction.

Bringing It Home

Peacemaking is a subtle and complex process that many women have had to learn because, unlike men, they cannot count on their physical strength to combat enemies and bullies. So, women learn to use brains, not brawn, to resolve dangerous situations and avoid physical contact. Furthermore, as mothers, we have to develop peacekeeping abilities in our homes. Otherwise there would be continuous screaming, slammed doors, and hurt feelings.

You might be thinking, "I can mediate sibling rivalry, but how can I help the cause of world peace?" You may be thinking, "My children don't listen to me, so why would any politician take notice?" Don't forget that almost every volunteer for the Irish peace movement began by saying, "I'm just an ordinary housewife." Some were surprised to find they could give stirring speeches for the cause. Others simply added their voice and bodies to the demonstrations. Movements need people in the spotlight and many more who are faceless supporters.

To get in touch with your maternal ability to settle disputes:

• How do you settle disputes in your family? Think about which peacemaking skills and strategies work well. Which have you acquired since becoming a mother? Think of ways you can use these outside the home.

• Talk with your children about war and violence in the news. Get them thinking about how people could solve their differences without fighting. If you raise children who can stand up for their rights without being aggressive, you have given them a gift—and the world one, too.

• How can you contribute to peace in your neighborhood, state, country, or the world? All of us can give a kind word, write letters in support of peace, and make some contribution. No matter how small, it all adds up.

chapter three

GIVING: HELPING PEOPLE CONSCIOUSLY

"Do you know what would have happened if it had been Three Wise Women instead of Three Wise Men? They would have asked directions, arrived on time, helped deliver the baby, cleaned the stable, made a casserole, and brought practical gifts."
—**Anonymous joke from the Internet**

Mothers give the gift of life and continue giving for the rest of their lives, not only to their families but also to neighbors in need. When my mother had a sick friend, she would bring over homemade brownies or a chicken casserole. She also volunteered to work at church suppers that provided fellowship for our congregation.

This tradition of helping has expanded rapidly in the last few decades. Mothers are extending their maternal caring well beyond their circle of family and friends by founding organizations that help thousands of strangers. They still cook church suppers, but also start soup kitchens and food pantries to feed the poor. They still help sick friends, but are also at the forefront of the organ donation movement, saving thousands of lives each year. In this chapter, you will meet several mothers who started soup kitchens on a shoe string budget and grew them into large organizations. Likewise, you will meet mothers who help others live, even though their own children have died.

In today's busy world, with so many dual-career families, the old sense of neighborhood has eroded. Often people feel alone on their own street, having never met most of the people who live nearby. The final story in this chapter introduces two women who brought old-fashioned hometown support back to a suburban small town.

The Loaves and the Fishes

I heard of so many mothers starting soup kitchens and food pantries that I called America's Second Harvest, a national network of food banks, and asked if Mother Power was fueling the growth of organizations combating hunger. The media relations manager said that while there were no hard data on that subject, "I would tend to think so. When I attend national and regional conferences, on the grassroots level, there are far more women than men on the front lines."

I could tell you many inspiring stories of such women: from the wealthy mother who started a soup kitchen after seeing someone searching for food in other people's garbage, to a group of mothers who did the same when they noticed people coming to their church who looked hungry. But I selected two stories that show how anyone can start small but make a big difference.

On Thanksgiving Day, 1989, Iris Sanchez was feeling very grateful. Although she was struggling to support her seventeen-year-old daughter and three-year-old grandson on a payroll clerk's salary in a one-bedroom apartment in Brooklyn, she realized that she was far luckier than the homeless people in her neighborhood. Furthermore, she felt safe this Thanksgiving: she had divorced her husband who drank too much and beat her on holidays. So, she bought an extra turkey, made sandwiches, and handed them out to thirty homeless men and prostitutes. Doing this felt so good to her, and made the people she helped so happy, that she began making soup every Saturday, giving away fifty to sixty cups to homeless or hungry neighbors.

Soon, volunteers began helping her cook each Saturday and her minister at Bay Ridge Christian Center agreed to donate money to pay for the food. They made sandwiches and soup, plus distributed clothes, blankets, canned goods, and "anything people gave us." "I was storing everything at my house," Iris told me. "So my pastor gave me a little room under the stairs at church for storage." Soon Iris took over an old trailer the church owned and expanded her programs and funding, getting money and food from various city programs and food banks.

Now, Iris's Mission of Mercy, which operates out of the church and trailer has become both a soup kitchen and food pantry. Volunteers still make the soup and sandwiches, and in addition, bags of food are given out to over four hundred families during the week. Iris, who was born in Puerto Rico and is Pentecostal, notes that the people who come for bags of food are diverse and include Russian Jews and Chinese immigrants. She is happy to serve anyone in need, and notes that the need is growing as welfare limits cut government support to families.

Iris retired two years ago at age forty-seven after working twenty-eight years for the phone company. Then she went to work full-time at Mission of Mercy. There, her life has expanded along with her programs. Her new husband helps staff the food pantry, and her grandson helps distribute the soup and sandwiches on Saturdays.

Iris has also started a summer camp that will serve eighty children this year, has a welfare-to-work training program, and is trying to buy a house to use as a shelter for homeless women. She says her approach is highly maternal. "Everyone calls me 'Mom' at the food bank," she laughs. "My husband says I have this 'mom thing' about always being protective and giving. My mom was always giving and taught us to share."

Several years ago, while working at the phone company and running the Mission, she began taking college courses part-time and recently received her bachelor's degree. She likes to tell people at the

Mission, "If I can do it, you can too. I never thought I was smart enough, especially with all the abuse in my life." Noting that some of the people her Mission serves have drug and alcohol problems, she is now working towards a certificate in substance abuse counseling.

Joan McGovern, who lives in White Plains, New York, also started a soup kitchen and food bank, the Lord's Pantry, for different, but equally maternal, reasons. "I had thirteen children," she told me. "One of my sons, Tommy, was gay."

When Tommy developed AIDS, Joan joined a support group at White Plains Hospital and became friendly with other mothers taking care of gay sons who were ill. "When Tommy died, so many people sent donations in his name to a place called God's Love, We Deliver, that I called up to find out what they did," she said. "It was an organization in New York City that delivers dinners to people with AIDS." When she told two of her friends in the support group, Anne Weiss and Fran Gray, they decided to start a similar service in Westchester County, where they lived.

Joan McGovern explained, "We felt that our children had received the best support and care. Fran was a nurse and she quit work to spend the last year with her Peter and nurse him. Same with Jimmy, Ann's son. We knew that there were lots of people who didn't have support— who had nobody. We felt we would like to do for other people what we had done for our own children."

As they were planning their program, Anne died of a heart attack, but Joan and Fran, both in their sixties, continued on. They contacted agencies that serve AIDS patients and offered to deliver hot dinners every day to anyone they referred. "My Tommy died June 7, 1990, and on June 6, 1991, we got our first client," Joan said.

At first, as the program grew, the two women bought the food and cooked the meals themselves, aided by twelve restaurants that also donated dinners. By the time they were delivering to thirty people a day, even though they were helped by volunteer drivers, the project had gotten too big to be run out of Joan's kitchen.

Joan recalled, "I had a friend, Phoebe, who was the cook for the Head Start program at my church, St. Bernard's. She suggested we ask the pastor if we could use the kitchen, since Head Start was finished at three each day. He agreed, so Phoebe stayed on and cooked the meals, and volunteers came in to help.

"It was like topsy, it grew! Never in our wildest imagination did we think it would get this big. We are doing at least ninety-five hundred meals a month [now their daily deliveries include cold breakfast and lunch for the next day along with a hot dinner five times a week]. The dinners are kept in special bags that keep them hot for two hours. We have two paid cooks, ten to twelve paid part-time workers, and I am the only paid full-time person. Fran died three years ago, so now I run it with my Board.

"The Board decided to pay me to run the Lord's Pantry full-time a few years ago. I had worked in real estate since I got divorced in 1979, and I tried to do both. But I had to give up real estate, because this became a full-time job. I was embarrassed to take a salary. I wish I could do it for nothing, but unfortunately I can't.

"In the beginning Fran and I were funding the Lord's Pantry ourselves. We were so ignorant, we were just two grandmothers who didn't know anything. Then we went to a meeting, and this gal got up from the Ryan White Title I Care Program. She said there was grant money if you wrote a proposal. I didn't know what a proposal was. So, one of my sons and a daughter and a couple of friends sat down with me and they wrote a proposal. They asked for $65,000 and I almost dropped dead. But my son said you have to ask for more than you think you'll get. We received $15,000."

The Ryan White program continues to support the Lord's Pantry. It also receives donations from many other sources.

Today, Joan and the Board struggle to keep the organization personal. She regrets that the program has grown so big that she cannot deliver meals. But she makes sure that she and another Board member speak on the phone to each client at least once every two weeks. "I miss seeing them," she says. "But we call them to see how they are doing.

"The face of AIDS is changing. Now we get mostly welfare people who have lots of problems. Some people say they brought this on themselves by doing things like sharing needles. So what? They need us more than anybody. No one will help them. One woman has five children, and we feed them all.

"They are such sad people. So hopeless. I think delivering meals every night lets them know we care. At Christmas they all get a present and a special meal. There is a florist who gives me her leftover poinsettias, so everyone gets a flower. We do the same thing on St. Patrick's day: everyone gets corned beef and cabbage with green ribbons on the bag and a carnation. We try to make it personal.

"I call running this operation my course in miracles, because whenever I think, 'I have no volunteers,' something happens and people turn up to see it through. I had to put God in the name of my organization, because I firmly believe that we are not doing this, we are just the vehicles being used. Sometimes I object to this. I say to God, 'You could try this with someone else! You could make this a little easier!' But, the Lord works in strange ways, and who am I to question?

"My son Tommy said, 'I'm just going a little ahead of you, Mom.' Well, I think he lied. I am seventy-six and this work keeps me busy and young. But I'm afraid of what will happen when I am not here. Who will run this? For now, it's good for me. I love my work."

The Gift of Life after Death

Joan found a way to give in her time of grief. Some of the following mothers did too—but in a completely different way.

A number of American mothers have recently taken a leadership role in promoting organ donations. Some made headlines when they rose above their own grief to give their dead child's organs to strangers. Other mothers made news when they donated their own kidneys to unrelated children. And finally, there are the less dramatic, everyday heroes who give their blood and bone marrow to help people like my son.

In 1994, Reg and Maggie Green from California took their two kids on a dream vacation through Europe. While driving in a beautiful but lonely area of Sicily, their carefree family excursion became a nightmare: bandits tried to stop their car with gunfire. Seven-year-old Nicholas Green was killed while sleeping in the back seat.

If the Greens had done what most people would do in that situation—lash out at Italian crime while taking their son's body back home—no one would have been surprised. Instead, they shocked Italy and the world by donating Nicholas's organs to seven Italians. Their act of extraordinary generosity gave life to five people and sight to two others.

A nineteen-year-old girl from Sicily was in a coma until Nicolas's liver saved her life. His heart was given to a fifteen-year-old Roman boy who had spent half his life in a hospital. The other recipients had less dramatic, but equally heartwarming recoveries. Italians, who had one of the lowest organ donation rates of all Western countries felt shame as well as gratitude. As one commentator wrote to the Greens in an open letter on the front page of a Milan newspaper, "I want to thank you—not only for the transplants, but for a lesson. Of generosity, of composure..."

Newspapers throughout Italy ran articles praising the Greens and noting the need for organ donations. Italian cities honored the Greens in various ways. In Rome, for example, they received the city's Gold Medal, an honor usually given only to heads of state. The Italian president and prime minister met with them. More important, emulating the Greens, Italians suddenly became more giving. Within days of Nicholas's death, organ donations in Italy quadrupled, and the ten thousand Italians waiting for transplants had new hope.

In Italy, a week after Nicholas's death, Maggie Green spoke to a reporter, saying she was "amazed what the people of Italy have done for us...The support we have received here has made a great difference. We have had the whole country grieving with us." She also reported a sense of peace that Nicholas, even in death, could help others. "It's not every child who can do so much for so many others by dying," she said.

Since then, Maggie and Reg have become spokespeople. They lecture around the world and donate their lecture fees (as well as money they received from a 1998 TV movie about their lives) to their Nicholas Green Foundation, which trains doctors in transplant surgery.

The movie, the media articles, and the Green's lectures have raised awareness of the need for organ donations all over the world. In the United States, such donations are increasing slowly but steadily. Like the Greens, other parents have found that when tragedy strikes and kills a child, they find some peace by donating organs.

Another mother whose personal tragedy became public is Tracy Robison-Sagers, an emergency room nurse in Utah, who made the news because, ironically, she was on duty when her ten-year-old son, Travis, was brought in, mortally wounded from a terrible accident. After two days of praying for a miracle, Tracy knew that the end was near and decided to help others live through organ donation.

When Travis died that evening, his heart, liver, kidneys, and corneas were quickly matched to save six other people. Instead of waiting for a child in need, Tracy decided to give the heart to a grandfather who was dying of congestive heart failure. Thinking of Travis, however, she made one stipulation: the grandfather had to promise that after the transplant he would take his grandson for a walk on the beach.

Like the Greens, Tracy has become active in increasing public awareness about organ donations, wanting people to know that every day over seventy-five thousand Americans wait for organs and every day ten Americans die waiting. Also like the Greens she has found some peace through her generosity. As she said, "Even after death, all of us still have a way of helping others. My son had a big heart. For me, it is such a miracle that it still beats."

These days you don't have to die to save a life through transplant programs. For example, a new surgical procedure allows people who are living to donate a kidney with few postoperative problems. This extraordinary gift of life had never been given to a stranger until Joyce Roush, who works for the Indiana Organ Procurement Organization, decided to be the first person to do it.

In 1999, Joyce, the mother of two teenage girls and stepmother to three others, made headlines when she decided to give one of her kidneys to a thirteen-year-old Maryland boy whom she had never met. Knowing that people could live normal lives with just one kidney, and that forty thousand people were waiting for a kidney donation, she hoped "others would make the decision I made."

Later that same year, Jane Smith, mother of a twelve-year-old boy and a teacher in North Carolina, learned that one of her students was suffering from severe kidney disease. When tests showed she was a match (meaning that his body would probably not reject her kidney) she also made headlines by offering to give her kidney to the boy. While many generous men and women will follow their example, to me it is no coincidence that the people who led this movement were mothers.

All around the world, there are many men and women who literally give of themselves, in ways that are less dramatic, but no less life saving. I became painfully aware of some of these everyday heroes when my son was dying of Hodgkin's disease (a cancer of the lymph system). The only chance to save his life was a bone marrow transplant. Since medical tests showed that no family member was a proper match, we had to rely on the generosity of strangers.

We learned that there are thirteen million people worldwide who have volunteered to give bone marrow, but even so, there was no guarantee to find a match. Our hospital contacted the national and international marrow donor programs and, luckily, several possible matches were found. I was amazed and grateful when the first potential donor contacted readily agreed to donate marrow for my son.

Throughout my son's six-month, final battle with cancer, he also needed blood and platelet transfusions. His fiancée and sister could make some direct donations, but again, we had to rely on the generosity of strangers anonymously donating to a blood bank. And once, after Christmas when blood supplies are notoriously low (everyone is too busy with the holidays to take the time to give blood and platelets), Jean Paul's health was damaged because he had to wait an extra day for blood.

What do donors, especially ones like Joyce Roush and Jane Smith, get out of such extreme giving? The knowledge that they are saving another mother's child. What did Maggie Green and Tracy Robison-Sagers get out of giving their sons' organs? The same thing, plus the knowledge that their boys' deaths were not in vain.

The recipients of all this generosity know they can never repay the debt, but some try. The grandfather who lives with Travis's heart says, "I thank that boy in my prayers several times a day." Maria Pia Pedala, the nineteen-year-old Sicilian who was in a coma, dying of hepatitis before getting Nicholas Green's liver, found a more unique, and quite maternal way of giving thanks. When she gave birth to a son several years after her recovery, she named him Nicholas.

The last few decades have brought remarkable advances in transplant technology that allow strangers to save each other's lives. However, with people working such long hours and moving frequently, the last few decades have also brought such a decline in neighborhood solidarity, that when a neighbor is in need, it's often a maternal stranger who helps.

Neighbors Helping Neighbors in a Small Town

This story shows how two mothers found a different way to help the sick—and show gratitude for their own recoveries.

Leafy, suburban Larchmont, New York, looks like an ideal small town, where everyone knows and supports each other. But these days, such community closeness is hard to find, even in a place like Larchmont. As one resident, Mary Stein, told me, "When our parents grew up, people lived in neighborhoods for thirty-five years and knew everyone. If someone got sick, neighbors would bring over food, babysit for the kids, or even offer a loan if needed. But these days, people move in and out. Everyone is so busy with their jobs or small children that you may not even know your neighbors."

Even so, bad news can still travel fast. It is not uncommon in a town like Larchmont to hear that the father of a child in your youngster's school just had a massive heart attack, or a mother a few blocks away was diagnosed with cancer. When Mary would hear such news, she would want to offer help, but usually didn't know the person. Mary's friend Kathy Staudt felt the same desire to give when she heard someone was sick, but felt awkward about approaching the family and offering assistance.

Both Mary and Kathy knew first-hand how emotionally and financially devastating it is when a family member has a catastrophic illness. They knew how even relatively affluent families could be strained to the limit finding all the help that is needed.

A few years ago, when Kathy was a young mother with three small children, she was diagnosed with Hodgkins disease, and spent a difficult year being driven back and forth to chemotherapy and radiation treatments. Mary, with four little boys, had spent a year doing the same for her husband fighting a battle with cancer.

They told me, "As mothers, we know what happens to a family when someone is ill—how hard it is to run the household and pay all the extra medical bills, how kids under stress need extra support and help with homework, how there just isn't enough of a parent to go around when tragedy strikes a family."

So, one day in the school parking lot, Mary told Kathy that she wanted to start a group that would organize volunteer efforts to help families with a medical crisis. And Kathy, very enthusiastically, said, "Count me in!"

They held a coffee at Mary's house, and invited ten people to brain-storm about what the group should do. All ten people were known to be real givers, but each had diverse skills and community connections. One was a former mayor: she knew everyone in town. Several were moms, known for their generous volunteer efforts in the schools or community. Two men, one a physician and the other a psychologist, had the necessary skills and expertise in their fields. All ten agreed that there was a need, and tried to define a mission statement for their group.

More meetings followed where they formalized their mission: "Larchmont Friends of the Family, Inc. is a not-for-profit, nonsectarian, charitable organization intended to assist families with significant ties to the Larchmont community. Formed by Larchmont residents, its purpose is to mitigate the trauma faced by a family with dependent children when a parent or child dies or suffers a catastrophic illness. Where needed, financial and support services and volunteer efforts will be provided on a short-term basis only and are intended merely to provide some stabilization of the family in the midst of a crisis until the family members are able to thoughtfully consider and adjust to their new realities."

They formed themselves into a board of directors, each with responsibilities that reflected their interests and abilities. For example, one person agreed to be in charge of fund-raising, another became the treasurer, and another organizes volunteer efforts. One drew up a form to assess the needs of families. Another agreed to get the legal help needed to be designated as a non-profit organization so that donations would be tax deductible and to get the proper insurance so that volunteers would be protected.

Kathy wrote a letter, which each board member sent to ten more friends. "We are a diverse community," says Kathy, "We have two temples, two Catholic churches, and two protestant churches, plus an international community. So, we wanted to reach out to all the elements."

That initial mailing brought in $16,000 in donations and a flood of volunteers. The $16,000 paid for insurance (they had to be covered if a volunteer slipped and fell), a Friends telephone line in the house of a board member, and a bulk mailing to every home with a Larchmont zip code.

Mary says, "We wanted to touch all eight thousand households, and we learned as we went along. For example, we found out we could buy mailing lists, but we needed to specify that we wanted both apartments and houses. We found out that we didn't need to stuff all the envelopes by hand—a local printer owned a machine that folds and stuffs very cheaply."

The first bulk mailing introduced the group and invited everyone to a town meeting about Friends of the Family. About 120 people showed up for a presentation by the board and far more people sent donations and offers of volunteer help.

About 150 volunteers are in the group Rolodex. The majority cooks or drives for families, but there are also lawyers, accountants, financial planners, social workers, and plumbers who give their services.

Decorators will make sick rooms look pretty. And a seventeen-piece orchestra volunteered to play at two benefit dinner dances. Merideth Viera, a friend of a Friend, volunteered to speak at a benefit fashion show and donated her winnings from *Celebrity Jeopardy* to the group.

Equally important are the outreach volunteers who notify Friends when they hear of a family in need. There are contact people in the small local factories, and in each congregation, school, organization, and government office in town.

Seven months after the initial brainstorming meeting, with all their policies and procedures in place, Friends began helping their first family. When I interviewed Kathy and Mary three years later, not one single day had passed without some local family receiving aid.

The first woman they helped had been sick since she moved into the community. Confined to bed, she was very lonely because she hadn't met anyone in town. Volunteers not only brought food for her family, but stayed to share a cup of tea with her. Because the woman was dying, a housekeeper was hired not only to take care of the house and two little boys, but also to provide a stable transition.

In another family, the father was extremely ill and did not want anyone to come into the home. The wife said she could handle everything, except she felt overwhelmed by laundry. So, everyday she left the dirty laundry on the porch where it was picked up by a volunteer, taken to a laundry, and returned clean and folded. Since both the ill and caretaking parent were preoccupied, Friends also offered to hire a college counselor to help one child and a tutor to help another.

In one family with a single working mother, Friends paid the rent so she could afford to stay home with a child who had cancer. In another very similar situation, Friends hired a baby-sitter to be with the sick child because the mother had to work to keep her medical insurance.

Larchmont is a relatively affluent community, so outsiders might be surprised that many families need financial help. Friends does not ask families to prove financial need, they just give what is asked for. Why? Mary, a nurse married to a physician, found out the hard way that even a family like theirs can be financially stressed by illness. "We had to hire a housekeeper to take care of the kids while I was taking my husband back and forth to treatments. That cost $700-800 dollars a week and was a burden for us. Much worse, there was one time when we were told by a medical facility that we had to come up with $23,000 immediately or they would discontinue my husband's treatment."

If one of the Friends families found themselves in the same situation, she says, "We couldn't give $23,000. But we can give $3,000 and that buys time to talk to the financial aid office at the hospital or to negotiate with the insurance company." (Friends has a three-month and $3,000 limit per family, with a second three-month/$3,000 extension available.)

How does Friends decide what to give? A two-person team is sent out to assess each family's need. After a discussion with three board members, a letter is sent to the family outlining the assistance to be provided. Everything is kept strictly confidential.

Larchmont borders two less affluent towns, so I asked why the Friends didn't offer aid to these neighbors. "We are not trying to be elitist," said Kathy. "But we can't solve everyone's problems. If we tried, we would be overwhelmed and drown. We are often helping five families at a time, and you run through volunteers pretty quickly sending three big meals a week to each family.

"We are just a group of neighbors and volunteers. But, the board recently voted to help two families a year with no significant ties to Larchmont, and we hope that our group will inspire similar efforts in other towns." They have recently written a pamphlet describing their organization for others who want to do so.

I asked what the hardworking volunteers received in return for all their giving. "Emotional and financial support," Mary said. "People who are givers get burned out when they try to help a family alone." Kathy mentioned that volunteers also know they are setting a good example for their children, and often have their kids help cook and deliver the meals. She smiled as she said, "Our children are very proud of us. My son John had to write a paper for school on someone he admires and he wrote it on me." That seemed to be the greatest gift this giver could think of receiving.

Bringing It Home

The ability to give consciously—giving with a clear eye as to whether the gift will help the person in need, not just assuage guilt, cover up conflict, or enable bad behavior—is a distinguishing characteristic of good mothers.

Most mothers give love, help, and support because they naturally care, and it feels good to be a helpful person. Good moms are careful not to give so excessively that they make their children overly demanding. And they don't give so much that they turn themselves into martyrs or doormats.

Likewise, when giving outside the home, they give as long as it feels good to do so. When it stops feeling good, they know they have given too much or in the wrong way. Too much giving, like too little, is toxic to the self and others.

It takes effort and awareness to find the right point on the long continuum between selfish and self-deprivation. However, finding that right balance of self-interest and generosity leaves a person feeling energetic, healthy, and effective.

If we all give what we can, we will make the world a better place:

• Not everyone can start an organization to help the sick or needy. But no matter who we are, we can all give a little. Some people can just give a few cans of food to a food pantry. Some volunteers only give a few hours a month. Others start a soup kitchen or a Friends of the Family in their town. At least put a "charity jar" in the kitchen so you and your children can put a small amount of money in on a regular basis—especially when you have given yourselves a treat. Then decide as a family where you want to give it.

• Very few people would feel comfortable giving a kidney, but there is also a pressing need for things we can all give with relative ease: blood, platelets, bone marrow, or stem cells. Know that when you give something as small as a pint of blood, or a little bone marrow, you may save someone's life.

• Food pantries and charities (except blood banks) are usually flooded with donations at Christmas and holidays. Don't stop giving then, but remember them in the slow summer months, too.

chapter four

EMOTIONAL: THE POWER OF HEARTFELT FEELINGS

"The prospect of taking the witness stand to testify frightened her.
She feared that she would lose control, break down,
cry uncontrollably."
—A Civil Action, **describing the concerns of a mother**
whose child contracted cancer from drinking
water polluted by toxic industrial waste.

Many boys grow up believing it is unmanly to show emotions, but girls are not so repressed. Consequently, most mothers hug, cry, and worry more openly than their mates.

At home, children see their mothers' freely displayed emotions as tangible proof of love. That's a big reason why mothers usually have closer relationships with their children than fathers. In the workplace, however, women have long been criticized for being too emotional. Until recently the rule of thumb was: for credibility, "act like a man" and don't let your emotions show in public.

Lately, mothers are coming out of the emotional closet. By showing how deeply they care about things outside the home, they are flexing their Mother Power muscles, because emotions, if used properly, carry enormous clout.

For example, the mother in the quote above, was embarrassed by the possibility of breaking down on the witness stand and crying when she talked about her child's death. She thought being emotional was inappropriate and would decrease her effectiveness. But the lawyers considered her one of their strongest witnesses because of the depth of her pain. After all, what jury would not be swayed by the honest tears of a grieving mother?

More and more mothers are learning to use—not hide—their strong emotions, because strong emotions are powerful. While it takes courage for grieving mothers to go public with their feelings, it takes an equal but different kind of courage for professional women to break the masculine code of conduct against displays of emotion. However, as more mothers join the professions, the restrictions against emotions are breaking down.

Sometimes it is hard to remember how rare it was to find female professionals before the 1970s. But it wasn't until the '70s that large numbers of young women started getting professional training. By the 1980s, it was no longer unusual to find female journalists, ministers, doctors, lawyers, and executives. As they became more secure, their masculine business suits with bow ties gave way to more feminine dressing. Then, as they stayed on the job after having babies, a greater revolution took place: professional women became secure enough to display maternal emotions and Mother Power on the job.

In this chapter, you will meet Shannon Carter, a successful entrepreneur in Cincinnati. At first, when she tried to persuade the male power elite to help her start a non-profit venture, they were dismayed by her fun-loving, affectionate manner. Rather than change her style, (which she credits for her success) she changed their attitudes. Her project, which helps impoverished schools, has become a national model.

Recently *TV Guide* ran an article about how women journalists are taking over the airwaves. They are getting both respect and high ratings because the public responds to their professional yet maternal, emotional approach. We will also look at some good examples of Mother Power on television.

Similarly, studies show that patients prefer female physicians because they behave in a more caring manner. As an example of what mothers are bringing to that profession, there is a story about a physician who is not only helping hundreds of families in Boston, but who has become a national advocate for children's nutrition. She credits her success to feeling maternal and angry when she treated malnourished kids—and then not being afraid to speak out about her feelings.

Doing Well, Then Doing Good

While Shannon Carter is a very emotional woman, she, like many high-achieving men, says, "I'm competitive, I'm organized, and I've got a good head for business." Her maternal approach becomes much more evident when she says that good business practices also involve giving and getting love, having fun, and being passionate about what you do. After building two successful businesses, she developed a non-profit, Crayons to Computers, which provides free school supplies to teachers in poor school districts. Through the power of heartfelt feelings, she convinced Cincinnati business leaders to give Crayons to Computers the support it needs.

When Shannon was at Wheaton College, she says, "I would go into Boston to the Pappagallo shop because I loved the shoes there. I bought them in every color." After graduation in 1972, she went back home to Cincinnati and decided to open a Pappagallo store there. "My father said, 'No way I sent you to college to sell shoes,'" she recalls, "but I had a passion for shoes and was determined to make it work." She borrowed money, bought an old Victorian house for the shop, and fixed it up on a shoestring budget. Within five years she was earning over $100,000.

Shannon used maternal skills to build her business, making it feel like a home to employees and customers. As she says, "Employees and people who came to buy were part of a family I created in the store. Most of the kids I hired were sixteen and on minimum wage, because that's all I could afford in the beginning. I was friendly and loving to them, and that made them loyal to me. My customers had true loyalty because they loved the product, but also because I made it fun for them to shop. I decorated the store in a Victorian manner and had lots of antiques around. The displays were user-friendly and everyone wanted to buy the display pieces. I did all the advertising by hand. It had a cutesy look—hand drawn and personal—a different look from other retail operations."

By 1985, ten years after she began, she had two stores, twenty-seven employees, and sales of over $3 million a year—but success was taking too much of a toll. She worked all week and "Sundays I worked on inventory and payroll. I had a second husband and a second baby and I didn't want to lose a second husband over this. I also had some employees with sticky fingers who ripped us off, and that took the fun out of it for me."

Shannon sold her business. Then she helped a friend open an antiques store and worked there part-time. She also organized and ran an antique festival that benefited the local children's hospital.

By the mid-90s she was bored. "The antique shop was slow compared to Pappagallo. My kids were in college and prep school, so I applied to Leadership Cincinnati, a program run by the Cincinnati Chamber of Commerce. It tries to identify potential leaders and programs that can help Cincinnati."

Business leaders from all over the city compete to get into Leadership Cincinnati, because of the prestige of being chosen and the networking opportunities. It is a year-long program where every month a different civic area is studied: government, the economy, social service, the arts, education, and health. The forty-eight participants then devise three ideas to improve Cincinnati and form teams to implement them.

Shannon first applied to the program calling herself an entrepreneur, but was turned down. The next year she applied calling herself a volunteer, and because the program looks for some diversity, she was accepted. She recalls, "All the other people were high-powered executives and I felt a little insecure."

When the group began seeking civic improvement projects, she recalls, "Someone had heard of a free store for teachers near Richmond, Virginia, called Crayons to Computers. I wasn't education-oriented, but the store aspect interested me. I had free time on my hands, so I flew down to see what it was like.

"Teachers spend a lot of their own money on school supplies—especially in poor school districts where families can't afford to buy them for their kids. On the other hand, businesses routinely give away or throw away a lot of stuff that is surplus or outdated or slightly damaged. A grandmother named Sally Keeler in Chesterfield Country, Virginia, found space in a warehouse and got companies to donate surplus stuff. Teachers who worked in the county could come and get it for free.

"I went down and saw the operation. It wasn't rolled out the way I would roll it out, but the concept was right. I came back and told my group, 'We're really going to make this work!'"

"The director of the Free Store, a food bank in Cincinnati, offered me thirty-five hundred square feet of their warehouse. Each member of my Leadership Cincinnati group was going to kick in some money and get the corporations they worked for to do the same—this is how we planned to renovate the space. But first, the board of the Free Store held a meeting with me and my board. The recently retired president of Krogers, Dick Bere, who volunteered as Operations Manager at the

Free Store, began bulleting me with questions. At the end, one of the guys on the board of the Free Store wrote us a check for $25,000. I burst into tears and said, 'We're pregnant! We're going to have a baby!' And the rest of my board said, 'Oh shit, Shannon. What are you doing?'

"I'm more emotional than the rest of them because they are all men. I was feeling good, but they were all acting so important. I'm big on hugs and big on emotion and all of them were just dead-center."

Shannon was feeling particularly emotional about Crayons to Computers because she had only recently become aware of how desperately it was needed. She had grown up in a wealthy family and had never before been confronted by raw poverty.

"I was naive and still in my Pappagallo phase when I visited a school as part of our Leadership Cincinnati program. A teacher was selling pencils to her students because they came to school without them. It was February and some of the kids didn't have coats. One boy took off his socks and put them over his hands when he went out to play because he didn't have mittens. I saw poverty for the first time—kids who couldn't afford pencils and coats. This was happening in my own backyard, when my kids were privileged enough to go to boarding school.

"My children had their own laptops in ninth grade, while these schools didn't have computers or the wiring or technical support for them. It's just terrible what's out there. I realized I couldn't change the world, but I wanted to do something to ameliorate the situation.

"The Kroger guy was watching over my shoulder. I said, 'We're going to start by painting the pipes in the warehouse green and purple and red.' He said, 'What? Nobody paints pipes in a warehouse!'" But Shannon wanted the space to look cheerful and welcoming.

"He said, 'I know a Kroger store that's closing down. I'll get you the shelves, but they need to be power-washed.' He was surprised when I rolled up my sleeves, and we power-washed them together. That was the beginning of our friendship. Now he is one of my best friends. He even signed on for color on the pipes and elsewhere."

As Shannon says, Crayons to Computers "looks like a cross between a Staples and a Pappagallo shop. It's very user-friendly and cozy—I made a warehouse cozy!—it's very cute and looks like a real store. The only difference is that here we give everything away.

"Before we opened our doors in February, 1997, we wrote fifteen hundred letters to the Chairmen of companies in the area. We got the lists from the Chamber of Commerce. We told them what we needed and that they would get a tax write-off. My buddy at the *Cincinnati Inquirer* (the local paper) planted a killer article about us and the television station ran stories, too.

"Corporations love the program because it cuts waste and they get a tax deduction for stuff they would throw away. The community loves it because it's great recycling of stuff that would otherwise go into landfills. I love it because it makes teachers and kids happy.

"In our donor packet, we have a teacher wish list: things like crayons, paper, glue. [Cash donations are used to buy these basic supplies, if necessary.] But we take everything." For example, one company with the licensing rights to Godzilla was left with 3.5 million dollars worth of unsalable party bags, wrapping paper, stickers, and merchandise when the movie bombed. They called Shannon and asked if she could take eight truckloads. She said, "Sure!"

Teachers use Godzilla for incentive prizes. Shannon barters it with other free stores around the country. For example, she trades it with, "a buddy in Orlando who has too much Disney stuff and one in Maine where we get lots of felt.

"A company gave us 250,000 ice cream containers when they changed their design. They became Easter baskets, Valentine banks, Mother's Day planters, and one teacher used them for barf buckets."

Another company that tried unsuccessfully to sell gift boxes of women's sanitary supplies over the Internet called and asked her to take seven truck loads of gift boxes, menstrual pads, and tampons. "When I agreed to take them, the administrator said, 'I love you! It would cost $250 a dumpster to send them to the landfill.' I sent out an email to health teachers and I can trade some to other places.

"Every day when the trucks show up it's like pot luck Christmas," Shannon says. "We have a paid staff of four and a half, plus hundreds of volunteers who sort the stuff and run the store. We give away $25,000 worth of stuff every day to 125 'shoppers.'

"We are open to teachers from 130 eligible schools (based on the percent of kids in free lunch programs.) They get to shop for free. Then we have teachers in another 250 schools where there are pockets of poverty. They can volunteer for three hours and then run around with a shopping cart and fill it up. All teachers write down what they take and their 'homework' is to have the children write thank-you notes to donors.

"By five every evening the store is a wreck, and we have to put it back together by two the next day. Every morning volunteers come in to do this. We give them coffee and donuts. We turn up the music and everyone wears their Crayons to Computers tee shirts and aprons. We have fun."

Shannon has gotten her once-stuffy board of business executives to have fun, too. "One Christmas soon after we opened," she says, "I thought, 'Let's shake up the board meeting.' So, I brought in a group of little kids who sang *Jesus Loves Me*. Tears were running down my eyes, but the Board were all sitting there dumb-faced. I thought, 'Come on guys, melt your hearts, this is the cutest thing I have ever seen.'

"The next board meeting I wrapped up little presents and put them in front of everyone with the board minutes. The presents were jock straps. Everyone was all embarrassed, but I said, 'This was one of our donations this week. We got one thousand of them. Gym teachers can take them for kids whose parents can't afford to buy them.' Finally they realized I am a no-nonsense person, and we can have a lot of fun."

Among the most unexpected donors to the program are prisoners. Shannon worked with the Ohio Department of Rehabilitation and Correction to set up Crafts with Conviction (her sense of fun again), which is now in twenty-three prisons. Male and female prisoners donate their time to make puppets and book bags out of her felt, flash cards and maps out of her posterboard, and a variety of other gifts and supplies. Prisoners gave a total of five hundred thousand hours from 1998 to 2001 and gained self-esteem, knowing they are helping poor children. For example, a man who murdered his wife has become their most productive craftsperson, supervising a group of men sewing for him. Shannon says, "He's become a very worthwhile human being, even though he's behind bars."

While the original Crayons to Computers in Virginia foundered after Sally Keeler moved away, Shannon's version has become a national model. Twenty-one other communities have replicated her program. Because Shannon believes most communities could use Crayons to Computers, she wrote a free how-to book for people who want to make it happen in their city.

While it is difficult work, Shannon says that, "Crayons to Computers is a feel-good program all around. My kids tease me, saying that I found Jesus in a warehouse. I didn't really find religion, but I found something. I'm a nicer person as a result of the program. I'm more open and giving and loving."

Caring about What You Report

By being more open about their feelings, the following women found, if not greater happiness like Shannon, at least greater success.

When *TV Guide* ran an article about news shows entitled, "How Women Took Over," they first cited Katie Couric's interview with

Michael Shoels, the day after his son was killed at the Columbine High School massacre. The article notes that she "never loses sight of the difficult questions," but "as he [Michael Shoels] struggles to control his grief, Couric does something no male reporter or anchor would ever do: she reaches over and holds Shoels's hand."

According to *TV Guide*, this "is part of a new style of reporting that has developed as women influence what we see on the news." But Couric's style is more than just feminine. As she says, "There is something about a maternal, comforting presence that is helpful."

Like all good mothers, her approach combines strength with kindness. "This is not to imply that women broadcast journalists are approaching their stories with handkerchiefs in hand," says the article, "Rather, it's a sense of compassion mixed with what Couric describes as *chutzpah* [a Yiddish word for nervy courage]."

That *chutzpah* was never more in evidence than when, during the 1996 presidential campaign, she nailed Bob Dole about the connection between his assertion that nicotine was not addictive and the large political contributions he was receiving from tobacco companies. Perhaps she was particularly emotional about carcinogens because her husband had colon cancer (the cause of his death in 1998, leaving her with two young daughters). Whether or not that influenced her line of questioning, she acted like a hard-hitting journalist, revealing Dole's dark side.

Her protective caring about her daughters has spread to children in general, inspiring her to coauthor several child-rearing books: *Raising Preschoolers: Parenting for Today*, and *Childhood Revealed: Art Expressing Pain, Discovery, and Hope*. Katie's recent children's book, *The Brand New Kid*, encourages youngsters to be nice to each other. She hopes if children are taught to be kinder to one another, this will reduce alienation and school violence, and she will never have to report on another school massacre like Columbine.

Couric's evolving combination of hard-hitting journalism and motherly concern helped make the *Today* show number one in morning ratings. This winning Mother Power combination has also made Barbara Walters such a long-lasting star, propelled Rosie O'Donnell's career, and is credited with changing the evening news programming, too.

Barbara Walters, one of the first female television journalists, has had enormous sticking power, in part because she comes up with news scoops during exclusive celebrity interviews. Again, according to *TV Guide*, media-shy celebrities trust her because of her "blend of maternalism and gentle persuasion."

Maternal talk show hosts like Rosie O'Donnell and Oprah Winfrey (not a mother, but maternal none the less) have shown that you don't have to be sleazy to be popular on daytime TV. Their uplifting, intelligent, and positive interviews are in stark contrast with many of their rivals, as my daughter and I found out a few years ago when we were home sick for a week together. We watched a lot of daytime shows, and most presented a view of life in America that was repulsive: it appeared that everyone on these shows was cheating on their mate, betraying their friends, and having babies that weren't properly cared for. Even worse, these shows implied that such behavior was, if not admirable, at least the norm. Rosie and Oprah's success is not based on such cynical, sleazy sensationalism.

Rosie says that having children changed her life. ("When my son Parker arrived, it was like the lights were turned on in my life.") That's no surprise to her millions of fans. So much of her show, from her famous Tom Selleck anti-NRA interview to her theater reviews ("As a parent and a mom and someone who loves theater, this is one show that should survive...") is fueled by her love of her children.

Having become a parent by adoption, she is very emotional about the subject. So much so, that, as a birthday present in March 2000,

Warner Brothers Television allowed her to forgo her normal celebrity focus for one show, and feature adoption instead. Her audience responded so well that she followed up several months later with a show about foster kids.

As I am writing this, Rosie is not only a single mother of three adopted kids, but also a foster mother. Plus she has opened an adoption agency in New Jersey (Rosie Adoptions) and says she will give up her television career to concentrate on that cause.

"When I have a baby who's hard to place and I find a family that's overjoyed with the child, it's definitely more fulfilling [than the talk show]" she says. Until she leaves her show, her fans will continue to love her not just because she interviews celebrities, but because she cares about more than just their glamour.

Women have long dominated daytime TV, so it is no surprise that Mother Power now influences daytime programming. But it took more than caring and *chutzpah* to make Mother Power part of the evening network news. Initially, the door was opened by the 1964 Civil Rights Act and a 1971 Federal Communications Commission ruling mandating equal employment for women. Then, the real breakthrough came in 1985 when women journalists complained to ABC about the lack of females on the evening news.

As women newscasters and reporters appeared more frequently, and as women rose to power in news management positions and aged into motherhood, they became more comfortable acting naturally and letting their emotional, motherly interests show. They began insisting that stories of concern to mothers be included in news programs. So now Mommy Issues such as child care, health, education, and the morality of business and politics now are being routinely scheduled as hard news these days, not just because they reflect the lives of female reporters and executives who fight for them, but also because women make up 60 percent of the network news viewing audience.

The TV battle is far from won. There is too much sleazy TV in every time zone, and Mother Power needs to clean it up. While we're at it, let's apply a little Mother Power to prime time, which, according to a recent article in *Working Mother* magazine, "doesn't get it when it comes to portraying real-life women." The homemakers are ditzy and the working mothers are "often job-obsessed, kid-neglecting harridans"...because..."people who create television shows are not living what they write," concludes the article. We've come a long way baby, and as soon as we get some more Mother Power writers, they will also.

Hunger in the Land of Plenty

Just as female newscasters are letting their emotions show, so female physicians are changing the stereotype of the strong, silent doctor. Dr. Deborah Frank is strong, but not silent. She openly expresses her heartfelt emotions in an attempt to help her young patients.

In the early 1980s, Deborah Frank's career path was leading to a lucrative private practice or a comfortable academic position. She was a young doctor with impeccable credentials: Harvard Medical School and work with the famous Dr. T. Berry Brazelton. "I was always interested in child development," she says, "and I thought I would spend my life talking to people about their amazing babies." Instead, she says she ended up talking about "deprivation, deprivation, deprivation."

Her life took that dramatic turn when she started wondering why so many of the inner city children she saw weren't reaching their intellectual potential. "It hit me like a blaze of light," she says, "It was malnutrition! Then I got really angry because kids were doing really lousy because they had been cut off of food stamps or WIC [Women, Infants, and Children's Supplemental Nutrition program]."

"I called a colleague at the Harvard School of Public Health and asked, 'Who should I contact about this?' He said to call a woman at the Food Research Action group who asked, 'Would you talk to a reporter?' Being young and naive, I said, 'Sure.' So, the next thing you know an Associated Press reporter was on my doorstep, and headlines reported, 'Boston Doctor Says Children are Starving.'

"I got into a fair amount of hot water with my hospital administration because the Federal Government was furious. But a very enlightened Massachusetts State Senator, Chet Atkins, held hearings and funded a study which showed that 10 percent of low income kids under five showed evidence of malnutrition." So, he funded a network of Failure to Thrive clinics in the state, and Deborah founded one of those clinics at Boston Medical Center in 1984. She never stopped being angry, because, despite such clinics, the problem has gotten worse.

Looking at Deborah, smiling kindly at one of her young patients, you would never know that she is such an angry woman. And she is careful never to direct that anger against her patients or her staff, because "I get genuine pleasure out of the families and the kids at the clinic. Even though the system is impossible, when an individual kid or mother or father perks up, that's great. I also like mentoring young doctors and bringing them along, knowing the torch will be passed and they will take it."

In a way, Deborah is glad to be angry. "If I wasn't so angry," she explains, "I would be despairing. It's the anger that gives me the drive...makes this scruffy little doctor from an inner city hospital in downtown Boston take on the Federal Government."

Most people believe the recent booming economy helped the poor, and that welfare reform made families more self-sufficient. Deborah and her colleagues know the opposite is true: the bottom 25 percent of the population is worse off today than it was twenty years ago, because of reductions in welfare and food stamps, combined with the rising cost of housing and fuel. In the last two years, her clinic has had a staggering 30 percent increase in the number of malnourished kids referred.

This is happening all over America, not just in Boston. "Today," she says, "One in four American children under the age of five can't be sure of adequate food everyday. Being a mother, it makes me even more upset to see these hungry kids."

Here's the typical child she sees: "He is an eighteen month old, a family cap child, which means he was born to a woman on welfare who got no benefits for him. When her oldest kid turned four, she had to go to work. She probably works evenings, and he is with some elderly, disabled relative or with the father who thinks it's not his job to feed children.

"The mother works in a hotel or fast food joint, but not full-time, so she doesn't get benefits. When the hotel is full, she works ten days in a row without a break, but when the hotel is empty, she doesn't work. She can't get food stamps when she needs them, because food stamps are predicated on your income last month, and last month she worked ten days and doesn't qualify.

"The child is not just malnourished, he also has some associated problem—food allergies, asthma, or developmental delay. I am telling the mother to take the child to the eye doctor, but she can't get off work to take him. She is a bit depressed and the older kid is probably acting up in school and that is worrying her, too. In addition, maybe her brother or uncle gets shot, and the whole family goes into a grief reaction, so things fall apart even more."

Deborah explains that impoverished mothers like that "have to make constant trade-offs: do I pay the bus fare to go to the doctor, or buy a quart of milk?" Deborah's "Heat or Eat" study showed that the number of underweight babies seen in emergency rooms increases after the coldest months in the winter, because moms have to decide whether to keep their kids warm or well fed. "So, whatever decision these women make, they are shorting their children someplace else and being 'bad mothers,'" she says.

"We see a very ethnically mixed group: Vietnamese, every kind of Latino and Central American, African-American, African-Caribbean, Irish, Italian, and refugee families from Africa and the near East. What the kid eats depends on what culture they are from, but they are all very proud of the fact that they don't let their children feel hunger. They fill their children up with very cheap, very dense, low-nutrient food. The classic is soda pop and french fries. If you are eighteen months old and you have your stomach full of McDonald's french fries, you don't feel hungry at all. You will go to sleep. But you don't have any nutrients.

"The kids I see at my Grow Clinic are only the tip of the iceberg—the ones who have been deprived so long that malnutrition has impaired their immune system and they have gotten infections. What I don't see are all the kids who are lethargic and crabby and can't remember that one plus one equals two because they are not getting enough to eat.

"I get mad at this incredibly wealthy society that lets its children be so horribly and unnecessarily deprived," she says. "On top of that when people go on and on about welfare reform, I get even angrier. I mean, one guy who was preaching fiscal responsibility, saying it was wasteful to spend money on poor kids, was lobbying like mad to get money for a new tourist center in Newport, Rhode Island where the mansions are. It's that kind of thing that sends me over the edge.

"I get mad at professionals who don't do their jobs: doctors who don't take a careful look at an inner city child, and Child Protective Services—I'm in a constant flame about them. I'm always writing furious letters to the Protective Services area director about what this kid needs and what you haven't done. But I also realize that it's an underfunded system with overwhelmed personnel, so I try very hard not to cream the individual caseworkers. This is all so unnecessary. I mean, you don't need an M.D. degree to see this is not proper care for which the Commonwealth is paying."

Deborah has learned that she must take on the government with hard statistics as well as strong words. She organized a group of colleagues who run Grow Clinics around the country, and they are collecting data nationally from pediatric clinics and emergency rooms. "The data is like, well duh, you cannot withdraw income maintenance support from families without making children hungry and increasing how sick they are. But you have to show this numerically, or no one believes you." She gives emotional but statistics-filled presentations at national conventions and in testimony before government officials. "I'm one of the doctors they wheel out to talk about childhood hunger," she says.

The question is how she fits the testimony and research into her incredibly busy schedule. In addition to raising her son with her husband, a rabbi, she sees patients, runs the clinic, trains young doctors, and also has to be a fund-raiser, because the state only funds a fraction of the services she needs to provide her patients. "I write grants because I have to pay for the doctors who work with me and my salary. The social workers and nutritionists who make home visits to families must be paid for with donated money." Those visits are key to helping families learn how to raise healthy kids, because often it is financially and logistically difficult for the families to travel to Deborah's clinic. However, the professionals who make home visits "don't fit into any medical model and no insurance will pay for it."

In the past when she would give one of her angry interviews to the press, "people would send me money," she says. "Being a well-brought up Baltimore girl, I would write them thank-you notes. I didn't realize this is called 'development' and 'building a donor base.' But now I have a wonderful group of private donors," and she can use every bit of help she can get.

Deborah's clinic is a model of how to help needy families. Not only does she provide basic medical care for children, but also the other

kinds of support poor families need. She explains, "We have five volunteers who have been with us for years and run a waiting room program for the kids. There is a lot of waiting since we are multi-
disciplinary, and patients have to see a lot of people. These volunteers
play and do crafts with the kids and chat with the moms. They model
good parenting behavior for the moms and their observations are very
helpful to us.

"Other volunteers work in our food pantry, sorting food and distributing it. We always need food, because the only time we—or any
other emergency food network—has enough is when a lot of people
give food at Thanksgiving and Christmas. Other volunteers scavenge
for clothes and toys."

Deborah realizes that few people who favor welfare reform or cutting social programs are consciously trying to hurt children.
Nonetheless, she says, children *are* being damaged because legislators
don't realize that poor families need at least the same kinds of support
as everyone else. She explains, "They have to realize that there are three
kinds of caregivers: the first kind, with adequate training, excellent
childcare, health insurance, and transportation can work in ordinary
jobs." This is what everyone—you and I and the fathers of our children—needs in order to work and raise healthy kids. So, isn't it amazing that everyone doesn't realize the poor need this too?

"The second group," Deborah continues, "can only work in supportive settings. I see a lot of moms like that. They are physically or
mentally unwell, very cognitively impaired or completely non-English
speaking. Those folk can't compete for a regular job, but could work in
a protective setting.

"With the third set of people, it takes all their skill and energy just
to care for their chronically ill children. For example, if you have a kid
with severe asthma, your child is up all night wheezing. Every time
your child is rushed to the emergency room, you get called at work and

you also have to keep all the clinic appointments, get all the medicine, and so on." Noting that it is almost impossible to hold a steady job and take proper care of an ill child, she says "we've got to make caring for the children the priority."

Deborah notes that "...asthma is extremely common and increasing in urban areas because of deteriorating living conditions: moldy houses, cockroaches and mice, bad indoor air, and toxic waste." While she worries about asthma as much as hunger she concedes, "I can only handle so many advocacy issues at once."

Deborah knows that, sadly, childhood hunger in America might not be wiped out in her lifetime. To keep from despairing, she thinks about the abolitionists she studied when she went to Quaker school in Baltimore. Many never lived to see the fruits of their labor, but they contributed to an important cause. She still remembers a quote from one of them, William Lloyd Garrison, who said, "I do not wish to think, or speak, or write with moderation....I will not equivocate—I will not excuse—I will not retreat a single inch—and I will be heard!" That inspires Deborah to use her intelligence, drive, anger, and Mother Power to make herself heard, too.

Bringing It Home

Mothers don't feel the need to be stoic and in control all the time. While we know that out-of-control emotions wreck plans and lives, we are learning that genuine emotions in moderation add credibility to a request or an argument. Just as our families are more likely to respond to expressions of honest emotional need and caring, people outside the home also tend to respond to heartfelt expressed emotion.

All around the world, effective leaders have one thing in common: whether they are male or female, whatever their cause, they convey that they truly care about what they are espousing. (Can you imagine following a leader who was dispassionate and didn't seem to care?) A mother's ability to express emotions and concern makes her persuasive, and gives her enormous leadership potential.

Every woman, not just in this chapter, but in the whole book, was spurred to success by her emotions. The same anger that makes you demand peace when your children are fighting, the same passionate concern that drives you to provide a safe, nurturing environment in your home, can be used to make our world better and more humane.

• Monitor your feelings when you watch the nightly news. Practice saying how you feel (not just what you think) about what is going on in the world. Harness your emotions by making one phone call or writing one letter to your political leaders to let them know your feelings.

• Is there a social issue or local problem that makes you angry year after year? Find out what others are trying to do about it and join the movement. It feels much better to take an active role than just stew or complain.

• Sometimes it is easier to express anger or negative emotions than positive ones. Be very generous with compliments and praise to family, friends, and strangers alike. Volunteers who are trying to improve society often get more complaints than compliments. Let them know you appreciate what they are doing. You will make their day!

chapter five

CREATIVE: USING WHAT YOU HAVE AND KNOW

"I had a hard time gaining credibility in the toy industry. For two years after I founded the company, toy buyers would say, 'Can you make it pink?' And I would say, "No, this is what girls like to play with."'
—Successful inventor/entrepreneur who designs electronic gadgets and toys with her daughter in mind

Our bodies create life itself. After that, the real creative challenge begins: coming up with effective ways to handle temper tantrums, answer children's myriad questions, and help them grow into responsible, loving, self-fulfilled adults.

Moms who value traditional roles take a creative approach to homemaking tasks like making meals and decorating the house. Meanwhile, more and more mothers are using their creative Mother Power to improve businesses, non-profit institutions, and the arts.

While every good mother is creative, many female creative artists are surprised to find that motherhood gives their careers a boost. For example, Isaac Stern said that violinist Anne-Sophie Mutter is playing with new depth since becoming a mother. And opera diva Renatta Scotto says she became a much better singer when she had children, because she didn't feel that every time she walked on stage her whole life was on the line.

With so many possible examples to choose from, I had to focus on several areas where mothers are being particularly creative these days. First, I want to explore how many successful writers are inspired by motherhood. Next you will see how one collector created an influential museum. Finally, since each working mother must create an identity for herself, and some prominent ones create new norms for their entire generation, I will profile how one First Lady—perhaps not the one you might imagine—did just that.

The Mother as Creative Writer

Society tends to treat mothers as mental lightweights, only interested in diapers, recipes, and baby food. Many women worry that they will lose their creative edge and become less serious thinkers after childbirth. For example, when author Jane Smiley was pregnant, she worried that motherhood would drain her ability to wrestle with important subjects. She wondered if she would only be able to write light family comedies like *Please Don't Eat the Daisies*.

Like many writers, Smiley had explored the subject of dysfunctional families in much of her work. For example, her first novel, *Barn Blind*, was about a mother who alienates her husband and children after one son dies.

However, after giving birth and switching roles from child to parent, she gained a whole new creative perspective on family life. Smiley found that, "Far from depriving me of thought, motherhood gave me new and startling things to think about and the motivation to do the hard work of thinking." She credits those thoughts with producing *A Thousand Acres*, a complex family saga that won a Pulitzer Prize.

While family life has always been grist for fiction writers, the everyday thoughts and feelings of mothers have rarely been respected as a proper literary subject for poets. Subjects like the humor of parenthood, a mother's connection to her little boy in blue jeans, or the death of a child's pet gerbil might be acceptable fare in a "ladies' magazine," but not the stuff of serious poetry journals. Not at least until Sharon Olds wrote about these subjects and made them so.

Sharon Olds, New York State Poet Laureate and winner of a National Book Critics Circle Award, says she became successful after she stopped trying to write like other poets and vowed to "just write my own stuff." That "stuff," according to *The New York Times*, "chronicles the daily life of a wife and mother not unlike herself....Only when she began to write about the passionate, messy experiences of childbirth, mothering, and sex, did she find her own voice."

She recently admitted in an interview that "[She has] a prejudice that narrative poetry is not as high an art as dense, mysterious, imagistic poetry." However, her skillful narrative poems about her children, her husband, and her maternal feelings not only attract scores of readers who readily identify with the subject, but literary prizes, too.

While neither a poet nor fiction writer, I found my writer's voice when I quit my job to stay home with my second child and start my private practice. Loving my children so deeply, I became upset about children who didn't have families, and families that couldn't have children. That led me to research the subject of foster care and adoption. Since building a practice is a slow process, I also had the time to pursue my lifelong ambition to write. Spare time for research and writing, plus maternal feelings, brought about a burst of creativity that lead to a number of articles in major magazines and my first book, *Successful Adoption*.

Other writers find their voice when fate does the opposite—forces them to stop being a stay-at-home mom and earn a living to support their kids. Bestseller P.D. James, for example, began writing her detective novels on a commuter train in the late 1950s. Her husband had returned from World War II so disturbed that he had to be put in an institution. She took bureaucratic jobs to support her kids. Stressed and needing a creative outlet, she began writing on her train ride to and from the office.

Similar circumstances in the mid 1970s forced Penelope Fitzgerald, heralded by *The New York Times* as one of England's finest authors, to begin her writing career. Her husband was dying of cancer. She began writing a novel as a way to entertain him—and sent the manuscript off to a publisher because she needed money to support her family.

But my favorite Mother Power writing story involves a spellbinding South African author, Sindewe Magona. Sindewe grew up penniless and disenfranchised in South Africa under apartheid. When she was twenty-three, her husband left her with three small children to support. Shortly thereafter, on one of the worst nights of her life, she found herself responsible for her children as well as several of her younger siblings. There was no food in her home and no money to buy any.

If being creative means coming up with ingenious solutions, using what you have and know, what do you do if, like Sindewe, you have nothing? Here's how she calmed the children and figured her way out of the crisis.

Putting a pot of water on the stove, she reassured the children that she would make soup. Throughout the evening she kept lifting the pot cover and saying the soup wasn't ready yet, as they drifted off to sleep.

Early the next morning, she went to the butcher and bought meat on credit—not to eat, but to cook and sell on the street. By becoming a sidewalk vendor, she earned enough money to buy more meat to sell and to feed her family.

Over the years, she found other creative ways to not only survive, but improve her situation. She furthered her education, and eventually joined the United Nations' public relations staff.

While still a young mother, she imagined that far in the future, her great-grandchildren would need to know what life was like in tribal South Africa, a supportive, communal existence that was all but destroyed under apartheid. So, in the 1990s, after work each night while her children cleaned up the dinner dishes, she wrote about her life and the history of her people for her imagined descendents.

As she writes on the first page of her book *To My Children's Children*, "Ours is an oral tradition. I would like you to hear from my own lips what it was like living in the 1940s onwards. What it was like in the times of your great-grandmother, me. However, my people no longer live long lives. Generations no longer set eyes on each other. Therefore, I fear I may not live long enough to do my duty to you, to let you know who you are and whence you are. So, I will keep, for you, my words in this manner."

This and the second volume of her autobiography, *Forced to Grow*, were inspired by her creative need to give something to her descendants. In the process, she gives inspiration to everyone, especially to other mothers oppressed by poverty and misfortune.

Creating a Collection, a Museum, and New Respect for Women Artists

The next woman's story is quite different. She made creative use of her wealth and high-powered connections.

Wilhelmina Cole Holladay, founder of the National Museum of Women in the Arts, is largely responsible for the growing respect for female artists. In awe of the creative spirit, she says, "If God speaks through humans, he does it through the creative instinct. Anytime someone goes beyond the learned or known and creates something new—whether it is poetry, art, or a child—it's awesome; it's God-like."

The museum she created evokes that sense of awe from the first moment a visitor walks into its huge, elegant entrance hall. The collection displayed inside proves that women have been creating beautiful, important work for centuries. But personally, I think her greatest creative achievement is the way she built a broad, powerful base of support for the Museum, so the art establishment had to acknowledge what they had overlooked in the past: the enormous creativity of women.

Wilhelmina Cole Holladay didn't start out with the idea of teaching the art establishment a thing or two. Far from it. When she and her husband, the head of the conglomerate Holladay Corporation, started buying art, she says, "We were just buying a few paintings for our house, and we tried to find material on a woman artist we had seen in Europe. We discovered that there was no material—none—on women in the leading art text in this country, *Jansen's History of Art*, which was used in practically every college and university." This omission sparked their interest.

The Holladays began to collect work by women artists. They also hired art historians to help them locate obscure and scholarly texts that contained information about women artists.

By 1980, the collection had grown to include five hundred works of art by women and a large research library. Nancy Hanks, the first head of the National Endowment of the Arts and a friend of Holladay, suggested that it become the seed from which a national museum might grow. So, they put together a committee of well-connected people to research the idea. They also contacted the Junior League, which started a project to identify works by women in private and public collections throughout the country, as well as train docents to lead tours of the collection in the Holladay's home. Inspired by the project, one of the docents offered to give two million dollars toward finding an appropriate building to turn the collection into a national museum. With this backing, Wilhelmina Cole Holladay was off and running, determined to build as broad a base of support as possible.

"I deliberately did not want to make this a one-person show, or have the museum named after us," she says. "I knew the more people

CREATIVE

involved, the more strength it would have. Without the help of thousands of people, corporations, and foundations, the museum wouldn't
be there."

True. But without Holladay's vast Rolodex of contacts—and the
creative ways she made people enthusiastic about the project—the
museum would probably have remained a small project.

"Mike Ainsley, who was the head of the National Trust for Historic
Preservation, was on our committee and found us a building," she says.
It had a majestic exterior and was just a few blocks away from the
White House, "but the first floor had been turned into a cinema that
functioned as a home for derelicts," she recalls. "It was in a dreadful
state of repair. You cannot imagine how bad it was—there were rats as
big as cats running around there, and the neighborhood was so seedy
we got the building for five million dollars.

"We were able to raise the money in various ways. We said anyone
who gives us five thousand dollars will have their names etched in glass
in the foyer forever. We built a constituency through that and raised
several million dollars."

Then Mrs. Holladay went calling on corporations—usually the
head of the art department and the head of the charitable giving. Often
they started with just the five thousand dollars necessary to get their
name in the foyer, but through her enthusiasm for the project, plus her
willingness to keep donors informed about all the progress the museum
was making, major gifts came rolling in when she asked for more.

"American Standard gave us the plumbing. AT&T gave the money
for our library, and Dupont gave us the carpeting," she says. "I went
around and stewed and fretted until they gave us things. Our greatest
corporate gift came from Martin Marietta, which gave a million and a
half dollars for our Great Hall."

The museum building was bought in 1983 and opened in 1987.
The two opening celebrations illustrate the creative ways Holladay

found to build support and gain credibility for women artists. The first opening exhibit, American female artists from 1850–1950, was drawn from collections around the country and underwritten for about half a million dollars by United Technology. (Holladay had invited the head of the arts for United Technology for tea at her home and a private tour of her collection.) When that exhibit went on the road to museums in San Diego, Milwaukee, and Hartford, a second celebration, underwritten by Phillip Morris, unveiled the permanent collection—the five hundred works given by the Holladays.

There was also a third, equally important celebration. "The year we opened," recalls Holladay, "Abrams [the publisher of *Jansen's History of Art*] called and said, 'Get up here and help us celebrate—we're putting women in the book.'"

In the beginning, while there were many supporters (the museum is one of the ten largest in the world in terms of membership) there were also many detractors. As Holladay says, "On one hand, the old dowagers said, 'This is some feminist thing,' and the feminists were calling us elitists. But I smiled sweetly and we did our thing and they have all come around. We have members from the most strident feminists to the most conservative grand dames. Art has unified them all, and I am so thrilled about that."

Almost three thousand works of art have been given to the museum, and it has gained support and influence in the art world. Now it is common for the most prestigious museums to hold retrospectives of women artists, and it would be embarrassing not to have women featured in collections.

Why was this not always the case? Why did *Jansen's* not mention women artists? Why did major museums have so few female artists in their collections? Holladay says, "I don't think anyone deliberately did this. My theory is that women lead fairly protected lives and the men who were writing about art went out and drank with the male artists and wrote about what they knew. If you are left out of the popular writing, you are soon forgotten.

"When it came to shows, museum directors wanted to show what was going to be popular. No one makes a great effort to show an unknown artist. And they had a long line of artists we were all dying to see: Cézanne, Degas, Matisse. But they are showing women now!"

While Holladay mothered her collection, the museum, and the reputation of women artists, she is especially proud of the way the museum reaches out to local children. As she says, "Most of the children in the public schools here in the district are underprivileged, and if we can give them an alternative to the streets and drugs, that's pretty maternal.

"Our library has a great emphasis on children. The director spent three years reading children's' books from all over the world and picked out any book where the little girl was the heroine.

"She contacted the artists who did the illustrations for the books, borrowed the originals, and did an art exhibition. We had all the books available in the library. And then we invited every second grader in Washington and brought them in class by class and read them stories from the books. We said, 'If you come in on any Sunday with your parents to read to you, the books will be out on the tables.'

"I went in the first Sunday, and there were six black families reading to their children. One little girl looked up and said to me, 'I brought my mother to our museum.' At that age, children begin to identify, and then if you can get them to love it, they will come to the museums and not be afraid."

Every year there are about eighty to ninety programs for children at the museum. Since there is no entrance fee, both children and adults know they can come as often as they want. (The museum runs in the black thanks to donations, membership fees, rental fees for private events, and a popular gift shop.) Furthermore, Holladay found a way to reach out to children all over the country. She says, "I discovered that the Girl Scouts were using Michaelangelo to teach about art. So, instead, we put together material for them and a beautiful book that teaches the terminology of art, shows them what to look for when they go to a museum, and tries to get them excited. UPS saw the book and wanted to reach rural children through it. So, we made the cover generic for them. This book has reached fifty thousand girls so far, but we will reach many, many more."

Wilhelmina Cole Holladay created a museum that provides artistic inspiration and role models for girls. The woman featured next, created a role model for all working parents—and a new way to behave as a First Lady.

First Lady, First Mother, and Fine Human Being

In the last thirty years, as more and more women entered the workforce and, even more revolutionary, stayed in the workforce after giving birth, each had to create her own new identity as a working mother. Very few of us had role models to show the way.

As a child I hardly knew any female professionals—only a smattering of teachers, librarians, and nurses. Few of them were mothers. In fact, my mother and her friends felt sorry for any woman who "had to work." So, I, like most of the other women in the last third of the twentieth century, had to create my own image of mother-on-the-job and my own way of balancing work and family.

Most of us did this in the privacy of our own lives. Our successes and failures were only known to—and only criticized by—our friends and family. We shared tips with other friends on how to pull off this balancing act, and devoured stories about how other women did it. By the year 2000, while each individual mother was still engaged in her own personal struggle to creatively balance work and family, it seemed that there were very few barriers left to be broken.

Then, in the first months of the twenty-first century, one mother broke new ground and became a very public role model. She created the role of working First Lady and new mother. She did this so well, using her pregnancy to further the rights of all mothers and fathers, that she stifled some of her harshest critics, while providing an inspiration for generations of mothers to come. She is Cherie Booth, wife of British Prime Minister Tony Blair.

When her husband became Prime Minister in 1997, Cherie Booth was a respected lawyer specializing in human rights and labor issues. She was also the mother of Blair's three children. Instead of quitting her job the way most First Ladies around the world have done, Cherie Booth made news by continuing to be a loving wife and mother, and professional in her own right. Not surprisingly, the British press roasted her for it.

In my office, I frequently hear how working mothers are hurt by criticism. I can imagine how difficult it would be having to withstand the barrage of public and very personal criticism she faced. As one reporter in London wrote, "For years, they criticized her hair, her figure, the cases she took on in court, the fact that she didn't curtsey to the Queen when she met her, the dowdiness of her clothes, and then, once she smartened up in deference to their criticisms, the excessive amount of money she spent on her clothes. But throughout all the attacks Cherie remained impressively good-humored and calm, and the mud never had a chance to stick."

The mud also had a hard time sticking because Cherie Booth refused to give interviews. She never expressed herself on policy or defended herself from attack. She simply continued to pursue her work, raise her children, and love her husband.

Then, at forty-five, she became pregnant with her fourth child and broke her self-imposed silence to promote a cause dear to her heart: paternity leave. In 1998, the European Union decreed that fathers had the right to take a two-week leave after the birth of a child. Yet only 2 percent of fathers had done so. European dads needed a strong role model to show them that "real men" take time off to care for their babies. Cherie wanted Tony to be that role model.

She told the press, "It is time that men start to challenge the assumption that the nurturing of children has nothing to do with them. Our children need their male role models as well as female ones." With that, public attention focused on Tony Blair to see whether or not he would take paternity leave.

In the end, he did not take full-time off. After all, he had to run the country. But, he quite publicly worked part-time after the birth of his child and shouldered responsibility for taking care of Cherie, the baby, and his other three children, too.

Several months later, Cherie Booth was in New York at a forum on human rights law. She was not only a featured speaker, but also a caring mother, slipping out of the conference periodically to breast-feed her baby. The conservative press, which had temporarily loved her when she was pregnant, was back to comparing her to Lady Macbeth.

Who knows if such criticism hurts her? She is back to her old habit of not speaking publicly about any subject, including her own bad press. As usual, however, while being a very private person, she is also a very creative role model for employed moms.

Bringing It Home

Writing teachers always advise students to "write about what you know." In other words, you will be most creative, credible, and successful if you mine your own experiences, feelings, and desires. Just as newswomen in the previous chapter became more successful when they stopped trying to act like men and let their maternal emotions come through, so it is with women in this chapter. They found success in diverse areas by letting their maternal feelings, desires, and passions guide their creative efforts. Each battled enormous odds, yet persevered by using what they had and knew as mothers.

You probably use your creativity every day. When you find a way to calm a crying child, when you make Halloween costumes, when you cook a delicious soup using leftovers, you are being creative. After all, creativity is simply being flexible enough to figure out how to solve a problem or achieve a goal. It is simply thinking, "How can I?" rather than "I can't."

Whether you have a fortune like Wilhelmina Cole Holladay or absolutely nothing like Sindewe Magona, the greatest thing blocking your creativity is probably self-doubt and pessimism. But undoubtedly you have an optimistic side, too. After all, no one deliberately brings a child into this world unless they have an optimistic spirit.

If your optimistic spirit has been dampened by the difficult realities of life, try to rekindle the hopefulness that inspired you to become a mother. Take time to allow yourself to dream about what you would like to create. Know that you can tap into your Mother Power to make those dreams come true. Remember that you, like the women in this book, can use your creativity to overcome every kind of adversity and disappointment.

• Look around your house for evidence that you are a creative person: plants, decor, recipes, clothes, games, art, or crafts. Feed this side of your personality by giving it time to play and perhaps some outside training.

• What would you do if you felt very creative? Would you, like the mothers in this chapter, begin to write...or display a collection...or find a better way to work and co-parent your

continued

105

children? Brainstorm to see how you can begin to do it now, just as you are.

• We are all creatures of our own invention. How would you like to change your life? Come up with some creative ideas to do just that—and make a step-by-step plan to achieve those goals.

chapter six

FAIR: TAKING TURNS HONESTLY

"If there was only one piece of pie left, I let one cut it in half, and the other have first pick."
—**My mother-in-law on how she kept things fair with her sons**

The symbol for justice is a woman holding a balanced scale. If you are a mother, you probably haul out that scale every day when your kids say things like "He won't let me play!" and "She's hogging the telephone!"

Child psychologists advise parents against being perpetual judges of fairness, but good mothers like to take an active role in making things fair, so this advice is hard to follow. In fact, these days more and more mothers are not only insisting that their kids be fair with each other, but also that the world operate in a more fair manner, too. They are doing this in the *house*...and also in the Senate.

Mothers' commitment to fairness is getting them involved in politics and non-profit organizations all around the world. This chapter shows some of the many ways mothers have become political. It also profiles a mother who is fighting to make a large industry more fair.

Political Mothers in the United States

Growing up in Baltimore, the only female politician I remember was Margaret Chase Smith, the Senator from faraway Maine. How times have changed. Now many elected officials bring maternal skills to the job. The mayor of my town, my state representative, my federal congresswoman, and senator are all proud mothers.

Male politicians often grow up knowing they want to run for office. Most female politicians in office today came into government more serendipitously. Typically they are drawn into politics after holding office in the PTA at their children's school or by working on some cause at the local level. Most are elected because there is a public perception that women, especially mothers, are honest and fair. Most are reelected because they care about getting a fair deal for their constituents.

For example, my congresswoman, Nita Lowey, has consistently pointed out how unfair it is for anti-abortion congressmen to also be anti-contraception. Nita, who wants every child to be wanted and cared for, sponsored "The Pill Bill," which would require health insurance companies covering federal employees to pay for contraception. As she tells them, "If you really want to reduce abortions, then encouraging contraception is just common sense."

When Viagra became available to help men have erections, Nita crusaded for another "It's-Only-Fair Pill Bill": any insurance company that paid for Viagra should also pay for contraception. Believe it or not, as this is being written, they don't all do it.

Mothers, like Nita, have come flooding out of the home and into politics, but their numbers thin out at the highest levels of government. As *Nine and Counting*, a book written in the year 2000 by the then-current female senators says, "Before 1992, only one married woman had ever been elected to the United States Senate. And before 1992, when Patty Murray and Carol Mosley-Braun were elected, a woman with children living at home had never been sent to the Senate. But with the elections of Mary Landrieu in 1996 and Blanche Lincoln in 1998, it's no longer unusual to come across preschoolers racing down the hallways of the Dirksen and Hart Senate Office Buildings." Each of these women have their own fairness issues, but for at least two of them, motherhood was one of the issues itself.

In 1980, Patty Murray was an apolitical, stay-at-home mom. When the Washington State Legislature cut funding for the parent-child education program that she and her two preschoolers attended, Patty, who loved the program, put her kids in the car and drove to the state capital to try to convince legislators to reverse their decision. Pigeonholing one legislator, she thought she was doing a good job of explaining her position. Then he dismissed her by saying, "Lady, that's a nice story, but you can't get the funding restored. You're just a mom in tennis shoes."

Determined that moms like herself needed more clout, Patty came home and organized a huge rally on the state capitol steps. She not only saved her beloved program, but began running for elective office as "just a mom in tennis shoes." That label became a populist rallying cry, proclaiming that she would be fair, honest, and caring.

Blanche Lincoln, the Senator from Arkansas, also found her maternal status being used against her. Blanche was a successful, young Congresswoman when, at thirty-five, she discovered that she was expecting twins. Deciding that the rigors of a rural reelection campaign (driving around in a flat bed truck) would be too much while pregnant, she chose not to run and was criticized by the opposition for using her pregnancy as an "excuse." After staying home for a year with her boys, she decided to try for a vacant Senate seat, and the opposition, being predictably oppositional, now questioned whether the mother of two young children could be an effective senator.

Blanche, like every other mother with a job outside the home, knows how hard it is to get up early every day, get the kids ready for day care, work long hours, and then try to have some family life afterwards. But Blanche, like Patty Murray, finds that motherhood gives her an advantage. As she says, "Sure, our life is hectic, but that's no different than the way it is for most working families today. I certainly have a better appreciation of what kinds of pressures they face. I tell them—'I'm just like you.'"

Rushing from packing the kids' lunch to a meeting at the Senate, she said, "It's hard to be high-and-mighty when you have peanut butter on your sleeve." And her inside knowledge of how families struggle and juggle these days makes her determined to get a fair legislative break for them.

Political Mothers around the World

All over the world, women are being elected to high office because, true or not, the public believes they are more fair and honest than men. Furthermore, there seems to be a growing political perception that mothers are the fairest of them all.

In the past, the few women who made it to the top rarely emphasized their maternal qualities, because they had to prove they were as tough as men. Margaret Thatcher certainly didn't show her "mommy" side, and grandmotherly Golda Meir went out of her way to let the public know she was a hawk. But these days women can act like mothers to their countries, because voters are looking for maternal caring, honesty, and fairness.

In 1999, Megawati Sukarnoputri ran on a reform ticket to be president of Indonesia, promising that, "We as government shall not be dishonest anymore to our people," and calling herself the "mother" of the students who led the initial call for reform. While she led in the popular vote, the national assembly named an ailing Muslim cleric as president with Megawati as vice president to succeed him. Her supporters rioted until she calmed the country by saying, "To all my children throughout the nation, I beg you sincerely to return to work. Your mother is standing before you." The crowds calmed down, knowing that the new president was so ill he would probably not be able to live through his five-year term, leaving their avowedly honest "mother" to succeed him.

Corruption scandals continued under the cleric. Ethnic and religious hatred threw Indonesia into turmoil. These problems may have been abated if Megawati had been allowed to claim her victory. As I write this, the cleric has been removed, and Megawati has assumed her rightful place. We can only hope that she will bring order, peace, and clean government through Mother Power.

In 1999, Panama inaugurated its first female president, Mireya Moscoso, who took the oath with her young son by her side. The themes in her inaugural address were the same as her campaign: the elimination of poverty and corruption, and the revival of a civic and moral spirit in her nation. Will historians conclude that she was more honest than her predecessors? Cynics say it would be hard to be less honest. Al Neuharth, founder of *USA Today*, wrote that if she can just run her impoverished and debt-ridden country "without Uncle Sam's parenting, she will become Latin America's biggest hero."

On a more local level in the villages of Peru, women were traditionally second-class citizens. Recently, however, as thousands became heads of families when their husbands were killed in the civil war, mothers began to feel empowered. At first, they exercised this power by hiding their sons to keep them from being forced into Shining Path guerilla armies. Then the women formed "mother's clubs" to run their villages, taking charge of food, supplies, and money.

These mother's clubs run communal gardens and distribute food donated by the government and charities. They form village banks to offer small loans to farmers and entrepreneurs. They are disseminating information more fairly, too: helping many women learn for the first time about family planning. As one human rights lawyer in Peru says, "In the past, women were subordinated, but now they play a central role and local services are delivered much more democratically."

Being a political mother doesn't just mean running for office. In 1999, an angry Thai mother demanding fairness tested the democratic openness promised under her country's new constitution. This mother, Sumalee Limpaovart, believed her six-year-old daughter was unfairly denied entrance to an exclusive, government-run school, where admissions are supposed to be granted strictly according to entrance exam scores. She did something previously unheard of in Thailand: she demanded to see the test scores under the new Freedom of Information law.

No one believed she would get the information. Her neighbors, believing corruption was a way of life, said, "Do you think you can change the system all by yourself?" She was determined to try.

Much to everyone's surprise, she succeeded. The scores were made public, creating a scandal: one third of the students admitted had failed the entrance exam, but had been accepted anyway because of their family's status or gifts to the school. Equally important, the fight for fairness spread. Soon, another parent filed a freedom-of-information challenge at a second school, and made it likely that all government run schools would be required to publicly report their test scores.

A Maternal Watchdog

Throughout this chapter, and the entire book, there are stories of mothers who, by becoming politicians or forming pressure groups, made laws more fair. However, as Sumalee proved in Thailand, fair laws are only effective if citizens insist that they be followed. Here is the story of how one American mother, Lisa Carlson, is spearheading a movement intent on making an entire industry, the $11 billion American funeral business, adhere to the laws that are supposed to make funeral practices fair.

You wouldn't think that someone who deals with death and funerals all day would have a great sense of humor. But Lisa has maintained her smile, her wit, and her smoky, throaty laugh, even though she learned in the most traumatic way possible that funeral practices were not always fair to the bereaved.

In 1981, Lisa Carlson's husband committed suicide, leaving her, a stay-at-home mom, with two small children to support. Still in shock from discovering her husband's body, the local funeral director asked $700 to cremate his remains. She didn't have the money. Desperate, Lisa began calling to find other alternatives and discovered a crematory that charged only $85 if she would handle all the details, including transporting the body. This do-it-yourself approach saved money, and, she says, was therapeutic.

Many people would have been traumatized by the idea of driving their husband's body to the crematory and planning the memorial service by themselves, but she found it helped her come to terms with what had happened, to show love and let go. It also began a long process that eventually turned her, according to the American Association of Retired Persons, into "the country's leading advocate for the rights of consumers regarding funerals."

Lisa became a teacher to support her children, but so many people asked her how she bypassed expensive funeral arrangements that she says, "I felt I ought to get that information out to the public. I went to the library, researched, and found that funeral laws were different state to state." She found that many states had laws, promoted by the funeral industry, that required people to pay for unnecessary and expensive procedures like embalming, and to buy coffins even if they were going to be cremated. So, she wrote a proposal for a book that would help people bypass such laws. She says, "I sent it off to twenty-six publishers, got twenty-six rejection letters, and put it away."

Lisa remarried, and in 1986, when her new mother-in-law died, her husband found it very satisfying to create his own do-it-yourself funeral. He made the coffin and dug the grave himself. This rekindled

Lisa's interest in fighting what she saw as unfair and overly expensive professional funeral services. She sees these feelings as very maternal.

"How I chose to deal with death mirrors how I chose to deal with birth. I wanted natural childbirth—wanting to be very much involved and be in control. I feel it is a fundamental right to have a baby the way you want and to be buried the way you want. I became enraged that the right to do so was limited by industry practices and state laws."

Lisa's husband decided to help her publish the book to empower others to create their own funeral arrangements without the assistance of costly funeral homes. They printed the book themselves and created a small publishing business. "My husband quit his day job, but I taught five years after that. We became very active in the small press movement," she says. Her book, *Caring for Your Own Dead*, caught the attention of the Funeral and Mortuary Society of America (FAMSA).

This was an organization representing self-help consumer groups around the country. As Lisa explains, "The memorial society movement was started in the late 1930s by a Unitarian minister in Seattle when the funeral industry was cranking up the price of funerals by requiring a pre-made casket and telling people that bodies had to be embalmed. The minister went to funeral homes and said, 'My people want a simple exit,' if you agree to do it for X amount, we'll send all our people to you. The movement spread up and down the East and West Coasts of America and into Canada." Many of the members favored cremation over burial.

FAMSA, after lobbying for ten years, finally forced the Federal Trade Commission to issue regulations to the funeral industry in the early 1980s. Basically, those regulations require that funeral homes must disclose in writing the prices for their services and consumer rights. Furthermore, they cannot force you to buy more services than you want to buy and they may not lie to you about state and federal regulations. The regulations also allow for direct cremation: funeral homes (or individuals) taking bodies to crematories without other costly services.

Lisa agreed to go on the national board of FAMSA, now called the Funeral Consumers Alliance (FCA) and in 1996, she became its national director. (The group changed its name because so many people thought FAMSA was an industry group.) She takes a very maternal, caring approach to her work, which she says is all about protecting consumers and insisting that they have fair choices.

Lisa operates FCA out of her home in Vermont, and the phone is always ringing. Many of the calls sound something like this, "My mom is dying and the funeral director is going to charge $6,000. What can I do?" "If I suggest direct cremation," says Lisa, "they are probably going to hang up. So, I start with asking what rituals are going to be important to the family. I also ask, 'Does your mom own a lot?' If the answer is no, I say, 'The very first thing you have to do is go shopping for a lot and get ready for sticker shock if you are not ready for cremation.' Most people these days don't realize that cemeteries often require a vault. And for-profit cemeteries are going to tell you that if you don't buy the marker from them, they are not going to take care of it for you. But they aren't allowed to highjack people that way."

Lisa wants to make sure people know that they can request anything from extended viewing hours at a funeral home to a simple graveside service, anything from cremation with extensive services provided by funeral directors to a direct cremation where the funeral home merely takes the body to the crematorium and the family plans their own memorial service.

Equally important, Lisa is intent on giving consumers emotional protection against the guilt they feel about wanting to save money on a funeral. Lisa's organizations encourage people to plan ahead and compare prices before a crisis, because grief-stricken family members rarely have the emotional resources to shop around after a loved one dies. Furthermore, some unscrupulous funeral directors prey on the bereaved by saying unfair things like, "I'm sure you want the best for your mother," when they are trying to sell the most expensive caskets and funeral plans. That line, by the way, is one Lisa likes to quote directly from an article in a funeral industry trade publication written to show funeral directors how to get grieving families to open their wallets.

"I was shocked to hear from one of my compatriots at the University of Kansas Center on Aging that 50 percent of widows are living on $10,000 a year or less," she told me. "If anything has helped fan the flames of why I do this, that statistic has made me want to get out there and make sure that people know what their choices are. Why are they spending $8,000–$10,000 to bury a husband when they could use that money to improve the quality of their lives?"

When I clipped some stories about Lisa and put them in my Mother Power files, I never thought I would use them myself. Then, in the throws of grief a few days before my son died, I went to the funeral parlor recommended by his hospice program. I knew we wanted direct cremation—to have the funeral home merely transport his body to the crematorium, file for death certificates, and then give us the ashes. We didn't want any "viewings" at a funeral home. We simply wanted a memorial service at our church that we would plan with our minister.

Stepping into the funeral home, I immediately had an uncomfortable feeling because the personnel seemed more like salespeople than grief counselors. The price for a direct cremation was going to be $2,500 and they told me I had to buy a coffin, because state regulations required that bodies be transported to the crematorium in some such container.

As a grieving mother, I was in no condition to argue. But I vaguely remembered the articles I had read about Lisa, who said such claims were illegal. So, I left and looked in the Yellow Pages, finding a nearby funeral home that offered direct cremation. That funeral director, who seemed much more professional and compassionate, charged $800.

When I told Lisa this story, she fumed. "New York state doesn't require people who want direct cremation to buy caskets," she said. "That wasn't just a lie he told to get you to buy a casket," she explained, "It is a violation of the FTC regulations and he should be charged a $30,000 fine. You should report that guy!" When Lisa gave me all the information to do so, I was glad to have such a strong, maternal woman on my—and every grieving person's—side.

Bringing It Home

When we grow up and become mothers, we go to great lengths to be fair and treat our children equally. Many of us dislike the competitiveness of modern society, and are uncomfortable with displays of wealth or success when friends and neighbors have less than we do. It is this natural sense of fair play and desire to share life's bounty that has created the gender gap in politics.

The gender gap and a growing sense of Mother Power have propelled many women into politics. It has inspired others to take their sense of fair play out of the home and insist that it become the norm in the outside world. How would you like to make the world more fair?

- Do you take a "fair share" of family resources for yourself? Fairness, like charity, begins at home, so be sure that you are fair with yourself in terms of time, money, space, play, and solitude. While it is impossible to be equal with everyone in the family, make sure that no one is really being short-changed.

continued

• Do you know anyone outside your home who is being treated unfairly? Is there anything you can do or any way to speak out and help this person? If not, a little extra kindness or empathy from you might make their life better.

• Is there any group that, in your opinion, is being treated unfairly? Come up with a way to help this group, either with time, money, or political support.

PART 2:

What Mothers Do

chapter seven

TEACH RIGHT FROM WRONG: ASSERTING OUR MORAL AUTHORITY

"Parents cannot help but teach kids their values, simply because children are bound to learn their parents' values by observing what their mothers and fathers do and hearing what they say."
—Thomas Gordon, *Parent Effectiveness Training*

If a child in the 1950s did something wrong, a mother would often say, "Wait 'til your father gets home!" The child would wait fearfully for father's return that night, because dad was the disciplinarian in most families. Sometimes he talked sternly about the infraction, sometimes a treat was taken away. Often the punishment was a spanking.

Today, with more parent equality (and so many absent fathers), the role of teaching right from wrong has largely passed from father to mother. We have become the moral authorities for our children. And, we are much more likely to explain the rules than spank.

As disciplinarians, mothers care as much about teaching right from wrong as punishing. Spanking doesn't convey our sense of morality to our children, so we would much rather explain that good human beings settle arguments peacefully and are kind to each other. We take to heart and try to impart that we *are* our brother's (and sister's) keeper.

Many of the women in this book have taken that message out of the home. They have stood up against military oppression and government corruption, saying that these are horribly wrong. They have insisted that common decency require safe streets, food for the poor, and family friendly working conditions in corporations. In fact, there are so many mothers around the world acting as moral authorities that it is impossible to include them all.

For example, in Africa there are mothers fighting slavery and genital mutilation. In Asia, mothers are trying to keep poor families from selling girls into child prostitution. And all around the globe, mothers are trying to outlaw spouse abuse and ensure that little girls are entitled to the same respect and education as little boys. With so many admirable mothers trying to teach the world right from wrong, it was very hard to choose examples for this chapter.

I finally decided to profile three American women, each very different from the other, but with two important things in common. First, they took the basic lessons in right and wrong that we teach our children—be nice to others and help someone in trouble—and insisted that society play by those rules. Second, no one would have predicted that they would become moral authorities, because they all were shy homebodies until life presented problems. Then, instead of backing away, ignoring the problem, or sinking into depression, they overcame their fears to help themselves as well as others.

School Should be a Safe Haven

Raising a family on a teacher's salary is never easy, and it is especially difficult in the expensive suburbs of New York City. But Bob and Evelyn Jackson found a small, old farmhouse there, not far from the high school where he taught English, and filled their home with secondhand furniture, books, music, and art.

When they discovered that their first child had severe learning disabilities, Evelyn went back to graduate school, trying to learn how to teach her daughter to read. Eventually, Evelyn became a reading teacher, and in 1985, took a job in an elementary school in the South Bronx—a forty minute commute from her home, and a complete world away.

While Westchester county, where the Jacksons live, is one of the richest in the country, the district where Evelyn works is among the poorest. Statistics provided to prospective teachers a few years ago showed that 42 percent of the families are on public assistance, 50 percent of the adults have not completed high school, 61 percent do not speak English at home, and more than 99 percent are minorities. New teachers were also warned that "daily, our students are exposed to overwhelming issues, such as drug abuse, violence, crime, unemployment, teenage pregnancy, homelessness, illness, and domestic abuse."

Evelyn found many of the parents working hard to protect their children from such a rough environment, but she found many others were either too absent or overwhelmed to do so. "There are very few fathers around," she told me, "and so many of the mothers are overwhelmed by the circumstances of their lives. Sometimes an old, sick grandmother is raising the children because the mother is too young and daddy is in jail." So, teachers like Evelyn step in and try to parent the kids.

Evelyn remembers when she started her job, "I was scared of the streets and the neighborhood, but not the kids. I felt like they were my children—most good teachers feel that way. But when I looked at what my own kids have and what I could give them, and I looked at what the kids in my school didn't have, I said to myself, 'I've got to fix this!'

"I noticed that some of the kids would be kind of raggedy or wear inappropriate things, like short sleeves when it was cold out, or dirty clothes with no buttons, or clothes way too little or big. One of my kids didn't come in for a big test, and when I asked her why, she said, 'My clothes were wet.' She simply didn't have extra clothes if hers had to be washed.

"Some of the teachers brought extra clothes into school and kept them in a closet to give the kids. I brought my kid's outgrown clothes, too."

The teachers also know that many of the children need other forms of motherly love. Evelyn cites this example, "There is this sweet little girl in second grade and when she sees me in the hall, she always runs up for a hug. I was upset that her mother is always so critical of her, saying her hair is messy or she doesn't read well. It turns out that the father died this past summer and the grandmother also died, so the mother is just overwhelmed. I'm not sure I'm changing the girl's reading or test scores, but at least when kids like that are in contact with me, they know I care about them and I am sorry they are going through what they are going through. And almost all of the kids here are going through something.

"When I first started working here, I was really shocked by the fights I saw when I had lunch duty. Teachers don't have lunch duty anymore, but in those days we did and I had to break up a fight every day.

"The kids didn't seem to have a way to solve problems without fighting. Everything was seen as an insult. They'd say, 'He said something about my mother…She looked at me in the wrong way…He touched my book…She touched my butt—whatever—and it would escalate into a physical fight." All this aggression not only created a tense atmosphere, but was physically dangerous. Evelyn remembers, "One kid banged another's head so hard his eyes got bloodshot."

She quickly learned that "The kids are told by their parents that in order to survive on the streets of the South Bronx, they have to be able to fight and act tough. Over the years, I have come to see that kids who don't present a tough image are very vulnerable. For example, there is a kid I teach who doesn't have that kind of arrogance. He isn't streetwise. He is a good kid who could blend into any middle-class neighborhood—and he gets creamed.

"His daddy is in jail, his mom is in the hospital, and he is being raised by his grandma, an old, thin lady who is overwhelmed. On Friday, she came to the school sobbing because he had been attacked by a group of boys on the street. They had thrown him down and cracked his head on the sidewalk and he was unconscious. The principal tried to help her."

Instead of getting burned out and cynical, or transferring to a safer district, Evelyn searched for something to give the kids a positive alternative to fighting, and teach them right from wrong. Four years after she began teaching, "A notice from the New York Bar Association came across my desk, offering a grant to promote conflict resolution in school." She applied for the grant, even though it was only $225. She used the money to research the legal system and create what she calls "The People's Court" to bring peer justice to violent kids in her school. Here's how it works:

In the beginning of each school year, Evelyn teaches a short course about the law to all fifth graders. Then she administers a mock "bar exam," which asks questions about the law and the courts. It also asks children to judge a case of two students who get into a fight.

The thirty youngsters who earn the highest grades become the staff of The People's Court, where students can bring complaints about anyone who breaks school rules against violence or theft. The court staff spreads the word to classmates and younger children that if someone bothers you, go to The People's Courtroom and ask for a complaint form. Then The People's Court students act as jurors and lawyers for both accuser and accused. Evelyn makes sure that "everyone learns to listen to both sides of the argument and think carefully about which side is to blame.

"A second grader asked for a form because a classmate threw green paint in his hair. A fourth grader came because another slapped him. Another was chased down the hall and fell, scraping his nose. Others have their lunch, money, or candy stolen. The important thing is that these incidents stayed incidents and did not escalate." 'Sentences' range from writing essays to 'doing time' with the strictest teacher in the school.

In 1997, Evelyn approached the Bronx district attorney who agreed to help The People's Court. Now, every Wednesday court members walk three blocks from the school to the Bronx courthouse where five assistant district attorneys give up their lunch hour to coach the students on how to be good lawyers and fair judges.

Evelyn used to be shy and self-conscious, so I inquired how she found the confidence not only to start this program, but also to ask the district attorney for help. She replied, "If you look at yourself and say, 'I'm shy and self-conscious' then you don't act. But if you look at the kids and think, 'They shouldn't be fighting,' then you can do these things. I don't want 'my' kids to end up in jail. I want them to be the prosecutors, not the prosecuted."

A fifth grade court member, Shana, explains why the program works: "I learned that if you feel like fighting, instead you can talk it out, think about it, write about it. Doing that helps you get your feelings out. You think about the consequences." Another member says he learned, "No one will get hurt if instead of using your hands or feet or a weapon, you use your brain instead." Evelyn hopes that kids like this will spread the word about The People's Court so other schools can teach a positive alternative to fighting.

Evelyn's enthusiastic concern for "her kids" ended up teaching a lot of people in my town a few things about right and wrong, too. You see, it is easy to forget how rough life is for other people if you live in a safe, comfortable place. But luckily, Evelyn is my friend and every time we got together, her stories about the kids in her school brought reality into my life. When my kids became too old to give their outgrown clothes to Evelyn, I put a notice in my church bulletin and many children learned that others needed the clothes they took for granted. Then we all learned not to take books for granted either.

Each year we have a church bazaar, and one popular booth sells second hand children's and adult books that families donate. Even though hundreds of books get sold, boxes and boxes of books are always left over. We were going to cart them out to the trash when I asked Evelyn if she could use them. It was as if I had offered her gold.

"There are no bookstores in our school district," she explained. "Many families don't even know what they are. The libraries are old and underfunded. While the kids are required to go there as part of their class experience, it is not part of their life experience.

"During my first Parent's Nights, I would say things like, 'It would be good for rhyming if you got a Dr. Seuss book,' but from their expressions I realized that was an unrealistic expectation. There are no bookstores to buy such books, and many don't have the experience to run to the library and get a book." When my church donated books, Evelyn said the kids could not believe they were actually being given a book to take home and not return. Many had never owned a book before. They were appalled that someone had thought of throwing books away.

Through Evelyn, we also learned that her kids need a lot more than just clothes and books. They need alarm clocks to help them get up in the morning. They need school supplies like pencils, crayons, paper, and glue. "You don't know what a difference this will make," said Evelyn when I handed over a bunch of lined paper pads that had been donated. "We have kids in homeless shelters who can't do homework because they don't have paper."

Like every good teacher, Evelyn's moral authority extends way beyond the classroom. As you can see, many people in my little town have learned a lot from her. We have learned that it feels good to share. We have learned to be more grateful for all that we have. Equally important, we have learned that only thirty minutes away, children are in desperate need. No one has to teach us that's not right. In fact, it is terribly wrong.

Kids Should Be Able to Trust Their Neighbors

Maureen Kanka thinks it is wrong for parents not to know when a sex offender moves into the neighborhood. If she had known the three men who shared a house across the street were paroled sex offenders, she would have warned her daughter Megan to stay away from them. When one of those men killed Megan, Maureen went on a crusade to insure that a similar lack of information would never again harm a trusting, innocent child.

Overcoming her fear of public speaking and a fear of driving alone, she traveled all around the country in her old sedan, rallying support for legislation requiring sex offenders to register with the authorities when they move into a neighborhood, and for the authorities to make that information public. Her story is important not only because such legislation now helps families all over the country. It is also important because by being honest about the fears and heartache she had to overcome, she makes all of us believe that we could rise to such a challenge too.

When the English Parliament was about to pass its version of Megan's Law, a reporter for the *London Daily Telegraph* seemed rude when he described Maureen Kanka, saying she, "should, by the odds, have remained the most ordinary of women. Her New Jersey home speaks of the modest, everyday comforts of the American middle class. She is wearing trainers and the loose tracksuit that stout women in the suburbs favor. On her sitting room wall is a simple painting of three children, their smiles as radiant as the amateur artist had the skills to make them. There is a girl, a boy, and then another girl, the youngest. In that painting lies the story of the transformation of Maureen Kanka into a woman of power. The younger daughter Megan is dead and everyone in America is now familiar with the awfulness of her fate."

For those not familiar, here is the story: on a warm July evening, Maureen cooked pancakes for seven-year-old Megan before letting her play outside. Later, when her husband Richard returned from a long day repairing air conditioning systems, they became alarmed when they didn't see Megan on the street with the other neighborhood children.

Searching the neighborhood, Jesse Timmendequas, who lived across the street, told the Kankas that he had seen Megan before dinner, but not since. Eventually, the Kankas called the police. A helicopter and hundreds of mothers and fathers joined the search for Megan. Jesse Timmendequas offered to get art supplies and make posters.

The next day when Megan's body was found three miles away, dumped in an overgrown section of a park, Jesse Timmendequas was brought to the police station for questioning since some of his statements didn't add up. The quiet neighbor admitted that he had lured Megan into his house, promising that she could play with his puppy. Then, after raping her, he strangled her with a belt, put her body in an old toy chest and dumped it. Feeling no guilt, he stopped at a convenience store to buy cigarettes and a newspaper before coming home and offering to help the Kankas.

Maureen was appalled to find out that Timmendequas was a twice-convicted child molester out on parole. Furthermore, his two roommates were also child molesters he had met in prison. She had warned Megan not to go with strangers who offered candy or a puppy, but never thought to warn Megan about neighbors. She felt it was deeply wrong that the authorities hadn't given her the information needed to protect her child.

Within days of Megan's death, Maureen was asking New Jersey Governor Christine Whitman, state representatives, and Federal Congressman Dick Zimmer to create a law so parents would be warned if molesters move into a neighborhood. Within months, she was traveling around the country, testifying before state commissions and rallying child protection groups, although she had no public speaking experience and was even afraid to drive alone.

Where did she get the strength? She says, "I would have died to protect my little girl and I didn't want another child to go through what my daughter did, another family to have the pain we did." She also credits her faith in God for helping her through her pain and fears.

"Looking back on those days," she says, "when I went out to speak, I suppose it was more heart-wrenching coming from the mother as opposed to the father. It was very natural for me to open up to everyone, because I was so traumatized by what had happened to Megan, and I wanted families to know that this could happen to others.

"Two New York assemblymen called and asked if we would help them bring the legislation to New York. My husband and I drove to New York City. It was horrendous, horrendous...we got lost for an hour and a half, but that started our working with other states.

"But my husband had to go back to work to pay the bills, so we agreed that I would work with whoever asked, because we both believed in this law.

"I had never done public speaking. I was petrified. I was a homebody who never went anywhere without my husband for the fifteen years we had been married. I was afraid to drive by myself, so I always had someone go with me.

"I remember going down to Maryland. I had to drive through a torrential downpour. There was flooding and I was late and a nervous wreck. I began testifying, but the committee members were standing around talking. They didn't have the decency to listen to me. I swore from that moment on, that if I went anywhere, because it was such an emotional drain for me, I would make sure that I would not be ignored. I began saying that if I come and bare my soul, I want people to have the common decency to listen to what I have to say." From that point on they started listening extremely closely.

Maureen eventually traveled to almost every state. While she is quick to point out all the support she received from family, friends, and child protection groups, it is clear that without her spearheading the movement, Megan's Law would never have passed. She used the moral authority of motherhood and her grief, sharing her story and her passionate concern that this not happen to others. This Mother Power swayed legislators and public opinion.

Her crusade was not without cost. Each time she had to tell her story, it reopened the pain she felt over her child's death. She also began receiving threats from those who felt she was being unfair to sex offenders who had served their time.

"We had threats on the telephone answering machine. I was petrified by several in the early months. Then I told my husband, I don't want to hear about them. I am not going to stop doing what I am doing, so I don't want to listen and I don't want to know.

"Part of the grief process was dealing with my children's fear. I couldn't reassure them because the reality was that their sister was raped and murdered by a neighbor. When my son asked if that could happen to him, I said yes, because I needed to be honest. But, I said that his mom and dad would do everything in their power to make sure it did not happen.

"That was the beginning of a major education process with our children—being open and honest and talking to them about dangerous people who are out there." That education process led Maureen to create a foundation that provides information to other parents about pedophiles and how children can protect themselves.

In 1996, after traveling to most states, Maureen Kanka went to the White House where she watched Megan's Law become federal law. She heard Representative Zimmer, the bill's sponsor, say, "The death of

Megan Kanka resulted in saving the lives of other children." In fact, it wasn't Megan's death, but Maureen Kanka's Mother Power that saved those lives...Mother Power insisting that it is only right for children to trust their neighbors—and very wrong not to know when they can't.

We Should Help Someone in Trouble

While some people question whether Megan's Law is double punishment for sex offenders, no one ever doubted Maureen Kanka's motives and moral authority. That gave her Mother Power. The next story shows how quickly a Mother Power crusade can derail if the leader's moral authority is questioned.

There are two kinds of Good Samaritan laws. The first kind protects professionals who aid those in need, such as a doctor who treats someone on the street having a heart attack. Many states have such laws.

The other kind of Good Samaritan law requires people to take some action to prevent or report a serious crime they see occurring. For example, if you see someone trying to rape or murder a child, you must do something to stop the attacker—even if only to call the police. This law is relatively rare. When Yolanda Manuel's daughter was raped and murdered, she was shocked to find out that it was perfectly legal when someone saw the attack and merely walked away without informing the nearby security guard.

For a while it seemed like Yolanda, a shy cafeteria worker from Los Angeles, was going to do what Maureen Kanka had done—make history by changing laws on the state and federal level through Mother Power. Yolanda spearheaded a brief but important movement for Good Samaritan laws. But the movement lost steam when she changed her focus.

She began by being intent on teaching us that it is wrong to watch a child (or adult) be harmed and do nothing about it. Now her story can also teach us a lot about how to gain and lose Mother Power: even the most powerless in our society can have enormous clout through Mother Power; a woman using Mother Power can quickly make an impact on society; but, maintaining her moral authority is the key to Mother Power's success.

In May, 1997, there was a shocking killing in a Nevada casino. Yolanda's daughter, seven-year-old Sherrice Iverson, was raped and strangled in the casino ladies' room by an eighteen-year-old boy, Jeremy Strohmeyer. Much of the initial publicity involved the fact that both the boy and girl had been with their fathers in the casino at 4 A.M. There was a lot of debate about parental responsibility and the fact that some casinos try to attract families with children. There were also news reports about the fact that Jeremy Strohmeyer's best friend, David Cash, had been in the bathroom for the first few minutes of the attack.

Yolanda, separated from Sherrice's father, kept her grief private until David Cash began giving shocking interviews, revealing the depth of what he had seen and how little he cared that a child had died. There were reports that he had seen Jeremy dragging Sherrice into a stall with his hand over her mouth. Other reports said that he peeked over the stall and saw Jeremy undressing Sherrice. Video cameras in the bathroom filmed him walking out without trying to do anything to stop the assault. Cash never tried to enlist aid from security guards, nor did he do anything when Strohmeyer told him that night that he had killed Sherrice.

All this caused a public uproar, but what really got to Yolanda was an interview Cash gave in which he expressed sympathy for his friend, but none for her child. "I'm not going to get upset over someone else's life," he told the *Los Angeles Times*, "I just worry about myself first. I'm not going to lose sleep over somebody else's problems." He also asserted that the publicity surrounding the murder made it easier to meet women at Berkeley, where he was a second year student.

When radio talk show hosts interviewed him, Cash asserted that

"There is no chance that I will go to jail, simply because I have done nothing wrong." In fact, he had done nothing legally wrong. There is no law that requires someone to try to stop or report rape and murder. But Yolanda Manuel, like many other people, knew that what he did was morally wrong, that it should be illegal, and that he should be punished.

The fact that he was free and bragging about not stopping the killing of her only child was too much for Yolanda Manuel to bear. She and supporters called a press conference, and she became an instant leader in the movement to create Good Samaritan laws, requiring witnesses to try to stop, or at least report, violent crimes.

"A shy twenty-eight-year-old from South Central, Yolanda Manuel makes a meager living as a public school cafeteria worker," reported the *New York Times*. "Yet anytime she clears her throat to speak these days, television news crews rush to capture her every word. Now she has become the spiritual leader of what she calls a campaign for justice to pressure authorities into bringing charges against Mr. Cash." She was also the titular head of campaigns petitioning the California and Nevada legislatures to enact the "Sherrice Iverson Memorial Bill" and Congress for a Good Samaritan law on the federal level.

She was too afraid of public speaking to appear alone at news conferences or on the many TV and radio shows that wanted to interview her, so she took spokesmen with her. Even though she often made grammatical mistakes, she conducted herself with such dignity that crowds flocked to her. For example, while some supporters tried to suggest that the killing had racial overtones (Cash and Strohmeyer came from wealthy white families while Sherrice was poor and black), Yolanda refused to allow the polarizing topic of race to enter the story. She would shake her head 'no' whenever race was mentioned.

Consequently, her cause drew widespread support. As the *New York Times* reported, "a coalition of supporters rare in this era of polarization: blacks, whites, Jews, Christians, Muslims, radio talk-show hosts, conservatives, and liberals" were pressing for Good Samaritan laws.

Her main spokesmen were male, but mothers flocked to her cause. She said they stopped her on the street, begged to sign her petitions for Good Samaritan laws, hugged her, and cried with her. "Mothers know what I'm going through," she said. "I'm never going to stop hurting. I've almost had four nervous breakdowns since Sherrice was murdered. I'm tired, so tired. But I got to keep going. I got to get justice for my baby."

A large, racially mixed coalition drove from Los Angeles to Berkeley, protesting that the university was allowing Cash to continue his studies. While many people spoke at the rally, once again, it was Yolanda's picture that made the news. Her few words, asserting that Cash's callous approach to crime was wrong and should be illegal made the headlines.

Public opinion supported her. Her campaign, begun in July, 1998, a few weeks before Strohmeyer was to go on trial gained instant momentum. When Strohmeyer pleaded guilty, avoiding a long trial, he accepted full responsibility for the crime, but asserted that Cash should have tried to stop him.

By September, a bill entitled the Sherrice Iverson Good Samaritan Law was signed by the Governor of California, making it a crime to witness the sexual assault of a minor without notifying the police. If Yolanda Manuel had stayed the "spiritual leader" of the movement, similar laws would probably have been passed around the country and on the federal level. But, her supporters felt she gave up the moral high ground when she joined Sherrice's father in a lawsuit against the casino.

The day before the bill was signed in California, one of her main supporters held a news conference next to Sherrice's grave to denounce Yolanda. He was incensed that Yolanda was suing the casino rather than denouncing a father who would have a seven-year-old in a gambling parlor at 4 A.M. saying, "Gambling was more important to Leroy Iverson than protecting his own daughter...Yolanda wants to make money off her child's death," he continued. "For Yolanda, this case isn't about justice anymore, it's about money."

While there is nothing legally or ethically wrong with Yolanda joining the lawsuit, by doing so, she gave up her moral authority and, as a result, her Mother Power. Without Mother Power, the community leaders and talk show hosts couldn't keep the momentum going for Good Samaritan laws.

Bringing It Home

Thomas Gordon, who wrote *Parent Effectiveness Training*, the classic book quoted at the beginning of this chapter, explains that our children learn right from wrong by observing us. The bad news is that they learn by seeing what we actually do, rather than by listening to our lectures. So, if we want our kids to be honest, they better not see us lying and cheating. If we want them to have a sense of justice, we better be just with them. All in all, if we want children to have good values, we must be proactive about our own, or they will discount us.

Children have an innate sense of right and wrong. Even when they don't act on their convictions, they want parents who will. They want us to be good role models. It makes them feel secure.

So, there is a triple benefit to acting on our Mother Power convictions: we might make a difference in the world; we will feel good about making the effort; and our children will respect us for acting on our convictions. After all, good parenting is all about setting a good example, and practicing what we preach.

• Put a copy of the Ten Commandments on the refrigerator door. Choose one to discuss at dinner each night. For example, is there any time when it is acceptable to kill? Is bearing false witness the same as lying? Is it ever acceptable to lie? Give children the right to explore their own sense of morality while hearing your point of view.

• Consider the wrongs you have done to others in your life. Is there a way to make amends? Don't be shy about letting your children know about this. It sets a good example. Likewise, consider mistakes you made in your life. If you can't correct them, perhaps you can be honest about them with your children, so that they do not make the same. (No one should ever tease or criticize someone who admits a mistake and genuinely tries to correct it.)

• What do you think is wrong about our culture, society, or the world? Take at least some small step to help make it right. You know the routine by now: a contribution, a letter to a political leader, or join a group that is trying to right the wrong.

chapter eight

NURTURE: CULTIVATING GROWTH

God could not be everywhere, so he made mothers.

—Jewish proverb

Even before our babies are born, we nurture them—our bodies keep them safe and nourished. After birth, nurturing requires more than just food and shelter. Landmark studies during World War II showed that babies in war orphanages, even those kept clean, warm, and properly fed, failed to thrive unless they were held and emotionally nurtured. This is something that good mothers instinctively understand, so they give their children lots of positive feedback and loving hugs.

Nurturing is a complex, never ending balancing act. Give too much and we stunt our children's growth. Give too little, and they will feel needy forever. The proper balance provides enough security and support (mixed with discipline, guidance, and expectations) so that children can flower into their own unique and independent selves. When mothers take these nurturing skills into the world, they make people and projects flower, too.

A well-known nurturing mother, Clara Hale, became famous after she started caring for babies harmed in utero by mothers with drug addictions and AIDS. She and her daughter, Lorraine, created a Harlem institution, Hale House, which provides much-needed nurturing to the neediest children. Despite scandals that have hit Lorraine and Hale House later discussed in this chapter, the legend of Clara Hale and the need for others to continue her work lives on.

Jo Luck continued and expanded a different sort of nurturing institution: the Heifer Project, which sends farm animals to poor families around the world. She has used Mother Power to nurture both those families and her organization.

An entirely different kind of nurturing is needed in the arts. Every writer, artist, dancer, or actor needs someone to notice their talent and help it along. Daryl Roth, who discovers and produces Pulitzer prize–winning plays, credits much of her success to being maternal with the creative people she hires.

Hold Them, Rock Them, Love Them

Clara Hale's life was one of hardship and poverty, and yet late in life, she became nationally known in a way that amazed her. Cited by Ronald Reagan in his 1985 State of the Union address as an "American heroine," she told reporters, "I'm not an American hero—I'm simply a person who loves children."

Common wisdom and psychological research shows that cold or abusive parents tend to raise children who become cold or abusive themselves. Luckily, there are exceptions to that rule. Some of the best parents I know grew up in dysfunctional families, but vowed to be loving and stable with their own children. Because they have kind natures and vow to be different from their own parents, they became the kind of parents we all wish we had. Clara Hale's innate kindness made her the loving nurturer her own mother was not.

Clara's mother, who was cold and unloving, but hardworking and industrious, died when Clara was sixteen. Since Clara's father died when she was nine, she lived with relatives while completing high school and then married. When Clara was twenty-seven, her husband died of cancer, leaving her a widow with three children to support in Harlem.

At first, she earned money cleaning houses during the day and theaters at night, but she hated leaving her children with baby-sitters, so she decided to do what she loved—be with children—and became a baby-sitter herself. She took in seven or eight neighborhood children each day while their parents worked.

Eventually, she became a licensed foster parent, and raised forty foster children. Her biological daughter, Lorraine, remembers, "She never yelled or screamed, but simply offered us the lessons she had learned in life." Those lessons included the importance of school and good behavior. All forty foster children graduated from high school, and many earned college degrees.

By 1969, Clara was sixty-five and retired from foster care, but she still baby-sat for six children in her apartment each day. Lorraine was driving home after visiting Clara one afternoon and saw a heroin addict nodding off while sitting on an upturned milk carton, oblivious to the crowds on the sidewalk. What caught Lorraine's eye was a baby's tiny arm sticking out of the dirty blankets on the woman's lap. Lorraine couldn't get the image out of her mind, so she circled back to find the woman.

Lorraine asked the woman about her living situation and the health of the baby. Then, spontaneously, she scrawled Clara's address on a piece of paper and stuck it in the woman's hand saying, "Go to this address. My mother will help. She loves babies and it would be a chance to get yourself together." The next day the addict showed up at Clara's apartment. Shocked, Clara called Lorraine and said, "You better come back here!"

Clara had taken in many children over the years, but never one off of the street. After serious consideration, she took the baby on the condition that the mother get drug treatment. Word quickly spread through the drug world in Harlem that Clara would take in addicts' babies. Within three months, there were twenty-two babies living in Clara's five-room apartment.

Twenty-two babies sounds overwhelming enough, but these were not just ordinary infants. Addicts' babies are born addicted too. They cry more frequently than healthy babies, kicking and screaming for months as their little bodies go through withdrawal. They have diarrhea and vomit their food. Clara Hale held the babies, rocked them, and told them she loved them. Neighbors and volunteers from the community came in to help, but Clara was the main source of nurture. She even kept some of the babies in her room all night so she could be there if they needed her—and continued this practice until a few months before she died at age eighty-seven.

Lorraine wrote a grant proposal and received $50,000 from the city, so she and her mother could buy a five-story brownstone in Harlem and establish the first home for infants of drug-addicted mothers. She quit her job as a school guidance counselor and earned a doctorate in child development and child psychology.

By 1973, Clara and Lorraine incorporated as the Hale House Center for the Promotion of Human Potential. Lorraine was in charge of administration. Clara was in charge of the babies. Known as Mother Hale, many people thought she was a saint.

Over the years, heroin, crack, and AIDS swept through Harlem and other ghettos. In the '80s the "border babies" crisis hit the papers: newborns who were left to languish in expensive hospitals when their drug-addicted parents abandoned them. City officials were happy to transfer those babies to Hale House. Over one thousand babies found shelter with Mother Hale, who tried to reunite them with their parents as soon as possible.

When the border baby crisis waned, the city decided that infants were best cared for individually in foster homes, rather than in group homes like Hale House. There were also some conflicts between Hale House and the city about record keeping. Eventually, Hale House stopped receiving government funds and referrals, but there was still a tremendous need for Hale House services. For example, many addicts and prisoners who couldn't care for their babies, but didn't want to officially place them in foster care, left their babies in Clara's care.

Private donations flowed in, more than compensating for the lack of government funds. Spike Lee, Mariah Carey, John and Yoko Ono, Lena Horne, and Tony Bennett are just a few of the prominent people who became Hale House contributors and supporters. In addition, volunteers came from all over the world to help cuddle and care for the babies.

In the late 1980s, the Hale House budget was only $200,000 a year. By the time Mother Hale died in 1992, the budget had grown to $3.5 million a year and programs had expanded to include housing and training mothers after drug treatment, apprentice training for local youths, and a home for mothers and babies with AIDS. Lorraine took over Hale House, vowing to continue her mother's loving tradition.

It is difficult to be the daughter of a saint. Lorraine, who was the primary spokeswoman for the humble Mother Hale, remembers giving stirring speeches while her mother sat quietly beside her. Afterwards, however, everyone swarmed over Clara, thanking her for her wisdom and ignoring Lorraine. It also must be hard to keep your head and your ethics when celebrities pour money on you. Last but not least, it is very difficult not to burn out when working with addicts.

In the early years of Hale House, the mothers typically were women who had only been using heroin for less than a year. It was easier for them to kick their habits and reclaim their babies. In the later years, the typical mother had been using drugs for years and was street-hardened. Hale House gave the babies a loving, supportive respite, but then they were reclaimed by mothers who often sank back into addiction, neglecting and abusing the children. In the promotional packet of material that Hale House sent me, there was an article where Lorraine admitted "fatigue and diminished sympathy for the recalcitrant mothers."

Burn out is one thing, but fiscal mismanagement is another. In 2001, the *New York Times,* which, like the rest of the world, had been a big fan of Mother Hale, ran a series of articles about financial scandals at Hale House. Clara Hale had always lived very modestly and frugally with the babies. Lorraine was paying herself $200,000 as Hale House director and her husband $100,000 as director of public relations. While not in the spirit of Mother Hale, there was nothing illegal about those salaries. More inappropriate was the fact that Lorraine admitted borrowing over $100,000 from the charity to renovate her suburban home, and other funds were reportedly used to finance her husband's unsuccessful Broadway play, while houses bought to shelter needy clients were never properly used. Furthermore, $43 of every $100 raised for Hale House was paid to a consulting firm.

Lorraine was forced to resign from Hale House. A new board of directors was installed and charged with the task of bringing proper fiscal management to Hale House and restoring the values of Mother Hale.

While there is sadness and outrage that the legacy of Clara Hale has been tarnished, she continues to be a role model and inspiration. She is part of the long, great tradition in black communities of taking in and nurturing children in need. Hale House, an institutional embodiment of this tradition, will not be allowed to die.

Whenever the leadership in an organization changes, there is always the danger that the health and reputation of the organization will be damaged. On the other hand, there is the chance that the new leader will guide the organization to greater growth and service. Jo Luck is an example of a woman, who not only kept a nurturing institution true to its humanitarian roots, but also made it grow through Mother Power.

Passing on the Gift

The Heifer Project was started in 1944 during the Spanish Civil War by an American relief worker, Dan West. Dan, a farmer and devout member of the Church of the Brethren, ladled out cups of powdered milk to hungry children. Haunted by having to decide who would go hungry when supplies ran low, and upset that parents had to beg for handouts, he asked his friends at home to donate heifers (pregnant cows) so the destitute families could produce food for themselves. Each family that received a heifer agreed to pass along the gift, by donating the heifer's first healthy female offspring to another family.

Dan's small effort grew into an international operation. By the time Jo Luck joined the staff in 1989, millions of small farmers on five continents had been helped to self-sufficiency. She told me, "The reason the Heifer Project has lasted all these years is the same reason that Mother Power works: it's about empowering and nurturing people, helping each one to become their best."

Jo Luck (who always uses both her names) is a real believer in maternal management, and she wants to make very clear what that entails. "A lot of people think of mothers as mother hens, and mothers are very protective," she explains. "But protection is just one tiny aspect of mothering. You see mother birds nudging the little ones out of the nest, making them fly. Mothering, parenting, being a CEO—leadership of any kind—involves empowering people to be the best they can be, and to be kind."

The Heifer committee that initially hired Jo Luck to be their International Program Director, was searching for someone who was bilingual, with experience in international management and animal husbandry. Jo Luck had none of those qualifications and suspects that she was included in the five final candidates merely as a token woman. However, she came with a strong track record of inspirational management in various non-profit and government jobs. Her dream was to work to end international hunger, so during her interview, she convinced the committee that they had plenty of bilingual animal husbandry experts on staff. What they needed instead, she said, was someone who could manage a diverse staff all over the world, "someone to pull them together, be their cheerleader, empower them, be the glue and the fun."

Once hired, "I started traveling around the world to villages," she told me, and as the first female in her job, she obtained a new and important view of the problems. "Men in my role had gone out and talked to men in the villages. The women were too shy to talk to a man. But when they saw a woman coming to their village in a leadership role, and when they found out I was a mother, they were very curious and wanted to talk to me."

By talking through an interpreter, to both the men and the women in the village, Jo Luck learned a key fact: it was the women, not the men, who took care of the animals and the gardens. "For forty years we had been training the men, but the women were the ones caring for the animals and never got the training."

Since it was unheard of to train women, she had to be particularly persuasive with village leaders and sensitive to local customs. She gave this example of a meeting that took place with the chief of an African village: "I said, 'Wouldn't it be great to train the wives?' And he said, 'No, no, no. Women don't get training.' So I said, 'I am in your culture and a guest in your home and country, and I would never suggest anything that was inappropriate. But I was thinking that you could probably double the offspring and triple the liters of milk.' I talked economics, and he was adding it up in his head.

"I said, 'You are the chief. You could set an example and just try it.' So, in about three months, they were training the women and what that did to the economy was unbelievable."

By talking to the women, it also became clear that cows often created as many problems as they solved. In Uganda, where water was scarce, women were grateful that cows provided nutrition for their children, but challenged because they had to transport so much extra water for the new animals. By encouraging the women to come up with a better plan, they realized that goats provide milk and meat, drink less and also could walk along the small local paths carrying the firewood and water women had been balancing on their heads.

In the early years, the Heifer Project replaced cows killed in war. Now Heifer works in forty-seven countries around the world providing twenty-three species of animals, everything from water buffaloes to chickens and rabbits. "We don't work with individual families. A whole community has to invite us in, because that way they will be stronger sooner and more self-sufficient," says Jo Luck. Each community, assisted by local Heifer Project experts, decides what kind of animals would be most helpful.

"In places like India, camels can be milked, can travel far with little water, and can be used for transport," says Jo Luck. "In Peru, Guatemala, and Ecuador, cattle can't get up and down the mountains or live above the timber line. And cattle can be very destructive. So, we have reintroduced the llama and alpaca. Their little hooves are just right for the environment. When they eat, they just nibble. They don't pull up roots like cattle."

Under Jo Luck's leadership, the Heifer Project has become intent on repairing the environment as well as the local economy. She gives an example of how the Heifer Project helped a small village in Honduras. "It was located on a slash-and-burn hillside. Everything was the color of dirt. The children were hungry and sick.

"We began with a specialist sitting down with the people and asking them about their goals. They had to elect a leader for their Heifer project and a treasurer. Then we went through a checklist: what is the environment? What will animals do to the environment? How can we improve the environment? Would it be good to plant trees? To plant living fences rather than cut down trees to build fences? How are you going to pay for the care of the animals? (They put 1 percent of their income in a savings account.) This process can last months or years until they are ready to receive the animals. We are out of there in three to five years, but we want to be sure the process will continue.

"The village in Honduras had about two hundred people and we gave them six goats. They had to select the families that would receive the first goats, and the next six families to get the pass-alongs. We don't pick—they decide who deserves the goats. Then we bought the animals as nearby as possible because shipping is expensive.

"We taught them to build pens with slats to collect the urine and manure for fertilizer, and to make bio-gas with it to use as a heat and energy source so they don't have to cut down trees. They planted trees that are nitrogen producing to improve the soil.

"I went back to the village three years later, and there had been such a transformation! It was green. There were trees. Children wearing colorful ribbons were giving the goats some exercise walking along paths in the hills. They had outdoor cooking areas, so they didn't have to cook indoors and choke on the smoke. They were using the gas. I was elated. But I hadn't done it for them. They had done it for themselves.

"It's like being a mother—you give all the tools, education, and support you can. You empower them. But, then you have to let them do it. And, you are proud of them because they have done it themselves."

When Jo Luck was promoted to President and CEO of the Heifer Project International, she applied this maternal management style and the staff loves her for it. Everyone I spoke to at Heifer had positive things to say about her and the whole program. As one man told me, "I am happy to wake up each morning and go to work. Everyone is so happy to work here. They like the people they work with and they feel good to be doing something about world hunger."

Soon after assuming leadership, Jo Luck realized that the Heifer Project lacked the kind of endowment that would ensure the program's longevity. Many new leaders bring in expensive fund-raising consultants or replace the existing development staff. Not Jo Luck. She increased the endowment from $4 million to $38 million by empowering the existing staff and donors.

While she appreciates every Sunday school class that raises $20 for a flock of geese, and people like the eighty-two-year-old woman from Indiana who scrimps and saves to give a cow each year, she recognized "we had to get some bigger gifts. When people give $25,000 to $50,000, think of how many villages that touches." But how to find such large donors?

"We took a lot of our older donors who had been giving for years and made them trustees," she explained. "They felt like it was part of their legacy to build the endowment. We also took people who were retiring from Heifer, and asked them to stay on part-time or as consultants to call on celebrities and major donors. After so many years with Heifer, think of the stories they can tell people." Those stories, plus the love the staff feels for Jo Luck and the Heifer Project, built the endowment and insures that the Heifer Project will be able to nourish impoverished families for decades to come.

The arts give a different kind of nourishment. Here is how Mother Power nurtures the creative spirit in the arts.

Mothering Creativity

There are far more people who want to be actors, writers, artists, singers, and dancers than there are jobs and contracts. Unfortunately, some people who succeed in these highly competitive fields treat newcomers with rude rejection, or exploit them with demands such as the infamous "casting couch." Luckily, others enjoy giving a helping hand. Here are two women who take a maternal approach with newcomers.

Barbara Kingsolver, who often writes about nurturing, maternal women in her novels, used the initial payment she received for her book *The Poisonwood Bible* to fund a perpetual $25,000 prize for "the literature of social responsibility": fiction that addresses the issue of prejudice, the need for economic or social justice, or "the moral obligation of individuals to engage with their communities in ways that promote a more respectful coexistence." Every other year, her Bellwether Prize will not only give a previously unpublished novel recognition, but also a contract from an established publishing house.

Kingsolver feels lucky being able to write "socially engaged" fiction, which she thinks is supported more by readers than the literary establishment. So, as she explained in a radio interview, "When I was lucky enough to get this big chunk of money, I wanted to support writers who are trying to do what I was trying to do ten years ago—establish myself as a writer of conscience…there is nothing better to do with money than to try to make the world a little better."

The most overtly nurturing, maternal woman I found in the arts is Daryl Roth, producer of Broadway and off Broadway plays, four of which have won Pulitzer Prizes. Daryl has everything: beauty, brains, success, and a generous spirit. As she welcomed me into her office with a view of Central Park, her friendliness and unpretentious nature were evident.

She told me how she was raised in New Jersey by parents who loved the theater. They often brought her and her sister into Manhattan to see plays and musicals. "When I was old enough, I took myself. I read plays all the time, but I never wanted to be an actress or a tech, so I didn't figure out how to get involved until much later," she told me. "I raised my children before I started working in this field."

She began as a volunteer. One night, at a dinner party, she sat next to a man who was the president of the Board of the City Center, a performing space for the arts in Manhattan. Daryl was so interested in what he did, that he asked her to join the musical theater committee. After two years, she was invited to join the Board.

"I would go to the theater almost every night—to little theaters downtown and I would hang around and say hello to people in the lobby. Often they were connected to the theater, and I got to know a lot of people. I always tell young people this is the best way to educate yourself.

"One night, I heard a cabaret act. It was just a string of songs, each one about a life transition. I approached David Shire and Richard Maltby who wrote it and asked if I could do something with it." She helped turn it into the 1988 off Broadway musical revue *Closer Than Ever*.

Since then, she has produced seventeen other plays. Four of them: *Proof, Wit, How I Learned to Drive,* and *Three Tall Women,* have won Pulitzer Prizes. One critic said that *Three Tall Women,* written by Edward Albee when he was out of fashion, cemented both his career and Daryl's.

"There is no way to train to be a producer," she told me. "You just do it. You learn as you go. Some people start by working for a production company or by working in general management. I didn't do any of that. I came from raising my children and running my own interior design firm...two strong places to come from. I designed offices, but running any kind of business is servicing clients, and a producer services the playwright, actors, director, and the audience.

"Raising a family you learn to do everything and keep your life going, to take care of everyone's needs and your own. As a producer, you have to take care of people and make sure they feel valued, supported, and loved. You have to make sure they feel part of the family, because any production feels like a family unit for the time you are together."

Many actors have told me about the family feeling that develops between cast members during a production. But they have also told me that a neurotic or overly demanding producer can make it feel like a dysfunctional family. Daryl Roth, however, revels in acting like a good mother.

"When I started working in the field," Daryl said, "People would say, 'She's just a housewife from New Jersey.' But I decided to turn it around and make it my strength." In almost every interview she gives, she is quoted as saying that she takes a maternal role as a producer. "I've always said that the reason I have good relations with people in the theater world is because being a producer is a very parental role," she told me.

"In the beginning, I was also called a dilettante. It hurt me, but it also fueled me and gave me tenacity, because I needed to prove that was not the case. I wanted to make a career out of this."

There was also a rumor that she was using her husband's money to fund her productions. "I had a nest egg. I used the money from my business, my mom put some money in, my sister put some money in, my dear friend put some money in, and my husband put some in, too. From the beginning I have put my own money into my productions, because I realized that people would feel more comfortable if I had my money at risk with their money. Many producers put up the seed money originally, and then try to lay it off on an investor. I just feel better with my investor relationships if they know I am working really hard on this and have money in it."

Raising the money to fund a production is one of the most important aspects of being a producer. But producers like Daryl, who specialize in producing new work by new playwrights, also have to find the director, manager, actors, theater, set designer, ad agency, and just about everything else. She says that the most important part of being a producer, however, is finding the project, and now that she is successful, many people send her scripts. Non-profit theaters also come to her with their small productions, asking her to help take them to larger theaters and larger audiences.

Daryl told me some of the ways she acts like a mom: she sends birthday cards to everyone in her productions or has birthday cakes at the theater after the show. She also helps with personal problems. For example, she arranged extra time off for one of her actresses with a sick mother. Furthermore, she established the Daryl Roth Creative Spirit Award that gives financial support to two young actors, writers, or directors who want to work on a specific project. The award includes the promise of a theater where they can do a reading or workshop.

Daryl's twenty-five-year-old son, Jordan, who has begun producing shows himself, has been allowed to watch her work for years. He came into the interview to tell me how he has seen the maternal quality in her work. "The level of support and safety she provides is very unusual," he said. "Safety is important in the beginning when you are finding what you want to do with the show—you need a safe environment to explore and not feel judged. When the show begins to run, there is a feeling of being truly supported, which is unusual in this business when actors and directors are replaced right and left if the show isn't selling enough tickets. She emerges from every production, whether it has been a flop or a success, with two or three life-long friends."

"By acting as a mother as well as a producer," Daryl added, "it frees the cast to do the work and not feel the weight of the world on their shoulders. A star can feel, 'Oh my god, there are millions of dollars and everyone's job depending on me.' Sometimes you are out on stage and the theater is only half-filled. Those are the times you want to come off stage and see your mom."

But Daryl doesn't just mother the stars. "Last night at *The Allergist's Wife*, we had two understudies playing parts. I go to my plays a lot and last night I just didn't feel like going. But I went because I wanted them to know that one of the producers was there to see what a good job they are doing. I didn't want them to feel like second fiddles."

If and when those understudies become stars in their own right, they will probably remember Daryl's kindness and want to work with her again, just like all the other actors, playwrights, directors, and set designers she has helped to become well known. They are all loyal to their nurturing theater mom who helped them grow their talent.

Bringing It Home

As mothers, we don't just protect our helpless infants, we foster their growth. We encourage strength and independence so our children can go off into the world—knowing they can always come back for nurturing as needed. But since the need for maternal nurturing tapers off over time, you might think about investing some of yours outside the home. The women in this chapter used their nurturing skills in many ways. How would you like to use yours?

There are over half a million American children in foster care. Few of us can help as many as Clara Hale did, but just providing a little nurturing for one lonely child is important work. Similarly, with all the hunger in this country and around the world, if all of us help just a little bit, it will add up to a lot. The Heifer Project estimates that the thirty cows the eighty-two-year-old Indiana woman has donated over the years have multiplied to at least twenty-one thousand cows by now.

On the other hand, perhaps your nurturing ability is being displayed at work. You don't have to be as wealthy and successful as Daryl Roth and Barbara Kingsolver to encourage the growth and ability of others. In most workplaces, there is someone who acts like a mother hen—remembering coworkers birthdays, lending support when others are discouraged, being concerned if someone feels sick. Those women are often the glue that makes the office feel like a family, and they deserve credit for keeping up morale. Farther up the hierarchy, maternal managers like Jo Luck make organizations grow to full potential.

How do you use your nurturing ability? Nurture your own dreams and aspirations and see how they can grow.

• Do you know a child who is not being properly nurtured? Is there any way you could spend more time with that child and provide some of the loving care that is missing? Many of my patients have told me that having a kind, nurturing neighbor or aunt made all the difference in their lives.

• Do you have a friend who is having a hard time or is trying to tackle a project that seems overwhelming? What could you do to help? When my son was sick, friends would occasionally drop off some soup or dinner. Just knowing that someone cared made us feel emotionally as well as physically nurtured. Similarly, when I was struggling with this manuscript, several friends read it and offered constructive criticism. They nurtured this project, just when I needed it the most.

• Do you know an organization that should expand? Do you know a small business that has a great deal of potential? Consider joining, making it grow, and growing with it.

chapter nine

COMFORT THOSE IN DISTRESS: THE ART OF HEALING

Who ran to help me when I fell
And who would some pretty story tell
Or kiss the place and make it well?
My mother.

—Jane Taylor

My psychology program required students to begin seeing patients after only one semester of graduate training. I was terrified when my first patient walked into my office. I didn't believe what the professors said: just listening to a person can be therapeutic. The professors told us not to give advice—just listen and try to reflect back what we heard the person saying. They told us that by giving patients a safe place to explore their feelings and by clarifying their situation and thinking everything through with them we could be helpful. I was amazed and relieved when it worked!

Why should I have been surprised? The most comforting thing my mother and father did for me was just to listen and care about what I was saying. By listening uncritically, they let me know that I was smart enough to solve my own problems. It was also comforting to know I could get their advice, if I asked for it.

Over the next few years, the professors taught us other techniques to help patients, so by the time we graduated and became full-fledged psychologists, we could do far more than just "active listening." But even today, after many years in practice, I still find that offering a comforting maternal ear is therapeutic.

Sometimes it is painful to lend a maternal ear in the home or in the office. It is heartbreaking, for example, when mothers have to listen to children who have been bullied. And sometimes, if we hear that our children are being harmed, we have to go way beyond just listening; we have to take strong, active steps to insure their safety.

In this chapter, you will read about mothers who have taken active steps to comfort not just their own children, but children and adults all over the country who have been victimized or harmed in various ways.

Helping a Child Survive Harassment

Perhaps the most extreme form of harassment in the United States occurred when schools were being integrated. Angry crowds of adults and children screamed insults and threats at the few black children brave enough to run the gauntlet into white schools. The black parents, who had to trust federal marshals to physically protect their children, found a variety of ways to emotionally comfort their youngsters.

Robert Coles, a Harvard psychiatrist who studied the situation, says the comfort and support the children received when they returned home each day allowed them to withstand torment. He was particularly impressed with the case of one six-year-old girl, Ruby Bridges, who, in 1960, was the only black child court-ordered to integrate an otherwise all-white elementary school in New Orleans.

Ruby's father had been a farm worker until he moved the family to New Orleans and became a janitor. Her mother was a housewife. The family was poor, but they had strong faith and values. They "were proud that their daughter had been chosen to take part in an important event in American history," wrote Coles, who reported that church was an important part of the Bridges's family strength. He quoted Ruby's mother as saying, "We sat there and prayed to God that we'd all be strong and we'd have courage and we'd get through any trouble, and Ruby would be a good girl and she'd hold her head up high and be a credit to her own people and a credit to all the American people. We prayed long and we prayed hard."

They taught Ruby to say the following prayer before she walked through the taunting crowd as she went to school each day, and before she had to face the crowds again at the end of school: "Please God, try to forgive those people, because even if they say those bad things, they don't know what they're doing. So, You could forgive them, just like You did those folks a long time ago when they said terrible things about You." By teaching Ruby this prayer they also taught her to not take the insults personally.

While Ruby's parents clearly encouraged her to be in a situation where she would be bullied and harassed daily, her mother also gave her an escape, if needed. During this terrible period Ruby told Coles, "Momma says if it gets real bad, we can always go [to grandfather's farm]. She says her daddy is the strongest man you can find. She says his arms are as wide as I am, and he can lick anyone and his brother together. She says not to worry; we have a hiding place and I should remember it every day." When people know they can leave, paradoxically, it often gives them the courage to stay.

No wonder Coles credits the resiliency of students like Ruby in large part to the backing of their mothers. As he wrote, "However impoverished and lowly their position in American society, Negro mothers are generally warm and affectionate." After grueling days at school, such warmth and affection helped the children recuperate.

Almost forty years later, another black southern mother, Aurelia Davis, of Forsyth, Georgia, discovered that her ten-year-old daughter,

LaShonda, was being harassed at school in a different way. She soon realized that more than maternal affection was needed to comfort her child.

In December, 1992, a boy who sat next to LaShonda in her fifth grade class began making repeated sexual threats and comments to her. He also began to rub himself against her and try to touch her breasts and genital area. When LaShonda told her parents about this, her mother complained to the teacher, assuming the boy would be controlled and the problem would cease. Instead, the problem seemed to be ignored.

Aurelia repeated her complaint and also spoke to the principal. The boy went unpunished, and it took three months just to honor LaShonda's request to have his seat moved away from hers.

Meanwhile, LaShonda was suffering in many ways. Before the harassment, she had been getting *A*s and *B*s. With the taunting, she couldn't concentrate and began failing tests. She screamed in her sleep, "Mommy please help me," while having nightmares that the boy, who chased her at school, caught her. Her father even found a suicide note.

Aurelia, a hospital file clerk with only a high school education, began going to the library after work to research sexual harassment. In May, she went to the police, and filed a criminal complaint against the boy. He pleaded guilty in juvenile court to sexual battery and wrote a letter of apology to LaShonda.

While the problem with the boy ceased, Aurelia was angry that the school had allowed the situation to go on for five months. She hired an attorney to sue the school for a million dollars, knowing that if she won, all schools would have to provide a harassment-free environment or face financial liability. The suit went through the federal courts and finally, in September, 1998, the Supreme Court agreed to hear the case.

When people asked Aurelia how she found the courage to fight so long, she said, "It didn't take courage to do this. It took anger, pure anger. My daughter wasn't taken care of, and they should pay for it...I didn't set out to make a landmark ruling, but if that's what it takes to make schools liable, that's what it takes." She wanted to require "schools to have a responsibility that schoolchildren will be both served and protected."

The justices seemed skeptical. They questioned Aurelia's lawyers sharply on how to draw the line between harassment and garden-variety teasing and flirting. But in May 1999, the Supreme Court sided with Aurelia Davis. They agreed with a lower court ruling that acknowledged students have a right to look to teachers for protection.

Thanks to Aurelia Davis's lawsuit, schools can now be held accountable for student sexual harassment. All schools have to come up with clear policies against such harassment and procedures for complaints.

By the time the Supreme Court ruled, sexual harassment had become widespread in schools. "Hostile Hallways," a 1993 Louis Harris poll for the American Association of University Women (AAUW) found that 85 percent of girls and 76 percent of boys in grades eight through eleven say they have been harassed. The majority of students have been the object of sexual comments and have been grabbed, touched, pinched, or brushed against in a sexual way in school.

The big surprise in the study was that boys were harassed almost as much as girls—and half of all girls and two-thirds of all boys said they had been perpetrators as well as victims. The difference is that girls are more likely to be harassed repeatedly, and to feel self-conscious and lose confidence in themselves because of it.

If this is such a common part of school life, should we just accept it? No. Psychologists (and all good parents) know how important it is for children to have the basic right to keep their bodies private, and not have to submit to unwanted touching or humiliation. "The kind of violence we see on television, in newspapers, in movies sends signals that behavior which is hurtful to others is not wrong," said Anne

Bryant, the AAUW's executive director. *Because* the behavior has become so common in schools and in the media, we have to fight against it.

Some conservatives saw the ruling as "gender politics" and "boy bashing," noting that while boys are often physical bullies, girls harass in verbal ways: name-calling, shunning, and starting rumors. True. But why should we tolerate either? Currently, spurred by the spate of school shootings perpetrated by children who have been bullied, parents are trying to force school systems to outlaw not just sexual harassment, but all kinds of bullying. While some over-vigilant schools will punish kids who are just being playful, strong steps have to be taken to make schools the safe havens all children need.

Repairing the Emotional Damage of Crime

When a person is the victim of a violent crime, it can feel like there is no safe haven. The whole world can seem dangerous. Family and friends, who often are in a state of shock themselves, may be too upset to think cooly about what to say or do. They may even find it too painful to listen to what happened. That's why victims' assistance services have sprung up all around the country.

Karel Amaranth directs Victims Assistance Services, one of the largest and most comprehensive agencies. She told me that services for victims began as a grassroots movement in the late 1970s and early '80s, after the women's movement focused on the trauma caused by sexual assault and domestic violence. It soon became clear that everyone—men, women, and children—are traumatized after being victimized by violent crime. "This agency, for example, was started by an individual whose aunt and uncle had been murdered," she explained.

"These grassroots organizations had an impact, and under President Reagan the Victims Rights Act was passed. It provides money for victims' assistance—not from tax money, but through federal criminal fines." For example, fines collected from pharmaceutical companies the federal government sued go into this fund as do the proceeds from selling drug dealer's homes and cars. The fund helps groups that range from MADD chapters and agencies combating domestic violence to victim's services offered through district attorneys' offices. An agency like Karel's, which has several offices in New York, uses such funds to provide counseling, as well as practical assistance that can range from changing door locks to giving rape victims forensic exams.

Whatever the crime, whether the counselor is male or female, Karel says there is a maternal quality to comforting victims in distress. "Victims services and motherhood are both empowerment models. There certainly is the nurturing component to help our clients grow, just like we want to see our children grow. We must be supportive and caring and teaching, just as parents are with their children. But it is very important for us to lay out the options, directions, and opportunities, and allow people to choose what is best for them."

Then, the most difficult part of being a counselor (or a mother) is to step back and let the person make their own decisions—and mistakes. "It is very difficult to see people make decisions that are not good for them," says Karel. "We experience this particularly with domestic violence victims. We may work with them extensively and feel that they have grown beyond their abusive relationship, that they are ready to go out on their own. Then they see the guy in court and they say, 'I love him and don't want to prosecute.' It is not just dropping charges, but going back into the violent relationship. Or in cases of elder abuse where the elderly person is not going to kick out their son or daughter, even though that child is being abusive, even though we have set out their options. In cases where there is violence, it is very difficult to back off and respect those choices."

However, when counselors see clients go back into relationships that will predictably continue to be violent and dangerous, they may not give up hope. "It often takes several tries to leave. It can be a long process of two steps forward and one step back. We have a project called The Hope Chest that recognizes that getting out of an abusive relationship is a process," explains Karel.

"We help people develop their own hope chest—whatever they might need—so if things get violent, they can pick up a bag (or have the bag in the back of their car or in our office) and leave with their children on a moment's notice. Things that might go in the hope chest are immigration papers, prescriptions, children's school records, a phone card, some traveler's checks, or a bus ticket. It is all very carefully planned with safety in mind."

Victims of domestic violence are just one kind of client that Karel's agency helps. Every kind of violent crime produces trauma. "There are lots of kinds of victims, and the pacing is different with each individual. However, with all victims of crime the important first step is just to be there and listen to what they have experienced and where they are. Eventually they need to get in touch with what their strengths are. Then we help them lay out their different options and alternatives. We help them make plans and facilitate those plans. But everything is very personal and individual based on each person's personality.

"Some people just want to tell you the basics and get on with filing for Crime Victims Board compensation or other steps to make things better. Some just want help to get justice or vengeance. They may come back months or years later to get some comforting. Other people need to express all their feelings before they can even think about what they want to do.

"Beyond this, here are some of the services we provide: in rape, a nurse will do a forensic exam and collect evidence. Many victims appreciate the sensitivity of that exam and the comfort of finding that they are medically okay, but they never want to use the forensic evidence to prosecute.

"With homicide victims, sometimes the first thing we need to do is help the family make funeral arrangements and deal with the financial aspects of it. We can contact the Crime Victims Board for an emergency check so the funeral director can get on with the funeral. We hold a vigil for homicide victims every year. That is one of the hardest things I do—setting it up and spending time with the families. It is very emotional. But it is comforting for people to know that their loved ones are memorialized."

Karel says that the best part of her job is being creative, inventing new ways to serve victims. For example, when she heard that some female prisoners had been raped, she not only created a program to help them, but also a way to get it funded.

Rape is common in prison, but unfortunately, it is often neither stopped nor treated. The Federal Victims of Crime Act only can help "innocent victims of crime," and even though the prisoners were raped by guards, since the victims were prisoners, they were not considered "innocent." So, Karel found private funding and she and the staff went to the jail after work.

"We did not go in with a bleeding heart approach or a punitive approach," she says. "Instead, we gave an eight-week presentation on what is victimization. This had a very powerful impact, because many inmates hadn't grasped the fact that they have really harmed people with their crimes. On the other hand, many people in jail have been victimized themselves. We talked about victimization. Then they talked and revealed their own victimization. We finished with a panel where four to five people who had been victims of crime talked about the impact it had on their lives."

The program was such a success that Karel now runs it not just for female prisoners, but also for men and adolescents in correctional facilities. The county now funds this work and she planned to present it at a national convention shortly after our interview.

Karel is concerned that victims do not know assistance services are available to them. She has tried a variety of outreach methods including brochures and even ads in movie theaters. She also tries to keep in close contact with police departments. She says that anyone who needs a referral to a victim's assistance service can contact the National Organization for Victims Assistance at 1-800-TRY-NOVA or at www.try-nova.org.

As a psychologist, I know how personally upsetting it can be when listening to a patient who has been the victim of a violent crime. So, I asked Karel how she and the staff who are caring, maternal people can hear such things all day, every day.

"I work very hard as the director to provide as much support as I can for my staff," she replied. "Because of strict confidentiality, staff can never go home and talk about what they have heard with their friends and family, so we talk together about the awful things we see—that is an important part of team building."

Having a personal therapist is helpful, she added, plus "You have to have a life outside of this and a perpetual recognition of how difficult the work is. I know that if I am going to be in this for the long haul, I have to take good care of myself. I know when I have to take myself away—go home for a bike ride, take my kayak out on the river, be with my family, take vacations.

"Whether it is working with victims or being a mother, I tell people that flight attendants give us the most important information: if there is an emergency, you must put on your oxygen mask before you assist someone else. If you don't, you might save someone, but then you are gone in terms of being able to help anyone else. Take time to make sure that you are breathing well and breathing good air."

The Pain that Never Ends

When Migs Woodside learned about a huge and previously hidden group of victims, the children of alcoholics, she felt obligated to start an organization to help them. She also found that wherever she goes, she has to comfort the adult children of alcoholics.

Migs, the dynamic founder of the Children of Alcoholics Foundation, says that whenever she is in a plane, restaurant, or public place carrying material marked with the name of her organization, people come up to her and say, "Can I talk to you?...Will you meet me?...Can I see you?"

"This is such a widespread problem," she told me. "There are twenty-eight million children of alcoholics in the United States, seven million are younger than eighteen. The remainder are adults, carrying their own pain and scars and worried about their children because we know there is an inherited susceptibility."

Many people have told Migs painful stories, and I asked what she says in return. "Hopefully I say things that are useful and comforting: you didn't cause it. You can't cure it. You can't control it. It's not your fault. Take the attention off the alcoholic and put it on yourself—you must get help."

You might expect that Migs started the foundation because she was the child of an alcoholic. Not so. In fact, she started working in addiction services as a fluke and was the only person in her office that had no personal experience with the problem. From that unlikely beginning, she came to be one of the foremost experts on addiction in the country.

"After I graduated from Vassar, I married and taught school for a year until I had my first child. Then I did a lot of charity and volunteer work, but I didn't want to make that my life. So, when my children were six and ten, I told everyone I knew that I wanted to work. A friend of mine was the medical/psychiatric supervisor of Daytop Village, a residential therapeutic community for heroin addicts. He rarely went there because he had a psychiatric practice, so he wanted me to be his eyes and ears.

"I was the only 'square' on the staff, the only one who had never done drugs. Since addiction had interfered with their education, they needed me because I was so literate. I did everything from talking to the parole board and probation officers to writing up notes of meetings."

That initial job led to others in the field, and by the late 1970s she was consulting to the Senate Sub-Committee on Juvenile Delinquency about narcotics issues. When she worked on the Runaway Youth Act, she discovered that there were children who were living alone on the streets, yet were not runaways, so were not legally eligible for services. She began going to agencies around the country to find out about homeless youth, and what she found shocked her.

"We knew there were kids in New York City living in doorways and alleyways and train stations, but there were also eleven-year-olds prostituting themselves in Seattle, and homeless kids living in cars in the suburbs. I interviewed these young people many nights. The main reason they couldn't go home was that someone in the house was drinking and being verbally, physically, or sexually abusive. Often the parents had told them to leave.

"In the suburbs, in middle-class, two-parent families it tended to be parents who said, 'I worked hard. I got mine, now go! You're sixteen, we've had enough. Get out.' In cities it often had to do with a single-parent family where there was a new boyfriend or girlfriend in the house and it was upsetting the homeostasis—particularly if mom's new boyfriend had, as they would say, his 'nose open for a young girl.' Mom would throw out her daughter, not the guy. These kids had no place to go. The common thread in these homes was alcoholism—these young people were children of alcoholics.

"They were so pitiful. They really touched my heart. All they wanted was for someone to open the door and give them a chance. They wanted to live in a single room with a hot plate and work in a fast food operation. But this is quite difficult when you are fifteen or sixteen. So, I wrote the report that lead to including homeless youth in the Runaway Youth Act.

"Governor Carey of New York asked Joe Califano to study heroin in the state. Joe included alcoholism in the study, because he had gotten interested in that subject when he was the Secretary of Health, Education, and Welfare under President Johnson. When Joe asked me to help, I proposed to study the children of alcoholics, because we knew they were not getting help."

Migs went out and talked with counselors and kids living at home with a parent who drank too much. She saw the pictures children drew of their life at home. "They were so heartbreaking," she said. "One was a picture of parents fighting and dad drunk with the child cowering in bed, listening. (Parents believe the children don't know what goes on, but the children hear everything.) Another had parents with guns fighting. One was titled, 'When Mom Hit Me with the Spatula.' There was a beer can saying, 'Now I've got your mother!' and one called, 'A Day in the Life,' which had five panels: mom trying to get up in the morning, mom taking pills and alcohol with coffee, mom going back to bed, the little girl in pigtails bringing mom her tray, and mom slumped over in the chair with the little girl standing next to her. I get chills thinking about that one, because when is that girl ever going to get any attention herself?

"Alcohol takes over the whole family and the children's lives. One pitiful aspect of this is when I asked the youngsters, 'What do you want for yourself?' all they could see was themselves in relationship with the alcoholic parent. They would say things like, 'When my mom stops drinking...' or 'When my dad gets better...' They had no hope, no dream, no future. They couldn't separate themselves at all.

"To listen to these young people talk touched me as a mother—to realize that my children had a future, my children had possibilities, and

I am doing everything I can for them, but these children are abandoned and neglected even though it may look like they are living in an intact home. The parents were in a fog, and the children never knew when the alcohol would kick in. These parents were very abusive and said things like, 'I drink because of you.' Children love their parents and believe it is their fault. They needed help.

"Governor Carey held a press conference about the Children of Alcoholics report. There were a great number of reporters, which was a surprise to me. First, we showed a film—a very poignant film—of children and what happens to them at home and how they run away in the middle of the night because their parents are drinking. Then he released the report to the press.

"The next morning I started looking for an article in the B section of the *New York Times*, but didn't see anything. Then I saw it was on the front page.

"There was an avalanche of calls from all over the United States and Western Europe and wherever the *Times* was seen. People called the governor's office and my office saying, 'I think my dad's an alcoholic, how can I help him?' 'My mom drinks too much and I can't bring friends home. She puts her elbow in the grapefruit and lies there drunk.' Spouses began calling asking what they could do about their husband or wife, saying they were worried about their children. Adult children of alcoholics called to say what had happened to them."

The calls continued. In fact, they have never stopped. In preparation for a Governor's Conference on the subject Migs, Governor Carey, and Joe Califano asked a number of prominent people to join an honorary sponsoring committee, just to lend their names to demystify alcoholism and the stigma surrounding it. People like Sherry Lansing, Paul Newman, Rod Steiger, Barbara Walters, and Hugh Downs joined the committee even though many had no alcoholism in their families. They agreed because it was a hidden problem and a good cause.

In addition, Migs recalls, "We set up a panel of programs and invited social service agencies to advise us on the nature of the problem, because we did not want to set up new bureaucracies. There were plenty of bureaucracies in place already. We also developed a show of children's artwork.

"The conference was widely reported, and the avalanche continued. I was going off to do a consulting project at Brown University, but the calls and letters didn't stop. So, Joe Califano and some of the social service people and I got together. We decided we had to set up some kind of organization, because we had stimulated this outpouring and it was irresponsible to walk away when there was all that suffering.

"In 1982 we set up a 501 (c)3 [a non-profit] and made it clear we were not trying to compete with existing organizations. We just wanted to give referral help and develop educational materials for the vast number of people who were and still are contacting us. We also wanted to develop material for any group that is in contact with children of alcoholics—physicians, school nurses, teachers, and psychologists."

Migs was the head of the foundation. When I asked her what she did, she laughed and said, "Everything! Anybody who starts an organization had better be prepared to Xerox. I did program development, fund-raising, hiring staff, organizing staff, replying to letters and phone calls, a lot of media, and talks to professional groups."

One thing the foundation did not have to worry about was funding. Many from the star-studded group that had originally helped publicize the conference stayed on to help and still continue to do so. Plus, "Joe Califano moved in a world where there were foundations, and my husband was the CEO of a major corporation, American Can, which gave us access to people who could help," she explained. "My husband and I moved in a world where there were other CEOs, but we never received funds from American Can because that would have been a conflict of interest."

For years, Migs Woodside ran the Children of Alcoholics Foundation and also handled the many obligations of a CEOs wife. She remembers being on a business trip with her husband in Korea, and regularly calling the office at 2 a.m. Korea time, so that she could comment on everything from proposals to graphics. While she gave her husband a great deal of support, he was extremely proud and supportive of her work, too.

Then in 1993, Migs's husband was diagnosed with a lung disease. It was thought that a different climate might be good for his health. She tried running the foundation from their new home in Arizona, but decided "it was unfair to try to supervise and run an operation long distance. I decided what was the most important thing in my life, and it was Bill Woodside."

She found a successor and also moved the foundation under the umbrella of Phoenix House, a drug treatment program in Manhattan. Now Phoenix House handles all the administrative functions, permitting the Children of Alcoholics Foundation to concentrate on programs and program development.

"I think all founders have a problem giving up their creations, but I knew it was healthier for the foundation if I did," she says. She remains connected by being on the Board of Phoenix House, and has started a new, philanthropic life in Arizona.

While alcoholism is still widespread, Migs's work to publicize the impact on children led to a far greater openness on the subject. The small explosion of books in the 1980s on the issues facing adult children of alcoholics was largely inspired by her work. And while seven million children are still trapped in homes with an alcoholic parent, at least schools and the helping professions can get materials from the Children of Alcoholics Foundation to let those children know they are understood and not alone.

Bringing It Home

The helping professions—teaching, nursing, social work—have always been predominantly female because they require healing, comforting maternal skills. These days even the traditionally male helping professions like psychology and medicine are tipping female.

Why are we so good at helping and healing? While many of us have been lucky enough to have comforting fathers, the basic comforting skills have been considered maternal. They are part of our "tend and befriend" instincts.

You probably do these things every day with your children. If not, don't despair. Even if they are not part of your natural instincts, they are skills you can develop. Everyone who is in training to be a psychotherapist is, hopefully, learning those skills right now. Parent education classes usually teach them, too. Here are some ways to use and improve your comforting, healing skills with or without classes:

- You don't necessarily have to do anything but listen and be there. For example, if you have a friend or family member who has a difficult appointment with a doctor, a lawyer, or the court, just going with them and quietly sitting beside them can be a very comforting act. (I will never forget the people who came to visit when my son Jean Paul was in the hospital.) It is comforting just hearing a friend genuinely make such an offer.

- Does your child's school have a program to combat bullying and harassment? It should include clear, reasonable guidelines for distinguishing acceptable from harmful behavior. It should include a simple, safe method for a student to lodge a complaint, and should set reasonable guidelines for punishments

continued

173

that fit the crimes. If not, offer to help the PTA or principal create such a program. Also, arrange to have one of the Children of Alcoholics Foundation art shows at the school. (If you think the problem does not exist in your school district, you are fooling yourself.) These shows help such children know they are not alone.

• Many organizations train volunteers in counseling techniques that comfort people in distress. Such volunteers do everything from answering telephone hot lines to working with troubled households sent by family court. If you would like to get such training, prepare for a lengthy search. Begin by calling your local family court or chamber of commerce to ask if they know of such training opportunities. Also, look in the Yellow Pages under Social and Human Services, which lists private, public, and government agencies. Call the ones that sound interesting to you and ask if they train volunteers.

chapter ten

SEE THE GOOD IN OUR CHILDREN: THE UNEXPECTED PERKS OF UNCONDITIONAL LOVE

No mother has a homely child.
—**A Dictionary of American Proverbs**

A friend told me about a VIP breakfast that honored successful women. One honoree was Barbara Corcoran, chair and founder of the largest privately owned real estate firm in New York City. Everyone at the breakfast knew how difficult it is to start from nowhere, as Ms. Corcoran did, and rise to the top of the cutthroat real estate field.

Barbara's success is attributed to her creative approach to advertising, promotions, and programs. For example, she started "The Corcoran Report," a widely quoted source of data about real estate sales. She was also one of the first realtors to go online.

When Barbara Corcoran accepted the honor, she revealed that as a child, no one except her mother would have predicted her success. She said her mom saw her talents when the rest of the world thought she had none. Here is a capsule of the story Barbara told: she was a dyslexic child who did poorly in school. Even though she was one of ten children, her mother listened empathetically when little Barbara would come home, upset by problems at school.

If Barbara failed a test, her mother would say, "Don't worry. You will be successful because you have a fabulous imagination." If no one picked her to be on their team, her mom would say, "Don't pay any attention to that. You have a fantastic imagination."

Barbara held on to her mother's words and began to think that maybe her imagination was something special. Her imagination began to foster dreams of success—and later created innovative ways to make those dreams come true.

Every child, at one time or another, feels shame about being unpopular, unsuccessful, or "stupid." Those are universal feelings. Good parents have come to terms with their own issues like this, so they can be empathetic when their children struggle with the same. Then, like Barbara's mother, they can point to some real reason why their child will be able to overcome difficulties in the future.

Lately, the most popular children's books are written by mothers who, understanding those universal childhood concerns, write stories to help kids cope. Bestselling authors Judy Blume and J.K. Rowling create modern heroes and heroines: kids with flaws and fears who are successful in spite of their failings.

On the other hand, what do you do when you discover that your child is struggling with a problem that you can't identify with...a problem that many people believe is not only abnormal but immoral too? In the last few decades, as homosexuals became more open, their parents had to cope with that painful reality. So many mothers learned to accept their gay children that they have forced society to become more accepting also.

The last example in this chapter deals with mothers who have seen the good in children who have "special needs"—older children or children with disabilities who need to be adopted. Many of these children have been removed from their birth homes because of abuse and neglect. Often they languish in foster care for years. Mothers around the country have led the movement to find loving adoptive homes for them, and have had great success.

The Flawed Hero

I bet that as a preteen you had a hard time seeing the beauty of your body. Instead, you were probably thinking your breasts were too small or too big…or your butt was too skinny or too fat. I bet you secretly obsessed over your menstrual pads, explored your body, had sexual thoughts, and fervently prayed that your heartthrob would notice you. Perhaps you can still feel the hurt of mean things someone said to you many years ago. For a long time you may have thought you were the only one who felt this way.

How do I know? These are universal experiences. We all had them, and our daughters do too. But, thanks to Judy Blume, our daughters know they are not alone. She tells our girls the truth: they are good girls even if they think "bad" thoughts sometimes; bad things happen to perfectly nice girls; and things will probably get better.

In the 1970s, Judy Blume broke new ground when she made children's writing realistic. She acknowledged that childhood and adolescence is not the sweet experience adults want to pretend it is. She addressed in fictional form the day-to-day angst that kids really feel.

My daughter, Nicole, and her friends read every Judy Blume book many times. Nicole says, "Even though I developed early and most of the girls in Judy Blume books were shy and undeveloped, I could always relate to them. They were always going through some coming-of-age experience that I was going through—or hoping to go through—like dating, kissing, getting your period, or growing breasts. The books were so real that I couldn't believe an adult wrote them."

Other kids say the books were lifesavers. As one girl told me, "I was a very large child with braces and bad hair. I was always made fun of. I thought I was just some freak, and felt that everyone else was so happy.

"Judy Blume's *Blubber* was about an overweight girl. I must have read it fifteen times. It was so great to be able to read about someone else's problems like mine. I remember using some of her comebacks to kids who teased me.

"Judy Blume made it seem like everyone was being made fun of by someone, which was a comforting thought. Her characters were always able to come out on top at the end." Now this girl is a beautiful, college senior who has just accepted a great job offer. She credits Judy Blume for helping her hold on through the rough spots growing up.

How could Judy write with the mind of a kid? She remembered what it was like to be a small, skinny late-bloomer. She remembered that before she became outgoing, she was shy and fearful. Most important, she remembered how painful those feelings are. Instead of being one of those adults who insist that childhood is the happiest time of life, she decided to write about things that make perfectly normal kids feel rotten.

Judy was a twenty-seven-year-old mother when she began to write. For two years she received rejection slips. Then she found a publisher who understood and encouraged her. "I felt only that I had to write the most honest books I could," she explains on her website, "It never occurred to me, at the time, that what I was writing was controversial."

Blume's honesty included not just the thoughts and fears, but also the real words and phrases kids use. Many adults were shocked and tried to ban her books. Others, including critics and children's literature prize committees, applauded her talent. More important to Judy, kids recognized her as someone who really understood them—someone who understood that good kids could have "bad" thoughts, and even do "bad" things—someone who understood that nice kids are often the target of mean teasing.

Judy Blume has written twenty-two books, which have sold more than seventy million copies around the world in more than twenty languages. Because young readers feel that she really understands them, thousands write to share their concerns and feelings with her each month.

Where does she get her ideas for books? "Ideas come from everywhere," she says. "Memories of my own life, incidents in my children's lives, what I see and hear and read—and most of all, from my imagination."

Her first book, *The One in the Middle Is the Green Kangaroo*, dealt with the lonely feelings of being a middle child. Her second, *Iggie's House*, concerned the relationship between black and white kids. Her real breakthrough, however, came when she wrote her third book, *Are You There, God? It's Me, Margaret*. She says, "I let go and this story came pouring out. I knew Margaret. When I was in sixth grade, I longed to develop physically like my classmates. I tried doing exercises, resorted to stuffing my bra, and lied about getting my period. And like Margaret, I had a very personal relationship with God that had little to do with organized religion. God was my friend and confidant." Some parents where shocked by Judy's honest portrayal of a sixth grade girl's thoughts, but girls loved the book and became loyal Judy Blume readers.

Her children inspired several of Judy's most important books. The character Fudge from several of her books, including *Superfudge*, which has won more than thirty-five prizes for excellence, was based on her son. An incident from her daughter's classroom, where the class leader victimized another child, inspired *Blubber*. Judy says, "When I began this book I was determined to write the truth about the school bus culture in the language of that culture. Some adults are bothered by the language and the cruelty, but the kids get it. They live it."

Judy was upset that her daughter's teacher lacked the skills and awareness to prevent the victimization. She is pleased that some school districts use *Blubber* in teacher training to help prevent such situations in the future.

The reality Judy Blume uses may seem worlds apart from the fantasy in J.K.(Joanne) Rowling's bestselling Harry Potter series. However, the two authors and their books have a lot in common. They allow kids to deal with universal fears and to see the good in themselves when they are feeling bad.

Harry Potter is an orphaned young wizard living with people who misunderstand and mistreat him. Since most children worry about losing their parents, and wonder how they could ever survive on their own, fantasy stories give children a safe way to explore such fears.

Like Blume, Rowling's success is due to an understanding that good kids often feel lonely, alienated, and unpopular. Both authors know from their own lives that pain is part of growing up, and convey this to their readers. More importantly, the books convey the message that even children who feel miserable sometimes can eventually become popular and successful.

Joanne Rowling's story is the stuff of legend. As a teenager, she watched her mother begin a ten-year battle with multiple sclerosis. As a young woman, divorce left her on welfare, living in an unheated apartment in Edinburgh with her baby. Writing in coffeehouses, while her infant daughter slept next to her, success seemed as much a fantasy as Harry's wizardry.

After several rejections, a British publisher bought her first book. One year later, the American publisher, Scholastic, bought the rights. After they published the book and promoted Harry Potter, and it grew into a massive bestseller, she was making millions.

Joanne brought her own knowledge of the fear of a parent's death, plus the loneliness and pain of poverty to her young character, Harry Potter. Even though the Potter series is fantasy, as her agent said, "It really comes out of the playground," because Joanne is a master at listening to the way kids talk, and knowing that even happy kids feel lousy some of the time.

Harry may have superhuman powers, but real-life children identify with him, because he has the same feelings and problems that they do. Like all children at one time or another, Harry feels lonely and misunderstood. He is excited by the prospect of going places alone, yet afraid of getting lost. He is afraid that he will not measure up in his new school. He is intimidated by the rich kids, feels stupid in class, and is disliked by "mean" teachers. Weren't you, too?

Even though Harry is weak, skinny, and poor, he finds ways to triumph over evil, cope with betrayal, and overcome a series of trials and adversities. In one hundred countries around the world, kids feel that if Harry can overcome his problems, they can, too. He inspires them to feel that weak kids can also be strong, and kids who aren't the brightest can still be smart and successful.

In short, Rowling, like Blume and good mothers everywhere, helps kids see the good in themselves.

Shocking Cher

Can you imagine having Cher as your mother? She is by all accounts loving, but she also wears revealing clothes, dates young rock stars, and has a flamboyant lifestyle. If you were her child, you would think there was nothing you could do to shock your mom, right? Not true. Cher's daughter, Chastity, wrote a book, *Family Outing*, about something that would shock and dismay most mothers, even Cher: finding out that their child is gay.

Chastity was a beautiful blonde baby that Cher used to dress in frilly clothes. As soon as she could pick her own clothes, however, Chastity became a tomboy who dressed in a masculine manner. Cher was embarrassed that her daughter was "marching around in combat boots." Then, when Cher realized the issue went far deeper than just style and clothes, she was distraught. "I cried myself into a stupor," she says. Then, "I tried to figure out what I was going to do about it."

Like most parents in similar situations, she discovered that she couldn't do anything about her daughter's sexual orientation, so she had to do something about her own attitude. "I tried to figure out what was making me so upset," she says. "I realized that as a mother, I felt so responsible. It also reflected on me in some kind of way: on who I was in the community." However, she also recalls thinking about Chastity, "You were my child, and I loved you."

That mother love propelled her into therapy with her daughter. It took a long time for Cher to fully accept Chastity as a whole person. "As my mother came to terms with my sexuality," Chastity writes, "we became closer than we'd ever been before." These days, Cher has even become an activist for gay rights, because when she realized Chastity and others "didn't have the same rights as everyone else, [she] thought that was unfair."

Cher's first public involvement with gay issues occurred in 1997, when she spoke at a ceremony sponsored by a support group for the families of homosexuals, PFLAG (Parents, Families, and Friends of Lesbians and Gays.) PFLAG is often the first place bewildered parents find understanding when they discover the truth about their children's sexuality. It was, as you may have guessed, started by a mom.

While homosexuality is still a deep, dark secret for many people, it is clear how much has changed when you read the history of PFLAG on their website. They explain that seeds for the organization were sown when in April, 1972, the *New York Post* published a letter from Jeanne Manford, whose gay son had been badly beaten at a protest while the police stood by. "I didn't think anything of it, but I guess it was the first time a mother ever sat down publicly and said, 'Yes, I have a homosexual child,'" recalls Manford.

Two months later, Manford and her son, Morty, marched in New York's gay pride parade together. Manford carried a sign that read, 'Parents of Gays: Unite in Support for Our Children.' The crowd screamed, yelled, and cried as Manford approached. Initially, she thought they were cheering for Dr. Benjamin Spock who walked behind the Manfords, but as people began to crowd around her, she realized they were reacting to her.

Immediately, people began calling Jeanne Manford. Homosexual men and women asked her to speak with their parents. Parents wanted to share experiences with her. Radio and television reporters requested interviews. In March, 1973, a meeting of twenty people who had gay children was held in a Methodist church in Manhattan. That was the beginning of PFLAG, which now has 440 chapters worldwide and over eighty thousand members.

I have three friends whose sons revealed they're gay. After a period of upset and distress, their families are still close. In each case, not atypically, the fathers gave tacit acceptance. The mothers, however, have become more outspoken in support of their sons. One of those friends, Marlene Shyer, has even written a book, *Not Like Other Boys*, with her son, Chris, about how they painfully came to terms with his sexual orientation.

Marlene, the author of eleven other books, including the well-known *Welcome Home, Jelly Bean*, didn't want to write *Not Like Other Boys*. She knew it would take an enormous amount of work, especially since Chris had never written anything except school papers and business memos. She worried that few people would buy the book. So why did she agree?

Chris was insistent and, Marlene says, "his motivation is sublime. He feels he has a mission, a selfless mission, to help adolescents avoid the suffering that he went through—the terrible self-hatred, the fear of being found out, the humiliation and scapegoating that occurred in his high school years."

Furthermore, Marlene wanted to help other parents avoid the pain and self-blame she felt from the time Chris was very young, because he was different from other boys. She told me she was always distressed that "although Chris had a father and older brother, he always seemed more interested in my activities and was particularly interested in watching me put on jewelry, cook, and bake. Most worrisome was his predilection for playing with the neighborhood girls instead of joining the games of the boys outside.

"I barred him from 'lady' activities, promoted friendships with boys his age, took him to three different psychotherapists, encouraged his father to become more involved with him and tried to teach him to throw a ball. I even took him to a neurologist to find out why he couldn't participate in ball sports.

"I had the incorrect notion that when you have a baby you have total control over what your child will be—one misstep and you have completely ruined the recipe. You have added the wrong ingredient and the cake won't rise. I took my role very seriously as a mother and I wanted to do everything right. I had all these misguided notions."

Marlene's two most seriously 'misguided notions' were accepted as common knowledge when Chris was growing up: an overly involved mother combined with a distant father creates homosexuality, and therapy can 'cure' most homosexuality. Once she learned that neither assumption is correct, she was able to "recognize that no matter what his sexual orientation, my son is an absolutely splendid, centered, hard-working, and unusually decent human being."

Marlene also realized that another great fear—that the life of a homosexual is miserable—is not necessarily true. "I know that life is easier for a member of a majority," she says. "However, I note that happiness in an individual's life is not necessarily correlated to sexual orientation. Chris is lucky to have siblings who provide him with plenty of family life, and he has a very successful career. (He is an executive with a manufacturing company.) His nature is generally cheerful and resilient, which is the biggest plus of all."

I asked Marlene why it seems that mothers can accept their son's homosexuality more easily than fathers. "There are many enlightened fathers who accept their gay sons," she replied. "On the other hand, most daddies want a chip off the old block, meaning, someone just like themselves. For many, being macho also means fathering macho sons."

When Marlene and Chris's book was published in 1996 they went on a promotional book tour around the country. Marlene was overwhelmed by the reception she received, "Young men came up to me and said our book meant so much to them. They wanted to give our book to their parents so they and their parents would know they were not alone."

Like most books these days, *Not Like Other Boys* eventually went out of print, but the Shyers are currently having it reprinted through back-inprint.com. Marlene says, "This is my most important book, not just for parents of gay children. All parents have to cope with the feeling that their child is not perfect—and have to figure out how to do right by that 'less-than-perfect' child."

Less-Than-Perfect Child Adoption

Marlene wants to help other mothers see the good in their children, even when society doesn't. The following mothers try to do the same with a different group of undervalued children—foster kids who need permanent homes.

When I was a young psychologist, in the late 1970s, I worked in a county mental health clinic. Two of the young patients I saw there still haunt me. Both were handsome, preadolescent black boys who had grown up in foster care from the time they were babies. Bobby had been taken away from his neglectful, drug-addicted mother. Phillip's mother had placed him in foster care "temporarily," but rarely visited him.

Bobby had been raped by older boys in a group home. Phillip tried to commit suicide when his foster family decided they didn't want to care for him anymore. I was furious, because these kids could have had happy lives if they had been adopted as babies. No one seemed to realize that they needed adoptive homes even more than psychotherapy.

I researched why there were so many children like Bobby and Phillip growing up in foster care, while couples were traveling around the world, spending thousands of dollars to adopt elsewhere. I found that foster care agencies were reluctant to free children for adoption because they felt no adoptive homes could be found for "special needs" children, i.e. non-white, older, or disabled children. However, all around the country, concerned parents were not only adopting such children, but were starting agencies to help others do the same. Two of the great pioneers in the movement were Barbara Tremitiere and Sydney Duncan.

Barbara Tremitiere of Tressler-Lutheran Social Services in York, Pennsylvania, worked in an area that was rural, white, and conservative. However, she and one or two other social workers found adoptive homes for more than two thousand special needs children between 1972 and 1985. She attributed her success to her dramatic change in adoption procedures: she put potential adopters in training groups and allowed them, not the social workers, to decide whether to adopt or not. The role of the social workers was supportive, not judgmental. They wanted to educate the applicants about the difficult realities of special needs adoption and help them acquire the parenting skills necessary for success.

Barbara allowed the prospective parents to select the special needs children they could love. Throughout the pre-adoptive training period applicants had access to photo-listing books of children that were waiting for homes. Tremitiere said, "It is always amazing to see how their level of acceptance expands as they actually see pictures and read about specific waiting children. It is a constant reinforcement to my firm conviction that adoptive parents should select their own children."

A staff worker further explained, "By changing the process—letting applicants be in charge, but giving them good preparation—we've been successful. They are 'happy customers' and they send their friends in." This helped the organization grow.

Today, Barbara Tremitiere is still active in the cause. She is the director of her own agency, One Another Adoption Program, in Hallem, Pennsylvania. She has fifteen children, twelve of whom were special needs adoptions.

Sydney Duncan, director of Homes for Black Children, worked with a different population—urban blacks. However, she and Barbara Tremitiere had much in common. They both believed in the goodness of potential adopters and the adoptability of special needs children.

When Sydney founded her agency in 1972, there were large numbers of black children free for adoption and waiting for homes. She knew that black communities have a long tradition of taking in needy children; however, they rarely adopted through agencies because they found such agencies intimidating. So, she and her small staff made sure their agency was welcoming. They, like Barbara Tremitiere, put the emphasis on the applicants' capacity to nurture, rather than traditional adoption requirements like a bank account, home ownership, and no previous divorce.

Sydney contacted a professional public relations woman and reporters from local papers. Pictures of available children plus human interest stories about adoption began appearing regularly in every possible medium, from the radical press to in-house company publications at the Ford Motor Company. The publicity Sydney generated resulted in seven hundred applications in her first five months of operation. She had to stop the public relations campaign because she was overwhelmed by applicants. Homes for Black Children facilitated four hundred adoptions in its first three years of operation. Today, she and her agency continue to serve the cause.

I would like to report that there are very few Bobbys and Phillips in the foster care system anymore. Unfortunately, that is not so. As I write this, there are over five hundred thousand children living in foster care. Drugs, alcohol, poverty, and unplanned pregnancies have kept the numbers high.

Most foster children have been removed from their birth homes because of abuse and neglect. Many are growing up in foster care and suffering as Bobby and Phillip did, even though pioneers like Barbara and Sydney showed this is unnecessary, and laws call for adoption plans to be made after a child has been in foster care for two years.

Why are kids still living in the impermanence of foster care? Too many foster care officials are still territorial about keeping "their" children in foster care. Too many do not promote adoption because they still believe that no one wants to adopt "special needs" kids. There are also many who have a negative view of adoption, like the federal official who told me, "Every adoption represents a system failure. It would be an abomination to suggest otherwise."

While one hundred thousand foster children are free for adoption, many have suffered so much before they came into the system, and then suffered so much in the system, that their needs are extremely special indeed. Luckily though, there are still dedicated professionals and volunteers working to help them—but not enough.

Here is another story of just how much one dedicated mother can do for the cause: Janet Marchese has made it her mission to find loving homes for Down's syndrome children. Her non-profit service, A Kids Exchange, which she runs out of her home in White Plains, New York, has helped arrange four thousand such adoptions.

Janet and her husband, a police officer, had two biological children when they decided to adopt two young sisters from Korea. As they were waiting for the girls, their adoption agency social worker called to ask if they would care for a Down's syndrome newborn that had been left at the hospital by his distraught parents. Instead of providing foster care, they adopted TJ.

Shortly thereafter, Janet got another call about a Down's syndrome baby and decided instead of adopting again, she would be a match-maker with another family who had expressed interest in TJ. That one matchmaking effort was so satisfying that she went on to compile lists of people who have been approved by adoption agencies and want to adopt Down's syndrome babies. When adoption agencies hear of such babies, but have no prospective parents for them, they call Janet. Her matchmaking lists usually contain about one hundred prospective adoptive parents and twenty-five to thirty potential kids.

Everyday, many times a day, women call who are pregnant with or have given birth to a Down's syndrome baby. Janet talks with them about the joys and difficulties of raising a mentally retarded child. For the pregnant women, she explains that their options include adoption. She says, "I don't talk people into or out of anything. I tell them they must act based on knowledge, not fear, if they want to be able to live with their choice." She also counsels hospital and adoption agency pro-fessionals, many of whom are amazed to find that there are families eager to adopt mentally retarded children.

Janet charges no fees for her service, even though her phone bill can run $1,000 a month. She has worked as a waitress to cover the costs. Her husband has moonlighted as a plumber to do the same. Her matchmaking and counseling is often emotionally exhausting, but her reward is great: knowing she has made a big difference in the lives of many children.

Bringing It Home

Dale Carnegie's book, *How to Win Friends and Influence People,* is one of the biggest bestsellers of all time, because it reveals a basic truth about human nature: we are all longing for people to see the best in us.

Carnegie advised readers to find something they genuinely like about each person they meet and let it be known. Being such a positive person is the way to win friends and influence people, he said. Decades later, his book still sells because this advice is so sound.

Good mothers instinctively see what is good about their children. Looking at their kids through rose-colored (or I should say love-colored) glasses doesn't make them blind. They can see faults and discipline bad behavior. But good parents put the emphasis on the positive, not the negative.

That's one reason why mother love is so famous and effective. Who else thinks you are as wonderful as your mother does? Try to pass that blessing on to your own children. If so, your children will blossom in such a positive light. By taking this positive approach out into the world, you can make other people and other projects blossom, too.

• If you didn't have parents who saw the good in you, know that was *their* failing, not yours. You will have to work hard to be a loving mother to yourself, noting your good points instead of emphasizing the bad. We don't always have to love ourselves to love our children, but it certainly helps. If you see too much "bad" in yourself, seek psychotherapy.

• We all need to catch ourselves being critical to ourselves, our children, and others—and change that way of behaving. Usually, constructive criticism is the only kind that works.

• While the world does need a lot of repair, remind yourself of all the people who are working to make it a better place. Give them whatever help you can, even if it is only a compliment or a thank you note.

chapter eleven

ASK FOR HELP: THE COMMON SENSE APPROACH TO GET WHAT YOU WANT

"Many women not only feel comfortable seeking help, but feel honor-bound to seek it, accept it, and display gratitude in exchange."
—Deborah Tannen, *You Just Don't Understand*

Have you ever wondered why men love action movies where the hero, alone and heavily armed, battles his way through a horde of opponents? Rambo and others like him represent a quintessential male fantasy: being so tough and self-sufficient that no help is ever needed.

Likewise, have you ever been in a car with a man who got lost? You probably suggested that he stop and ask for directions, but he ignored you and kept driving around in circles. Most men feel it is a blow to their competence—and even their masculinity—to ask for help.

Often physically smaller than men and traditionally having the primary responsibility for caring for the children, women had to learn to ask for help. This is one of the primary skills for mothers' "tend and befriend" method of coping with stress and danger. And as you have seen throughout the book, the ability to ask for help has allowed mothers without money or powerful connections to change laws and build organizations that make a big impact on society.

In this chapter, you will see how one woman, Betty Mahmoody, became an international hero when she freed herself and her daughter from domestic imprisonment in Iran. If she had not been able to effectively ask for help, they would never have returned home. Then, back in Michigan, she asked legislators to help other women and children caught in similar situations.

You will also see how several mothers built a successful business that donates all profits to charity. Their margins are very high because they are so skilled at finding free help. Finally, even a mother like Bette Midler, who has lots of money and powerful connections, has to ask for assistance if she wants to accomplish a big task. Bette wants to clean up New York City parks. Since she doesn't like to impose on people, even she has to overcome some shy feelings to ask for the help she needs.

The Great Escape

Consider this hypothetical situation: Rambo and his daughter are being held prisoner by his wife and her family in Iran. What do you think he would do? The movie plot would probably have him steal some weapons and fight his way back home with his daughter strapped to his back. That might work in fiction, but in real life Rambo wouldn't stand a chance.

In 1984, Betty Mahmoody found herself in that terrifying situation—she and her daughter were being held prisoner by her husband and his family in Iran. If Betty hadn't found inventive ways to ask for help, she and her child would still be there.

Betty's story is the stuff of nightmares. It began happily in her native Michigan where she met and married a charming, prosperous physician, Moody Mahmoody, who had lived in the United States for twenty years. Moody was very assimilated and had a wide circle of friends. He became a seemingly loving stepfather to her two sons by a previous marriage. Betty learned to cook Persian dishes, and when she gave birth to a baby girl, they named her Mahtob, which means 'moon-light' in Farsi, the language spoken in Iran.

When the Iatollah Koumeni overthrew the Shah and set up an Islamic Republic, Moody suddenly became very interested in Iranian politics. He began spending time with Iranians in America who were pro-Iatollah. Then he decided Betty and Mahtob should join him in a visit to his relatives in Iran. After seven years of marriage, Betty trusted Moody, but something prompted her to make him promise on the Koran that they would all come home to Michigan after the two-week holiday.

After the two weeks passed, Moody announced that he had lost his job in the United States and the three of them were staying in Iran. Betty was made a virtual prisoner. She worried that she might never get to see her sons and her parents again. When she tried to argue with Moody, he beat her and threatened to kill her. She was forbidden to use the telephone or to leave the house alone.

Moody and his relatives watched her closely. Even if she could find a way of sneaking out of the house, escape from the country was impossible because the border guards and police required identity papers, which her husband controlled. If she had gone to the police, they would not have helped her leave the country, because in Iran it is illegal for a wife to leave without her husband's permission. Even if the police helped her escape because she was being beaten, Mahtob would not be allowed to go with her. In Iran, fathers always have custody of their children.

There was no American embassy in Iran. However, Betty's mother discovered that the Swiss embassy handled American affairs. She managed to get a quick telephone call past Moody, and told Betty the Swiss embassy address. A few days later, when everyone was napping, Betty and Mahtob snuck out and rushed to the embassy, only to find that the Swiss would not give refuge. Diplomats explained that as the wife of an

Iranian, Betty was considered an Iranian too and, therefore, was subject to local laws that gave husbands dominance. With nowhere to turn, she had to sneak back into the house and pretend she had never left.

After a period of depression, Betty pretended to accept her fate in order to gain a few freedoms, like the ability to go the market alone or to take Mahtob to school. Once she achieved those goals, she decided, "I would do whatever I could, talk to whomever I could trust, and sooner or later I would find the right people to help me."

Betty chatted with local shopkeepers, slowly revealing a few of her problems to some who seemed sympathetic. One agreed to let her use his phone. She also began making friends with some of the Iranian women at Mahtob's school and a few American mothers she met at the playground. It became clear that the only way to leave Iran would be through people who could smuggle her and Mahtob out of the country.

Betty met several Americans who offered to help her escape. Since they were amateurs, she had to refuse their aid, because if caught, she would have spent the rest of her life in jail. Professional smugglers were a problem, too. Most would take her, but not her daughter. And there were plenty of stories of smugglers who took money and then abandoned or killed their charges.

Finally, after eighteen months in Iran, Betty found a professional smuggler through a sympathetic shopkeeper. That's how she and Mahtob escaped in a grueling journey over the mountains to the American embassy in Turkey.

Reunited with her sons and parents, Betty and Mahtob had to live under assumed names, fearing that Moody would fulfill his threat to kill her or kidnap his daughter. Caught in a legal limbo, she was unable to divorce Moody, because under the existing American law, the courts had to notify him of the proceedings, and reveal her current address.

When Betty learned through the State Department that over one thousand women and children were being held against their will in

Islamic countries, she decided to tell her real-life adventure in the book (and later, the movie), *Not without My Daughter*. That book made her a hero and brought a flood of mail from women around the world who had similar stories. Many wrote saying that their husbands had abducted their children to a different country. Under international law there was no way to get them back.

So, in 1992, Betty wrote a second book, *For the Love of a Child*, about the problem of international child abduction. One group she featured in the book was the Mothers of Algiers, a group of French women married to Algerians who left France, taking the children with them to Algiers. Algerian law, like that in Iran, gave mothers no rights to reclaim their children.

Throughout the 1980s the Mothers of Algiers staged sit-ins at the French Embassy in Algiers, went on hunger strikes, and held protest marches in Europe, promoting their cause and asking the French government for help. Finally, in 1988, an agreement—the first effective child custody agreement between Christian and Muslim states—went into effect. It affirmed two basic principles: that children have a right to stay in the place they consider home, and that both parents have the right to regular visits with the children. Furthermore, the country where the parents were married has jurisdiction over any international custody case. Child abductions from France to Algiers virtually ceased.

Meanwhile, parental child abduction had become a worldwide problem. So, a Hague Convention stipulated that any child under sixteen who is "wrongfully removed to another country shall be promptly returned to the childhood place of habitual residence." In 1988, a year after *Not without My Daughter* became a bestseller, the United States became the tenth country to sign the agreement.

Betty still needed help. She needed to change Michigan state law so she could divorce Moody while concealing her whereabouts, since she was still afraid he would harm her or Mahtob if he discovered where they were living. She drafted a bill with the help of an attorney allowing such secrecy in an international divorce where risk could be substantiated. She asked her state representative to sponsor the bill and it was passed after she helped lobby for it. Through a similar process, she helped make international parental abduction of a child a federal felony.

Making Cancer History

There is no doubt that Betty's fame made it easier for her to plead her case and get the help she needed. But as you have seen throughout this book, even women with no wealth or fame can get a lot accomplished when they have a worthy cause and ask for help. The following story of the Children's Art Project is a good example.

These days, a number of fund-raising projects sell cards created from designs by children. Many copy the extremely successful Children's Art Project at M.D. Anderson Cancer Center in Houston, Texas. No wonder. The Children's Art Project, which grew from one young patient's Christmas card design in 1973, has become a $6 million business generating $1.5 million in profits that fund programs for children at the famous hospital.

What's the secret of their success? They use a lot of Mother Power that includes the ability to ask for a lot of help.

Shannon Murray, director of the Children's Art Project and a former marketing executive at Coca-Cola says, "Most of our twenty-six staff members are mothers, extremely talented women who could make a lot more money elsewhere. But this is close to our hearts, so we don't mind putting in extra time and making less, because at the end of the day we have made someone's life better."

Shannon and her staff run the Project as a business. Many similar fund-raising operations merely license their names or designs and collect 10 percent of the profits. Shannon's operation earns over 25 percent profit by overseeing the manufacture, sales, and distribution of most of their products. However, she and her staff of twenty-six could never run such a complex operation—producing and distributing year-round seasonal cards, plus an ever expanding line of gifts including paper products, silk scarves, and silver jewelry—without asking for help from volunteers.

Most non-profits use volunteers. What makes the Children's Art Project different is the extensive and creative ways the maternal managers at the Project ask volunteers, young patients, and the community for help.

Shannon estimates that 90 percent of the labor expended for the Project is volunteered. Most of the people who answer the office phones, pack and send the orders, teach art to the young cancer patients who contribute their designs, and even deliver the goods to retail outlets are not paid. This is how the Project can offer such high quality goods for such reasonable prices.

The products are sold in the hospital's gift shops, on the Internet (www.childrensart.org), and in two thousand retail outlets in six southern and western states. "While some businesses call and volunteer, most places, especially the grocery stores, are very much asked," Angela says. "We knock on doors and make appointments. Then our retail team works very hard to maintain relations with them and thank the store managers, because they give us the space for free and aren't remunerated for their efforts.

"A normal card operation like Hallmark has merchandisers who go to their retail outlets to straighten the cards and restock supplies three times a week. There's no way we could pay a system like that. So, we put pull-off stickies on our displays asking customers, 'Would you like to adopt this display?' Those volunteers are our eyes and ears, letting us know if the display fixture is broken or out of cards."

The success of the Children's Art Project is based on product designs that are not only attractive, but that maintain the character, flair, and innocence of children's art. Ironically, to keep the artwork looking naive, a lot of professional management and outside help is required.

Angela explains, "The process is very maternal. As mothers with our own kids, we are all very appreciative of the children's designs. We want to keep them childlike, rather than trying to make them glitzy, sophisticated, or perfect. Some people don't buy the products because of that look, but we've made a conscious decision to say that's who we are.

"Since this is a mother-run operation, people are very caring here. We ask for a lot of opinions and it can take a lot longer to make a decision because we are careful not to hurt each other. We are careful to reach consensus, and that is valuable because everyone has bought into the idea or project, so you run smoother in the end."

The first step is to ask the young patients in the art programs at the hospital to donate their designs. Then, Angela explains, "Each March, Cali Hatzisavvas, the staff member who oversees the art classes at the hospital, brings us about 170 pieces the children have created—pictures for Christmas, spring, and Valentine's. Then we have a volunteer appreciation meeting, and all our volunteers get together and vote for the top thirty to fifty designs.

"Then we put those designs in a card format and for several days we set up display boards in our retail outlets and ask customers which cards they would buy. A manager will go to our big corporate customers and do the same. We also ask our Internet customers to vote. All in all we try to get about one thousand votes. We bring that data back and make decisions.

"For the final design selections, the two managers who handle sales may disagree with the two artistic people who handle marketing. But, we work until we come to an agreement instead of one trying to dominate the other.

"We also ask for advice when we are at a crossroads in our business. For example, two years ago, we asked people in the community to set up task forces to advise us on five areas: the Internet, direct mail, retail, public relations, and finance/operations." This expert advice has helped profits grow 20 percent in the last two years.

Angela says, "We retain a great relationship with people on these task forces and in some of the retail chains that carry our products. For example, I ask a VP at Foleys to look at our designs and our positioning in the store. Also, every time we design a new catalog, I ask an outside designer to tell us if there is anything else that should be done with it.

"It takes humility to ask when you think you have done it right. But, you can't be an expert in everything, and you can get pretty isolated in here instead of being out on the cutting edge design-wise. So, asking for their opinions and help is real important."

In the early '70s, childhood cancer was usually fatal, so hospitals like M.D. Anderson used art as a way to divert the children away from their problems. But now 80 percent of pediatric cancer patients survive, and while art is still used as an educational diversion, it is part of an ever-growing focus on the future while the children are in for treatment.

Shannon Murray, explaining some of the nineteen different programs Project profits fund, says, "It's hard for kids to get back to school and friends after cancer treatment, and we don't want them to be behind. So, we have an educational program to keep kids up with schoolwork, plus field trips to help kids have fun and improve their self-esteem. We fund summer camp programs for patients and their siblings. And since cancer treatment can be a terrible financial burden for families, we provide up to eighty college scholarships for patients and former patients each year, too."

After helping the Project achieve much of their success, Angela confesses that two years ago, she considered getting a job in private industry. She says, "I went on a job interview with a company in a downtown high-rise building. The offices had big, beautiful windows and views [as opposed to the cubicles at the Project]. The owner of the company wasn't there. He was at his big ranch.

"I realized that I get to be creative and innovative at the Project. And since this is a mother-run operation, if you have to bring your kids into the office or take time off to see them in a Christmas pageant, everyone is supportive. But most of all, I realized that if I took that job with the beautiful office, ultimately what I would be working for would be to make that owner rich and support his ranch. Whereas now what I work for is to make money for the kids at M.D. Anderson." That worthy cause is what gives Angela and everyone else at the Children's Art Project the guts to ask for lots of help.

Bold and Brassy—but Occasionally Shy

A different worthy cause gives Bette Midler the courage to ask for help. Bette lived in Los Angeles with her husband and daughter until an earthquake in 1974 scared them into moving back to Manhattan where she had originally gained fame with her brassy nightclub act. "I love New Yorkers," she said. "I'm like them. I'm noisy. I have my opinions." But unlike New Yorkers in the 1970s, Bette liked things neat and tidy.

As she drove New York highways, she saw garbage and abandoned cars. When she wandered around the parks, she found them in appalling condition. "I was very disappointed in how parts of the city looked. People were throwing their garbage out the windows, leaving their lunches on the ground. I was so upset, I didn't sleep for weeks."

Why did she care? Bette has always been a neat person. Plus, her love of the environment goes back to her early days in Hawaii. "It was a hard childhood. We lived in a very poor neighborhood, which was very rough. But there was a great deal of solace from nature: the beautiful skies, the sea, the smell of the flowers, all those bugs and birds. I thought the whole world was like that. When I came to what they call the mainland, it was a complete shock to my system."

While building her career as a young, single woman, Bette didn't put too much effort into environmental concerns. But Donna Hanover, former First Lady of New York City, reported that after Bette's "marriage to Martin von Haselberg and the birth of their daughter Sophie, she [became] a committed family woman with serious concerns about preserving the earth for future generations." So, while in California, she took part in the Adopt a Highway program, where corporations or individuals can pledge to keep a section of a roadway maintained. "Then," Bette says, "because my daughter went to school in Coldwater Canyon, which had become a big dumping ground, I began to work with Adopt a Canyon, a project that involved going in and hauling out trash."

In both California and New York, thieves who stripped cars of valuable parts dumped the remains by the road. Contractors who didn't want to pay dump yards, and individuals who were too lazy to properly dispose of trash, threw everything from McDonald's wrappers to old refrigerators in secluded park areas. That made Bette hopping mad, and she says, "I realized I needed to do something—even if I had to pick up stuff with my own two hands." While she does pick up trash herself, she realized to make any appreciable difference, she had to ask for help.

First she called the Parks Commissioner in New York City to offer help and ask advice. He was impressed that unlike many V.I.Ps, she didn't want to concentrate on celebrated Central Park, or just build some monument to herself. She wanted to clean up park areas in the poorest and most forgotten parts of the city. Then, she called the California Environmental Project and asked their help to set up a program in New York, which became the New York Restoration Project.

While Bette provided the initial $250,000 to start the New York Restoration Project (NYRP), she realized that money was just a drop in the bucket compared to what was needed, so she got out her Rolodex and started dialing. That Rolodex was crammed with star-studded friends—but would you believe it was hard for her to make those calls? Just like you and me, she was shy about imposing on people.

"It would take a whole day, working myself up to make these calls," she remembers. "A lot of times, I'd end up talking to their secretaries. They'd say, 'Is that really you?' But then their bosses wouldn't call me back."

Many did call back and offer help. Jann Wenner, publisher of *Rolling Stone* magazine, for example, gave her free office space. Others like Candace Bergen and Rosie O'Donnell pitched in. Bette not only asked help for her project, but for Adopt a Highway, too. She is proud that she convinced Larry King to adopt a mile.

After NYRP hired a director and work staff, the first project they tackled was parkland on the Hudson River under the George Washington Bridge. On their first clean-up day in July, 1995, twenty thousand pounds of debris and abandoned cars were hauled away. One administrator was extremely impressed that after most of the press and public had gone away Bette stayed with her staff and continued to pick up litter for hours. She didn't ask people to do what she herself wouldn't do. In fact, cleaning up parkland became a frequent family project for Bette and her husband and daughter.

It may seem strange that a city as rich as New York needed such help. But, the problem was twofold. First, there is so much parkland in New York (twenty-six thousand acres), that it is hard to maintain it all. Much of it, especially in the poorer areas, had simply been abandoned to weeds and dumpers.

Some of Bette's early work was in a section of Riverside Park that runs along the Upper West Side of Manhattan beside the Hudson River. In the glory days of New York's parks, six workers were assigned to maintain each playground in Riverside Park. But, after years of cutbacks, the Parks Department only had eighteen workers to cover Riverside's entire 320 acres. Volunteers had tried to maintain some areas, including a group of mothers who adopted one playground. However, when Bette hired ten workers to not just clean, but also maintain the Northern region of the park, it made a huge difference.

The New York Restoration Project has grown into a project that employs almost sixty people and has a budget of $3 million. (Bette personally contributes about $1 million a year.) It has reclaimed and maintained about four hundred acres of parkland, and hauled away over three thousand tons (that's six million pounds!) of junk.

Bette spends up to 50 percent of her time working for NYRP. Furthermore, an assistant commissioner at the Department of Sanitation says that Bette constantly calls to report abandoned cars, graffiti, or tenants throwing garbage out of windows.

Recently Bette and the NYRP have expanded their scope to include not only large parks, but tiny neighborhood gardens, too. For years, New York City has had title to many small lots scattered all over its five boroughs, and has often allowed local residents to turn the lots into gardens. But, in 1999, as land prices skyrocketed, the city decided to sell 114 of those community gardens to developers. A coalition raised the money to buy all but fifty-one of the gardens and give them to the communities. At the last minute, Bette and NYRP stepped forward with $1.2 million to buy the remaining fifty-one.

Often, these gardens provide the only green space for a whole neighborhood, and the communities were grateful to Bette for saving their little patches of nature. "None of us expected the outpouring of love and gratitude over this gesture," Bette said. "I didn't realize how much emotion has been invested in these gardens. It made me think there's more to be done. I'd like to do more. We would like to begin a community garden movement. We're not exactly sure how."

No. But I'm sure she will figure out who to ask.

Bringing It Home

Thank goodness women don't mind asking for assistance! Can you imagine trying to raise a child and not being able to ask for help—or directions? Can you imagine the selfish children we would raise if we didn't ask them to give their fair share of help to the family?

Often we get shy about asking for help outside the home, because we are afraid of imposing. But asking people for help is a way of honoring them. It acknowledges that they have skills or strengths that are valuable and needed. If they feel your request is an imposition, they can simply say no. No big deal.

Asking for help is a key ingredient of Mother Power, because no one can accomplish anything important all by themselves. One determined woman can start a movement, a project, or an organization. But if that woman doesn't recruit others to her cause, it will wither and die. So, ask for the help you need. If you get turned down, just screw up your courage and ask someone else.

> • If you have trouble asking for help, consider some small task you have put off because you don't know how to accomplish it. Figure out who could help you do it, and ask for their help before the week goes by. If they refuse, so what? Just keep asking until you find someone who will help.
>
> • Is there an area of your life that is especially hard to manage? No one does everything well, and most of us have some trouble managing a big area like work, money, health, children, eldercare, or family relations. Think about all your friends and where their strengths match your weaknesses. Then ask for the help you need.
>
> *continued*

• Help for just about any problem is also available through self-help groups. Log on to www.selfhelpgroups.org or call Ed Madera, the extremely helpful director of the American Self-Help Group Clearinghouse. If the kind of self-help group you need doesn't exist in your area, he will help you start one.

chapter twelve

NAG: KNOWING WHEN NOT TO LET UP

Diligence is the mother of good fortune.

—Miguel de Cervantes

As mothers, it's a good thing we know how to ask for help. There's so much that needs to be done, and we can't do it all alone. So, we ask our children, "Please take out the garbage...Please pick up your room...Please walk the dog." But is there any family on Earth where one such request is enough? We usually have to ask, and ask, and ask. That's how we become expert naggers.

While no one likes being nagged, it's a useful skill that mothers employ to accomplish important tasks outside the home. It sounds more polite to call this skill tenacity or persistence. Here's how Diane Feinstein, mother, ex-mayor of San Francisco, and current U.S. senator from California, talks about it in *Nine And Counting*, "If you're serious about being part of government, you have to be prepared for the long haul. You have to be prepared to lose many of your battles the first, second, and third time around, and then get up and go back to work for the fourth time around. Sometimes it'll take fifty tries. Some things will still be unfinished when you die. But if you keep at it and lay the foundation and bring others in, they'll carry on."

This chapter features the stories of several women who had to be extremely tenacious to accomplish their goals. The first nagging mother, Thelma Toole, is an extreme example of all the parents who see their children's artistic talents and support them. All good parents applaud their kids in amateur talent shows, hang elementary school artwork in the kitchen, and read special compositions with rapt attention. Some of us even think our kids are talented enough to be professional. Thelma, however, was convinced that her son was a genius who committed suicide because publishers unfairly rejected his novel. Would anyone but a mother like Thelma nag publishers until the novel was finally printed? Was anyone but Thelma not surprised when it won a Pulitzer Prize?

The second two stories involve causes: one won and the other still being fought for by tenacious mothers. If you recently gave birth to your child without heavy medication, in a hospital that welcomed your husband into the delivery room and encouraged your efforts to breast feed, you probably don't realize that all those rights were won by thousands of persistent mothers, who forced the medical establishment to allow and finally even encourage those practices. You'll read how this mothers' revolution took place.

Finally, there is a Mommy Issue that is a work in progress: the gun control movement. Mothers are not only the backbone of grassroots organizations that support gun control, but they also created the breakthrough legal case that may end the flood of guns into our cities and schools. You will also learn why this war may not be won unless a million mothers become nags.

My Son, the Genius

All good parents are quick to see good qualities in their children—and let their kids know about them. But some parents go overboard. Reading how Thelma Toole described her son, John, you'll probably notice that she was a bit extreme. Thelma recalls, "The beauteous babe,

John Kennedy Toole, was born Dec. 7, 1937, in the Touro Infirmary in New Orleans. He had the alertness of a six-month-old infant, and an aura of distinction [that] I didn't label genius, but the years proved so." If Thelma didn't call him a genius at birth, she did soon thereafter, and later referred to "my darling's Mt. Parnassus brain and multiplicity of talents."

Perhaps she adored her son because he was born when she was thirty-seven, long after she and her husband had given up hope of having a child. Perhaps she spoke in such an overblown manner because she was a drama teacher. Whatever the reason, we all know that when mothers talk that way about their sons, it usually creates a credibility gap. People turn off and don't want to listen. But Thelma's extraordinary devotion to her son inspired her to nag and push the rest of the world into acknowledging his talent long after he died.

People who knew John Kennedy Toole remember him as a chubby, smart New Orleans boy with a good sense of humor. When he was only sixteen years old he wrote a novel called *The Neon Bible*. Since almost no one, especially if he comes from a family with little money and no connections, gets a novel published at sixteen, the manuscript stayed in a drawer for years.

But John's "Mt. Parnassus" brain did get him accelerated in school. By sixteen, he was also entering Tulane University. Since that brain was less prized by the army that drafted him, he was assigned to a typing pool in Puerto Rico.

By chance, other men with literary aspirations were in that typing pool. They formed a small artist's colony, and John wrote a second novel, *A Confederacy of Dunces*. It was a satirical comedy about the poor, white demi-world of New Orleans. The hero, a hugely fat young man, has a hard time making a living. For example, when he works as a hot dog vender, he keeps eating his products and profits—and then has problems with gas. Thelma thought the manuscript was great!

John was determined to get his book published by Simon & Schuster. He sent it off with high hopes, and began receiving letters from an editor there. For two years, the editor suggested changes that needed to be made, but never bought the manuscript. Finally, in despair, John asked for the manuscript back.

Now, most readers might think, like John did, that this means his book was a failure. But any writer will know that this story signals potential success. Here's why: novice writers believe publishers are interested in any manuscript that arrives by mail, but the opposite is true. Publisher's regard manuscripts that arrive "over the transom" (sent by an unknown writer, without the recommendation of an agent) as a nuisance. Usually those manuscripts sit in a huge pile, until some over-worked, inexperienced assistant takes a quick look before rejecting them. "Over the transom" manuscripts rarely get referred to an editor, and it is almost unheard of for an editor to spend two years making suggestions for improving the manuscript. While writers often feel such suggestions are insulting, the editor is showing that the project is worth an investment of time. Even if the editor ultimately rejects the project, another publishing house might be interested knowing that a major publisher like Simon & Schuster had almost bought it.

But discouraged, John put his manuscript away. Thelma was dis-couraged, too. "You can't stand the heartache of the correspondence," she later said, referring to the letters between John and the editor.

John, after earning a master's degree in literature at Columbia University, taught at several colleges. Then, in 1969, three years after asking for his manuscript back, he left his New Orleans home and dis-appeared for several months. Near Biloxi, he committed suicide.

Five years after his death, Thelma reread the manuscript for *A Confederacy of Dunces*, and decided it was a masterpiece. For the next seven years, she hounded publishers. As the *Los Angeles Times* later described her approach, "She peddled with the tenacity of a door-to-door salesman." She was a woman in her seventies, given to wearing excessive make-up, fueled by too many Hostess Twinkies, and obsessed with finding justice for her son. Most people, and all the publishers she contacted, dismissed her. But Thelma knew how to nag.

In 1976, she heard that the famous writer Walker Percy was teaching at Loyola in New Orleans and, as he describes in the Foreword to *A Confederacy of Dunces*, "I began to get telephone calls from a lady unknown to me. What she proposed was preposterous. It was that her son, who was dead, had written an entire novel during the early sixties, a big novel, and she wanted me to read it....And if ever there was something I didn't want to do, this was surely it: to deal with the mother of a dead novelist and, worst of all, to have to read a manuscript that she said was great, and that, as it turned out, was a badly smeared, scarcely readable carbon. But the lady was persistent..."

Thelma finally cornered Walker Percy in his office, and he figured the only way out was to read a few pages and break the bad news that the novel was unfit for publication. However, to his astonishment, he says that what he read made him, "grin, laugh out loud, shake my head in wonderment."

Still, even with Walker Percy's help, there was difficulty finding a publisher. At last, in 1980, Louisiana State University published the book, thinking it would probably only have regional appeal. Instead, much to everyone's surprise (except Thelma) the book received glowing reviews and won the Pulitzer Prize in 1981. Many people thought that Walker Percy's Foreword, telling of Thelma's passionate devotion to her son's cause, caught the interest of reviewers, the public, and the Pulitzer Committee.

But Thelma's devotion and success grew even more surprising. She began giving performances, acting out scenes from *A Confederacy of Dunces*. Then she decided that John's first novel, the one he wrote when he was sixteen, *The Neon Bible*, was also a work of genius. However, she felt it should not be published and celebrated until "*Confederacy* has had its share of glory."

Thelma became involved in legal wrangling with the relatives of John's late father, who, under Louisiana law, had some claim to John's estate. While she had brought *The Neon Bible* out of hiding, these wrangles kept it from being published until after her death. Finally, in 1989, it too was published to glowing reviews. In fact, a reviewer for the *New York Times* wrote, "*The Neon Bible* not only stands as a remarkable achievement for a sixteen-year-old writer, but it also serves as a testament (more valid than *Dunces* in this critic's opinion) to the genuine talents of Toole." Clearly, no one would ever have known about those talents if his mother hadn't been a genuinely talented nag.

Demanding a Better Birth

Thelma Toole's nagging allowed thousands of people to enjoy a wonderful work of literature. The following story tells how maternal nagging allowed millions of us to enjoy the birth of our babies.

When I was pregnant with Jean Paul in 1971, many of the young mothers I knew began telling me that I had to breast feed and 'do natural childbirth' because it was better for the baby. The idea of childbirth without medication was terrifying: I have always been a real sissy about pain. But because it seemed better for the baby's health, I searched for a doctor who believed in 'natural childbirth,' a hospital that allowed fathers in the delivery room, and a chapter of the La Leche League.

The benefits turned out to be as much mine as Jean Paul's. His birth was a highlight in my husband's and my life. I was grateful to the mothers who convinced me to be awake and aware during the whole process. Afterwards, breast feeding my newborn son felt wonderfully maternal. I had no idea until I started researching this book that my friends and I were part of a nagging campaign that changed the practice of obstetrics in the United States and around the world.

"It really was a mothers' revolution," explained Barb Kilpatrick, a registered nurse and childbirth educator. (She also explained that I should call the process 'prepared childbirth,' not 'natural childbirth,' because the techniques used to control labor pains are learned and do not come naturally for humans as they do for animals.)

"A wonderful American writer, Marjorie Karmel, was in Paris in the 1950s for her first pregnancy," Barb told me. "Her physician, Ferdinand Lamaze, had studied how Russians used psychological techniques for pain management and uterine efficiency in childbirth. He taught her those techniques, and she had such an amazing experience, that when she moved back to New York, she wanted to have her second baby that way.

"No one had heard of this technique, but she finally found a doctor who was willing to learn it from her. She wrote an article about her experiences in *Ladies' Home Journal*, and was deluged with letters from women wanting more information. So, she wrote a book in 1959 called *Thank You, Dr. Lamaze*, explaining to women how they could give birth to their babies without being 'knocked out.'"

Marjorie Karmel and physical therapist Elizabeth Bing founded an organization, which became Lamaze International, to promote the Lamaze method and train childbirth educators. But, the medical community was slow to change. Most obstetricians wanted women to be highly sedated for pain and given drugs that would make them forget most of the birth experience.

"When I was in nursing school from 1962 to 1966 at Bryn Mawr Hospital in suburban Philadelphia," recalls Barb Kilpatrick, "I never even heard of prepared childbirth. Most moms had general anesthesia for delivery. In the late 1960s, working as a nurse in San Francisco, I was not aware of childbirth preparation there either.

"I first learned of Lamaze when I moved to Bethlehem, Pennsylvania, in 1972. I was pregnant and met Lois Tarbell, the wife of one of my husband's colleagues. She was a nurse teaching Lamaze and a La Leche leader, too. Childbirth preparation was in its early stages in the Lehigh Valley, and the medical community was not sold on the idea of the fathers or significant others being trained as labor coaches.

"Mothers became informed about it by reading or by telling each other. They really had to search to find classes and doctors who agreed with the theory of being educated and trained prior to labor. The hospital where I gave birth had just started a six-month trial of letting prepared coaches (usually the fathers) in the delivery room.

"My husband, Craig, and I took the classes with Lois. We had a magnificent experience giving birth to our daughter Joy. The Lamaze classes educated us about the entire childbirth experience. They gave us a lot of psychological tools to handle the pain, and taught us how to work with my body and the forces of labor rather than tensing and fighting against them. Craig was taught to be my pain-control coach during the labor and delivery. It made a dramatic difference—I was confident and really looking forward to the birth. I didn't need pain medication or anesthesia.

"It gave us confidence to parent a new baby as well. We felt an instant bond with Joy. She wasn't a stranger. It was absolutely wonderful. I couldn't say enough good things about it. When our second child, Susie, was born three years later, we again used the Lamaze method and it was every bit as wonderful as Joy's birth.

"I began training to become a childbirth educator when Joy was six months old. I joined a group of nurses who were teaching the Lamaze method to couples who were delivering at many different hospitals in the area. We were not only nurses, we were also mothers who had Lamaze births. It gave us great credibility. At one time we were the largest group of independent nurses teaching Lamaze in America. We taught thousands of moms and coaches in the past thirty years. It has been the most rewarding thing I have ever done.

"We saw the movement begin slowly, but the more informed the moms became, and the more they chose doctors and hospitals who agreed with preparation for labor, the more it grew. As physicians and hospital nurses began seeing how well their prepared moms did in labor, they started to become advocates of Lamaze."

Today, most hospitals welcome the use of prepared childbirth and fathers in the delivery room. This revolution has been fostered not just by Dr. Lamaze, but by others, most notably the English physician Dr. Grantly Dick-Read who published *Childbirth Without Fear* in 1944, and Dr. Robert Bradley, who published *Husband-Coached Childbirth* in 1965. But, their advocacy of medication-free birth and the participation of fathers was largely ignored or fought by the medical establishment. It was the mothers themselves, as informed consumers and childbirth educators, who nagged, pushed, and convinced physicians and hospitals to allow a choice of birthing methods.

Seven mothers in Illinois who formed a breast-feeding support group in 1957 started a similar revolution. These mothers needed to share support and information because breast-feeding had largely fallen out of use. This small support group quickly grew into La Leche International, which now has three thousand chapters in the United States alone. Each year, American La Leche volunteers answer over seven hundred and fifty thousand telephone questions from anxious new moms. The persistence of La Leche League mothers in promoting what they consider to be a healthy start for babies and mothers, has brought breast-feeding back into wide use today.

Now that mothers have won the right to choose whether or not to use anesthesia, and whether or not to breast-feed, childbirth educators are needed more than ever. Barb Kilpatrick, who says she gets great maternal satisfaction from helping young couples, explains why, "Today, doctors are so busy. They don't have the time to sit down and explain to their patients what to expect in labor or to train them how to handle it. We give couples twelve hours of instruction that can make a big difference not just in giving birth, but in being parents as well. The couples learn to appreciate each other and bond together, working toward the peak experience of giving birth. It's a solid foundation on which their new family will be built."

When a group of Russian physicians visited Bethlehem recently, Barb Kilpatrick was surprised to learn that fathers rarely are trained to be the labor coach in the country where this all began. Perhaps American mothers have something to teach the Russians about nagging.

When Even a Million Moms Asking Once Isn't Enough

Overcoming the reluctance of the medical establishment to change its practices was difficult, but simple compared to overcoming the influence of the National Rifle Association (NRA). The battle for sensible gun control laws is still being waged, and to win it, American mothers may have to be more tenacious than ever before because of the force of the opposition.

On Mother's Day 2000, almost a million people gathered in sixty cities to support gun control. The Million Mom March in Washington, D.C., was a thrilling experience for me and my friends who caught an early train to be part of the occasion. Moms, dads, and kids of all colors, ages, and political persuasions made a huge, polite mixed bag of protesters. While participants looked happy as they milled around the Washington Mall, they showed their anger when speakers touched raw nerves: politicians being paid by the gun lobby to vote against sensible gun control designed to make our streets and schools safer. Anna Quinlen rallied the crowd, stating, "We are the women who fed our kids breastmilk and put them in car seats, so don't you *dare* tell us not to keep our kids safe!"

The event was an organizational miracle. One woman, Donna Dees-Thomases, a mother in New Jersey, saw pictures of the shooting at North Valley Jewish Community Center in Los Angeles. Seeing that the little children at the Center were the same age as her own, she decided it was time to stand up to the gun lobby. She called some of her friends, who in turn called their friends, and they formed the 100 Founding Mothers.

On Labor Day, 1999, the Founding Mothers held a press conference in Manhattan to launch their plan: gather a million moms on Mother's Day 2000 to demand that Congress stop stalling on "common sense" gun laws: mandatory safety locks, background checks at gun shows, licensing of handgun owners, and registration of all handguns.

That press conference was just the beginning. The Mothers had only nine months (a span of time they thought was symbolic) to organize a huge operation, so they had to ask for a lot of help! The Founding Mothers contacted other mothers all over the country, and everyone started recruiting more mothers in a classic grassroots operation. For example, I heard about it from a friend who faxed me a notice that was circulating in her synagogue, and I passed it along to the women I play bridge with, and they passed it along to their friends.

The event was a huge success. There were prominent politicians, celebrities, and almost a million committed attendees. However, a one-time event, even one as large as the Million Mom March, was not going to change politicians' votes, because politicians have to be nagged.

My friend, Barbara Hohlt, the chair of a grassroots gun control organization, knows all too well how much nagging is necessary. She told me from the beginning that while the Million Mom March would be impressive, it would not make any permanent change, unless those million moms stayed with the issue and continued to lobby for gun control legislation.

Barbara, who has been in the gun control movement for years, explained the history of the movement to me, "The first major effort in gun control was made in the 1930s when Congress, in response to gangland killings, required that people register to buy machine guns. They were trying to keep such weapons away from criminals.

"The handgun control movement was started after the assassinations of the Kennedys and Martin Luther King in the 1960s. Two large national groups were then formed in the early 1970s. One, the Coalition to Stop Handgun Violence, wanted to ban all handguns. The other, Handgun Control, thinks it is not possible to ban handguns, so simply wants to register all guns and keep them out of hands of people who might be dangerous. Mothers have been the grassroots backbone of the gun control movement, because they want to keep their children safe from violence."

Barbara herself is a good example. A lifelong desire to make the world a better place began crystallizing after her sons reached the teen years and she became upset about the violence on nearby city streets. Barbara's conscience began hurting and she was prompted to action when someone asked her, "What are you doing to make the streets safer for your kids?"

Shortly thereafter, in 1993, a teacher was shot while bicycling midday in a local park. Neighborhood women held a candlelight vigil. Barbara was invited to follow-up meetings that eventually lead to the forming of a non-profit organization, New Yorkers Against Gun Violence. Barbara left her well-paying computer job to take the unpaid position as director.

A tall, slender brunette, Barbara becomes uncharacteristically forceful when she gives a speech or press conference about gun control. She points out that while recent school killings have stirred the conscience of America, children being shot is a long-standing problem: fifty thousand U.S. children were killed in the last decade by guns.

The NRA fights any sort of gun control legislation as an infringement on personal rights, but Barbara notes that most dangerous items are regulated—everything from alcohol to children's flammable pajamas. She argues, if cars are registered, why not guns? If marriage applicants are licensed, why not gun owners? If aspirin bottles come with childproof devices, why not guns?

The public always has to be nagged to keep the need for gun control in their consciousness. Leaders like Barbara have to keep giving speeches, holding press conferences, asking reporters to cover the events, and coming up with dramatic representations of the problem.

One such representation has been the Silent March, a national event since 1994 started by two mothers, Ellen Freudenheim and Tina Johnstone. The Silent March collects shoes of people who died from gun violence each year (thirty to forty thousand) and displays them every other year. Barbara and her group collect between one and two thousand pairs of shoes as silent reminders of New Yorkers who are killed by guns each year.

In 1994 and 1996 the shoes were used to ring the entire Capital Reflecting Pool in Washington, D.C. It was a moving sight, since each pair represented a victim, and many had pictures and notes attached. In 1998, the shoes were laid out in front of gun companies. In 2000 they were taken to the Republican and Democratic conventions.

"You really have to prod the legislators," Barbara says. "You have to keep going and going to them. Politicians need two things to survive: money for campaigns and votes. Big rallies like the Million Mom March, or press conferences about the issue, can help change public opinion and the polls. Politicians care about polls because they need voters to elect them.

"But some take money from the gun lobby to finance their campaigns and keep their jobs. However, many politicians genuinely care about people. So, if we keep hitting them with lots of people lobbying, it shames them into doing something. Mothers who lost children to gun violence are especially good at shaming politicians—they get embarrassed to vote against gun control when parents who have lost a child talk to them. One or two crime victims can do a lot if they keep going and going.

"When I take high school kids to Albany to show them the legislative process, they think they can just go to a legislator, explain the need for gun control, and have the legislator say, 'I'll make that law tomorrow!' In reality, a law usually takes seven to eight years to pass, and you have to keep trying to win them over and win them over. It takes being on the phone all the time."

It takes tenacity of all kinds to sustain an organization like New Yorkers Against Gun Violence. "In the beginning," says Barbara, "we had to pursue people to get cheap rent for office space. A guy offered us an office for $450 a month, but I had to call him eight times. I have to call people and ask them to come in and make phone calls, to go up to Albany and lobby. I have to keep asking people for money, and it is hard for women like me to ask for money. It gets discouraging to have to ask and ask and ask."

Finally, however, the constant calls have produced income for a salaried executive director. Barbara hired someone for that role—someone who will share the prodding, asking, and nagging—but she will stay on as chair.

Was Barbara discouraged by results after the Million Mom March? Far from it. In New York, the legislature and Governor Pataki, who had resisted gun control legislation for years, read the polls and stopped stalling. In August, before the election, a comprehensive gun legislation bill was finally passed and signed.

As of this writing, gun control legislation remains stymied in Congress, but referendums to close the gun show loophole passed in Oregon and Colorado, showing that even states with large numbers of hunters and gun owners want sensible gun control. And in the Gore versus Bush presidential election, the popular vote, but not the election, was won by the candidate with the strongest gun control policies. So with a more nagging...

Lobbying is effective nagging, and lawsuits may be an even more effective form. "A group of mothers brought a suit that might set a precedent for many others," says Barbara. "Hamilton versus Accutek was the brainstorm of a mother, lawyer Elisa Barnes, who decided that guns were a public health menace partially because illegal guns are so readily available to teens."

In 1995, she brought suit against gun manufacturers, arguing that since guns were a dangerous product, manufacturers were responsible for distributing them more carefully. This suit along with others brought by state attorney generals under nuisance laws may finally result in effective gun control. But the NRA has convinced some states' legislators to make suits against gun manufacturers illegal, which only points out the need for more nagging in the form of lobbying legislators in those states.

Bringing It Home

There is an old saying, "The squeaky wheel gets the oil." However, we all know that a wheel that squeaks too much and becomes too annoying gets replaced or tuned out. So, mothers learn that nagging is an effective tool only if it is used sparingly: ask too often and our requests are dismissed as complaints and whines. But when the issue is important, we are tenacious and don't let up.

This tenacity is a key element of Mother Power. In our own homes, we have to persist: we cannot let our children see us as pushovers, especially where their health and safety is concerned. And in the outside world, anything worth having often involves a struggle.

Our capacity to nag and be tenacious, honed at home on the classic issues of doing homework before watching TV, eating vegetables before dessert, and looking both ways before crossing the street, can be invaluable when struggling to get what we want in the outside world.

As Diane Feinstein said, sometimes we have to ask fifty times. Sometimes we have to bring others in and turn the job over to them if all the nagging burns us out. But, eventually, given persistent Mother Power, we will get what we want and make the world a better place.

• There are ways to make your nagging more effective at home and elsewhere. For example, if you have asked a family member to take out the garbage, but the bag is still sitting in the kitchen, don't go into a long song and dance about how irresponsible the person is. Simply say in a neutral voice, "The garbage needs to go out." You may have to say it many times. (Psychologists call this the broken record technique.) You may have to let the garbage sit there and rot while you occasionally put on the broken record. But, the bag will be taken out eventually and slackers will discover that they cannot wear you down.

• If people complain about your nagging, consider whether or not you have unwittingly created their resistance by using unfair techniques like blaming, insulting, pushing, asking them to do something that is unfair, or being dictatorial by assigning tasks rather than including the others in a joint decision about what needs to be done. If so, apologize for your unpleasant approach and strategize with them about how to work more effectively as a team.

continued

• If, after such consideration, you decide that they are just slacking or unfairly resisting, don't let them intimidate you by calling you a nag. Explain why you think it is fair that they do what you want. Then explain (with a smile on your face and your tongue-in-cheek) that you are not a nag: you are merely tenacious.

chapter thirteen

DO IT OURSELVES: OUR IMMIGRANT/PIONEER LEGACY

"Necessity is the mother of invention."

—Unknown

Mothers are not too proud to ask for help or to nag if help is not given readily. If nagging fails, we are left with three choices: stew in anger, drop the subject, or do it ourselves. At home, where chores are supposed to be shared, mothers often do it themselves, since few of us will let the dog go unwalked or the garbage pile up for weeks. Increasingly, outside the home, mothers are taking a do-it-yourself approach, too. To assure their financial well-being, they are starting their own businesses. To assure the well-being of others, they are starting non-profit organizations. Our maternal ancestors would be proud.

As a nation of immigrants, we are descended from men and women with a vibrant do-it-yourself approach to life. My own family history has recorded some of the exploits of male ancestors—farmers, soldiers, and preachers—who arrived when America was a primitive place. The contributions of their wives go unrecorded, but are undoubtedly no less valiant. They had to be strong, courageous women to leave the relative comforts of Europe to come to a place where all those comforts had to be created. Those who came more recently, from a Europe that provided few comforts, also inspire me because they came with little except a determination to make a better life for themselves.

Until recently, women were encouraged to turn their back on this rich legacy of self-reliance. The feminine American dream encouraged the aspiration to become princesses and let men or servants do all the work for us. The feminine American stereotype held that we were too inept and helpless to think and do for ourselves.

But, times are changing here and around the world. Even in some of the most oppressive societies, mothers are trying to change the world by taking matters into their own hands. For example, in Afghanistan, women are defying their fundamentalist government and educating their daughters with the help of books and supplies sent by sympathetic mothers around the world. In Pakistan, a professor and mother, Najma Najam, founded her country's first graduate school for women in 1998. Government funding for this project was minimal—only an old building with no furniture and money for a staff of two. She had to "conjure up" a faculty when seven thousand students applied. She enrolled 350 students the first year, made room for one thousand the second, and hopes to serve six thousand in ten years.

In the United States, everywhere you look mothers are taking a do-it-yourself approach and starting organizations. Some are small and local. Others have grown into major operations. A typical small project, a pastoral care program at my church, was started by a friend while grieving the loss of her mother. My friend became angry that our minister never called to see how she was doing. She noticed many other parishioners needed a friendly call—the homebound elderly, the sick, and the bereaved—but weren't getting it either. On her way to chew out the minister, she stopped at the altar and heard a voice in her mind saying, "Do it yourself!" So, instead of berating the overworked minister, she started a group of volunteers to provide maternal, caring services: everything from rides to the doctor or a meal, to a visit to the sick or bereaved. Not surprisingly, my friend reports that by taking action to help others, she felt better herself.

Mothers have always created small projects like my friend's. What's different these days is how very many are being created, and how many are growing into large operations. For example, in this chapter, you will read about two women who started projects that have helped thousands of people. One woman, distressed to find that there were no services for her disabled child, started a summer camp for such children. Nothing new there—except this one small do-it-yourself project was the acorn from which an eighteen million dollar multi-service oak has grown.

The second mother had to go on welfare when her husband stopped paying child support. Unable to get her county prosecutor to help, she founded a self-help group to collect such payments. That small group has grown into 390 chapters nationwide, with forty thousand members who have initiated major legislative changes.

An even bigger socio-economic change is the number of mothers starting their own businesses. According to the Small Business Administration, women are starting companies at twice the rate of men. So, the third profile is one of those many women who gave birth to a baby and a business at the same time. In eighteen years, her business grew from a ten thousand dollar investment into a three hundred million dollar company.

The Adventure of Camp Venture

When Kathleen Lukens died in 1968, the *New York Times* ran a long obituary that began, "Kathleen Lukens, a more or less ordinary woman whose life had such an ordinary focus on her children it is a wonder how much people made of what she saw as routine maternal devotion." Strange that the *Times* could call "ordinary," a woman who built an eighteen million dollar organization that led the way in providing services to the mentally handicapped. However, it is true that no one, including her devoted husband John, who told me so much about her, would have predicted that her autistic son, David, would have inspired her extraordinary achievements.

David was born in 1961, Kathleen and John's fourth child. A handsome baby, he seemed to progress normally until he was about eighteen months old. Then he stopped talking and started acting somewhat bizarre. His loving, worried parents took him to a number of experts until they received a diagnosis: autism.

These days that diagnosis is terrible enough: 50 percent of autistic children never learn to speak, and few can ever hope to either live independently or relate in an affectionate manner. At least, however, professionals have learned that autism is a purely organic disorder. In the 1960s, they blamed the parents for causing autism by being cold and unloving.

"Kathleen was really into mothering," John remembers. "It broke her heart to realize that a mother's efforts weren't enough to turn David around. She needed help. We found an eccentric teacher who took him into nursery school."

When other children began kindergarten, the Lukens had David placed in special education classes. Kathleen described those early days this way, "David had rudimentary speech, some self-control, and a special education teacher, named Mary Bader, who really cared for him. He still slept only an hour or two each night, rocked endlessly, twiddled, banged his head against the floor and walls, destroyed the other children's toys, and responded catastrophically to any minor change. I lived in constant fear the special education administration would overrule David's teacher and expel David, the way it had cast out other children who were as difficult as he was."

Since it wasn't until 1975 that schools were mandated to provide special education for disabled children, Kathleen realized, "We parents did not need an ordinary kind of PTA, but rather an organized pressure group to keep our children in school."

She formed a PTA for exceptional children, which, John says, "was really a lobbying group because a lot of these kids weren't accepted even into special classes. This was during the Civil Rights movement and Kathleen made this problem a civil rights issue. She met other people in the same situation, but realized if she organized them and kept pushing school boards and agencies, she could change from a joyful person into a crank. So, she decided to do things for 'exceptional children' herself."

John continued, "Kathleen decided to start her own summer camp with the idea that no one would be excluded and no family would have to pay. She went to a man who was running for State Assembly and he promised that if he was elected, he would help her start her camp. He was elected and got her a grant. Then she went around to the five towns in our county and got a small grant from each town, based on the fact that there were kids in the community who were excluded from other programs. She was a very convincing speaker and did her homework. She would stay up half the night researching what she had to know."

When Camp Venture opened, John remembers, "It was a shoestring operation. Kathleen didn't know anything about running a camp. I remember the first day, trying to form groups with the 150 kids that showed up."

But Camp Venture thrived because there was a tremendous need for the service (three hundred kids enrolled the second summer) and Kathleen staffed it with caring people. Started in 1969, it is still in operation today. It was just the beginning of her projects.

John says that "Kathleen referred to people with handicapped children as handicapped families, and one of their greatest handicaps is that they can't afford to die. On every parent's mind is, 'Who will take care of my child when I'm gone?' So, she got into providing adult services, because the place they were supposed to go was Letchworth Village, which was a horror for lack of funding."

The Lukens lived in New York State in Rockland County, which was relatively rural even though it was less than an hour from Manhattan. Nearby, there was a large facility that housed mentally handicapped children and adults, Letchworth Village, which at one time had five thousand patients. John says it used to be so well-funded that the state paid four times what it would have cost to send someone to Harvard to house a person there.

Then came the financial crises in New York State and Governor Nelson Rockefeller instituted a hiring freeze in places like Letchworth. If an employee left, they could not be replaced. This put a severe strain on such institutions, because most had extremely high turnover. Kathleen and John saw the abominable conditions and were terrified that David might end up in Letchworth. For example, in one ward two attendants with a cart of food were allowed only one hour to feed one hundred patients who could not feed themselves. "The main cause of death was choking on food," says John.

Kathleen went to a press conference where Rockefeller was professing how much he loved children. Kathleen stood up and asked, "If you love children that much, then how can you allow them to die in their own filth in your institutions?" By the end of the day, an order went out approving the hiring of one hundred new attendants for Letchworth.

Still, Kathleen wanted to bring people out of institutions like Letchworth, and never have people like David sent there. So, she convinced the Sisters of Charity to donate land, cobbled together grants, and began building the first facilities in New York State that allowed handicapped adults to live independently.

Under Kathleen's guidance, Camp Venture grew into an $18 million operation that includes fifteen supervised group homes, four day service centers, a sheltered workshop where people learn work skills, and, of course, the original summer camp. The whole operation serves one thousand people a year with autism, Down's syndrome, and cerebral palsy. If, in retrospect, it looks easy to create such services, don't be fooled.

Kathleen wrote how hard it was for her to confront Rockefeller at his press conference in Albany, "In those days it was almost impossible for me to get away. The three older boys were in the throes of adolescence. The baby [their fifth and last child] was only seven. And, David was reserved for sitters who liked a challenge. Just upfronting the cost of a trip to Albany required budget tricks I was rarely in a position to play. Wherever I went, it had to count."

She also wrote about the stress of finding financing for all the various projects she started. Just because the state and towns promised funding for Camp Venture, didn't mean the money came on time. "Before the first pay day at the end of June, I appealed to our local bank to lend me $2,600 for three months and they agreed. At that time in our lives, my husband supported our family of seven on a salary of $7,000 and I was a housewife without a paying job. Yet a banker lent me $2,600 and when I repaid the bank in ninety days, he donated the interest to Venture."

She inspired many people to help her: wealthy mothers of handicapped children sponsored benefit luncheons and art auctions. She was a master at buttonholing politicians, and then giving them "Friends of the Handicapped" awards, so they loved her. Because she was good at public relations, when she started a new project, volunteers from all over the community showed up to help. As she wrote about one camp development project, "The response of the people of Rockland County dazzled and overwhelmed anyone inclined towards cynicism about the goodness of people. Nuns and atheists, hardhats and longhairs, Boy Scouts and politicos brought their own rakes and shovels, paintbrushes and sanders, seeders and lawn carts, and set to work methodically reclaiming the site for the children of strangers."

And yet, everyone was not so kind when Kathleen built housing for the handicapped. "The road to creating a new life course in our community for those who are different has been a hard uphill struggle though one that is personally rewarding. For while the community has provided thousands of volunteers and hundreds of thousands in contributions, it has also been the source of bitter opposition whenever we try to open a new home, despite our perfect record for living peacefully with our neighbors.

"Criminal charges have been made against me for violating zoning laws, my family's and clients' lives have been threatened, and I have even been knocked to the ground by an angry neighbor. To me, the greatest source of anguish in this work is the need for endless confrontation in order to be one's brother's keeper." But a keeper she was, creating a system of training opportunities and housing that took in anyone, regardless of their disabilities, and tried to make them as independent and self-sufficient as possible.

Kathleen reveled in giving them a community of their own. She wrote, "Camp Venture added a whole new dimension to our children's lives: friends. They would never be part of the team or the gang or the neighborhood set" in the outside world, but within the Venture projects, they found acceptance and companions. In the various supportive living arrangements she created, they blossomed: "Once fifth wheels in their normal families or ciphers in a massive institution, they suddenly found themselves to be not only individuals at the center of their own lives, but members of a valued group."

For years Kathleen ran the Venture operations as a volunteer, keeping management lean. John says that when she finally became its paid executive director, she made sure that the pay scale was narrow: the highest paid executives including herself made no more than four times the lowest paid workers. And as she wrote, "Parents dominate the board of directors where they think of every client as if each were their daughter or son."

When Kathleen was only sixty-seven, and enjoying running her expanding operation, she was diagnosed with brain cancer. Three months later she died, knowing that one of her sons, Daniel, would take over as executive director and John would continue to volunteer. John says that just before Kathleen died, she said there were two things for which she was grateful: her family and her cause—because both had given her life meaning.

Supporting Those Who Need Child Support

Kathleen's do-it-yourself project for her son eventually benefited thousands of families in Rockland County. Gerri Jensen's grew into an organization that helps many more all over the country.

Gerri Jensen of Omaha, Nebraska, was in many ways a typical American woman. She was married with two young children, had a house with a mortgage, and a part-time job. Statistics tell us that half of all marriages fail, so when she got divorced, that was not atypical either, nor was the settlement. He kept the car. She kept the house and mortgage payments. He agreed to pay $250 a month in child support, which was the national average in 1977, the year of her divorce.

For six months her support payments came regularly. Then they stopped. Unfortunately, having trouble collecting child support is typical, too. About half of all non-custodial parents do not pay all the support they owe, and do not pay on time. Statistically, that was and still is one of the main reasons why children live in poverty.

Even though Gerri started working full-time, when her husband stopped paying child support, she lost her house and had to move her kids back to Toledo, Ohio, where her parents lived. There she worked two jobs, hiring two shifts of baby-sitters, trying to make ends meet.

One night, when her son begged her not to leave for work, she decided her children were suffering from her being away so much. She quit her jobs and went on welfare. She says it was a very depressing experience.

As a welfare mom, she received grants and support to go back to school, where she earned her LPN (Licensed Practical Nurse) degree. She got a job paying $12,000 a year—enough to get off welfare, but not enough to pay for medical insurance. All this while, she had asked the Ohio Department of Social Services to help her collect the child support owed her, but nothing happened.

With her new career, in 1983, life seemed to go back to normal for awhile. Gerri even became a supervisor at the nursing home where she worked. Then she got sick and her son needed an operation. The medical bills for her three weeks in intensive care, plus her son's surgery put her $52,000 in debt. She had to declare bankruptcy and go back on welfare. She says the stress almost made her lose her mind.

Angry that unpaid child support payments could have made all the difference, she went to the County Prosecutor's office and demanded that he help her collect. She says he looked her in the eye and said, "I'm sick of you whining women. If you think you can do a better job tracking down these deadbeats, then go right ahead."

Gerri had only $13 to her name and a pound of hamburger in the refrigerator, but she spent $8 on an ad in the Sunday *Toledo Blade* that read, "Not receiving your child support? Call me." She had ten calls that Sunday evening.

Seven women and one man came to her first meeting in March, 1984. Within two weeks she had formed the Association for Children for Enforcement of Support (ACES) with fifty members. Two months later, two hundred had joined. Then Ann Landers mentioned ACES in a column, and letters came pouring in.

Members contributed their $5 fee to join this self-help support group, and pooled their experiences and knowledge. A Toledo-based group of lawyers, Advocates for Basic Legal Equality, provided legal advice, which ACES interpreted for members who were confused and frustrated by unhelpful bureaucracy. A grant from a group affiliated with the Catholic Church and another from the Department of Social Services allowed Gerri to move the ACES operation out of her kitchen and into small offices in a YMCA. She and the group worked on legislation, met with enforcement agencies, and protested in court rooms and outside judge's homes.

Such tactics began working for the members. For example, Gerri collected the $12,000 in back support payments owed her and her kids. But, when a judge offered to personally process any ACES application, the group refused. They wanted more equitable treatment not just for their own members, but for all parents struggling to get back payments for their kids. There were 5,500 such cases in Gerri's county alone.

Less than a year after that initial meeting, ACES had one thousand members in twenty-three chapters all over Ohio. Here's how a reporter described Gerri at that time, "Geraldine Jensen, who is less than five feet tall in her stocking feet, doesn't look threatening. But, when she gets on the subject of child support, her voice sounds as if it could knock down brick walls.

"Her attacks on the bureaucracy and determination to squeeze answers out of dry legalese have made her the terror of courtrooms and attracted nearly one hundred new members a month to a parents' advocacy group she formed eleven months ago."

Today, ACES has forty thousand members in almost four hundred chapters in forty-eight states. They disseminate self-help information and have successfully lobbied for legislative changes. For example, the Family Support Act passed by congress in 1988 included ACES suggestions for income withholding, mandatory guidelines, and paternity establishment. And in 1992, the Child Support Recovery Act passed by Congress made it a federal crime in interstate cases (once the hardest to collect) if a non-payor fails to pay for a year or falls $5,000 behind. Even with all these legislative advances, which have helped so many children, the problem of uncollected child support continues to grow. In 1994, nineteen million children were owed $34 billion dollars. That figure had climbed to $57 billion by 1999.

Why does this happen? There are many reasons. Sometimes a change in the father's (85 percent of non-custodial parents are male) economic situation makes it hard to pay. Often the father is angry at the mother, so he takes it out on the kids as well. Some fathers balk at paying because they feel the courts are biased against men. Others simply do not realize how much it costs to raise a child, or understand the consequences of having their child grow up in poverty. Unfortunately, there are also some parents who are simply irresponsible and refuse to take care of the children they brought into the world. Even ACES can't fix that, although they are trying.

Giving Birth to a Baby and a Business

When Rebecca Matthias made her own maternity clothes, she realized this little do-it-yourself project could become a business. But, as a young mother on a tight budget in Philadelphia, she never realized how big the business would become.

Rebecca remembers being inspired by a talk by Debbie Fields (the famous "Mrs. Field's" cookie lady), who told of raising her three daughters while building her multi-million dollar business from one tiny outlet in a strip mall in California. These days, Rebecca likes to give similar encouragement to young mothers, by offering her own story. She can laugh at her first clumsy attempts to combine motherhood and entrepreneurship, because she has become phenomenally successful.

Never heard of her? Well, while pregnant, it's a good bet you bought clothes in one her nationwide chain of stores: Motherhood, Mimi Maternity, and Pea in the Pod.

Many mothers are starting small businesses out of their homes these days. Some are experts in their fields. Others, like Rebecca, begin on a wing and a prayer. She had more courage than knowledge, freely admitting that when she started a mail-order maternity clothes business, "[she] didn't know anything about mail-order catalogs, fashion, or business, [she] just knew [she] couldn't find maternity clothes to wear to the office." So, in 1981, deciding that other women had the same need, she quit her job, stayed home with her new baby, and used $10,000 in savings to start her business.

Every new mother can identify with Rebecca's first buying trip to wholesale maternity clothes manufacturers. She was treated as a nobody as she pushed her baby in a fold-up stroller, carried a diaper bag instead of a briefcase, and got breast milk stains on her blouse. But, she was a persistent nobody.

Buying a few pre-made items, including a sample jumper and jacket she planned to manufacture herself in wool, she put together a four page, black and white catalog, placed small ads in the *Wall Street Journal* and *New Yorker*, and waited for orders to roll in. To save money, she and her husband moved into an apartment in her parents home in Philadelphia, and as her business grew, she stored her inventory on racks hung from the apartment ceiling. When she bought her first computer, the apartment/office was so crowded, it had to be installed in the bathroom.

The good news and bad news of working out of her home was that the kids were always there. She could address catalogs and pack and send merchandise while being a full-time mom. On the other hand, while having a phone conversation with someone eager to connect her with an investment banker, she saw her son crawl over and pop a cockroach into his mouth. Like every work-at-home mom, Rebecca was a quick thinker. She calmly told the contact, "Let me get back to you," and raced over to rescue the baby.

After four years as a small but growing home-based business, she began to think big. She moved her operations out of her apartment into an "amazingly crappy building" with cheap rent. She also decided the least expensive way to expand rapidly was selling franchises for retail stores. Luckily for her, a revolution was taking place as more and more professional women stayed on the job during pregnancy, and bought their clothes through these stores and her catalogs. Soon her company was racking up yearly sales of over a million dollars.

By age thirty-five, she had three children (including a baby who came to the office with her) and a multi-million dollar operation that manufactured and sold maternity clothes in six hundred stores nationwide. Quite a do-it-yourself project.

Rebecca's frequent lectures and the book she wrote, *Mothers Work*, not only tell her story but offer practical advice for starting a business, raising capital, and avoiding the costly mistakes she initially made from inexperience. She cautions mothers who want to start a successful business to focus all their energy on family and business, instead of letting their do-it-yourself instinct run amok: to become financially successful, Rebecca advises, "Prioritize your life and get rid of extraneous activities," like cooking and entertaining, because "you have bigger fish to fry."

Bringing It Home

Parenting is largely a do-it-yourself project. Even if you read extensively on the subject, since there is so much conflicting advice, each of us has to figure out how to do it ourselves.

In fact, all of life is a do-it-yourself project. Becoming who you want to be and getting what you want out of life is largely up to you and your own ingenuity. For example, once I realized I wanted a successful career, a graduate degree, and a balanced life with kids, I also realized I would have to figure out how to get all these things, because no one was going to hand them to me. Good thing my Cinderella fantasy died early. After mourning the lack of a fairy godmother, I set to work on a do-it-myself plan.

The same thing holds true when we look outside our own lives. Gandhi said, "You must be the change you want to see in the world." He was right. We can't count on others to make the world a better place. We have to do it ourselves. By tapping into our Mother Power, we can do just that!

- What have you been waiting too long for someone to do for you at home? Set a deadline and tell them you want it done by then. If they won't do it, accept that you have only three positive choices: forget it, find somebody else to do it, or learn how to do it yourself.

- It can feel great to be self-reliant, acquiring the skills you need to accomplish what you want by yourself. On the other hand, too much solitary do-it-yourself is a recipe for burnout. Plus, nobody likes a martyr. If you are feeling like you have taken on too much and you cannot hire someone to help you or find someone to share the load, here's the plan: instead of feeling burdened by the long list of everything you have to do, analyze the list and strike out everything that isn't absolutely necessary now. Mumble "*Manana*" or "Forget it!" to yourself as you lighten your load.

- Think about how all the women in this chapter—and most of the mothers in this book—started small and grew. What have you been asking business, social, or political leaders to do? How can you begin to take the bull by the horns and do it yourself?

.

PART 3:

What Mothers Need

chapter fourteen

TO TAKE TIME OUT: A MOTHER'S SENSE OF PRIORITY

"When my kids kissed me impetuously, I would never have said, 'Later. Now go get washed up for dinner.'"
—Erma Bombeck, *If I Had My Life to Live Over*

Back in 1951, *Newsweek* put Millicent McIntosh on the cover, declaring her newsworthy, not because she was the president of Barnard College, but because she combined marriage, career, and children. In an era when most women sought college degrees so they could raise educated children, Dr. McIntosh encouraged them to juggle children and careers. Her advice was generally ignored.

It wasn't until Betty Friedan wrote *The Feminine Mystique* in the 1960s that such an idea entered mainstream thinking. In 1960, only 32 percent of all married women were employed, the statistics not showing whether they had children or not. By 1970, 40 percent of married women with children were in the work force, and by 1999 that number had jumped to 62 percent. Women now make up 46 percent of the workforce, and it is the huge influx of mothers—especially well-educated mothers—that has been the biggest change.

Many mothers have brought a maternal style to management, a style that can nurture both projects and people. However, the bigger impact, experts told me, of the huge infusion of mothers throughout all levels of organizations has been to make employers and the whole country focus on the balance between work and family life.

It is hard to maintain a balance when employers are demanding longer hours. (According to the International Labor Organization, Americans now put in the longest working hours of any industrialized nation.) Research shows that these long hours are equally troubling to men and women, but men are made to feel unmasculine if they object. So, mothers have become the dominant force opposing the workaholic, family unfriendly demands made by corporations and organizations.

Working mothers have forged new ground by inventing ways to have successful careers and time for their children. They are doing this in three basic ways: choosing to work for companies that have family friendly policies, starting their own businesses so they can have control over their hours, and being a major force in the work-at-home trend.

Family Friendly Companies

Lisa Benenson, editor-in-chief of *Working Mother* magazine, told me that "the impact of mothers in the workplace has been tremendous, largely in terms of work-life balance. Work-life balance was a phrase that wasn't even in our vocabulary before mothers started coming into the workforce in such great numbers that [they] required a whole rethinking of the way we work and the way we live our lives.

"When we started our Best Companies for Working Mothers list sixteen years ago, there were only thirty companies on the list and the benefits noted, like maternity leaves, were targeted only at mothers. What's happened in the years since is the recognition that work-life balance affects everyone. The impact of mothers in business served as a wake-up call to employers that work-life issues are important if you are going to get more out of employees in the long run.

"Now we get hundreds of applications from companies and the

competition is stiff for our 100 Best Companies list. Sixty-six percent of the companies on our list offer on-site or near-site childcare or childcare referral, as opposed to 16 percent of companies overall. Ninety-nine percent of the companies on our list offer some sort of flex time, compared with 60 percent of U.S. companies overall.

"Companies have found that for every dollar they spend providing childcare, they get back between three to six dollars in employee retention and less lost time," says Lisa. Why such large returns? If people can't come to work because of inadequate childcare, the costs are extremely high to hire and train permanent or temporary replacements.

Similarly, companies documented that they receive a big return for a far less costly benefit: offering flex time (which can mean anything from letting employees come in late if they need to take a child to the doctor, to letting employees work forty hours a week in four days instead of five). "Flexibility is the single most important benefit for working parents. It makes a tremendous difference knowing that you can go home if you need to, or have a morning off," says Lisa.

"People often say that small companies can't make our list because good benefits are more difficult for small companies to offer. But small companies can provide tremendous benefits through creative use of people on their staff," she contends. "For example, we function like a small company, and we practice what we preach in terms of flex time. Four of my senior editors are on part-time schedules and two others telecommute.

"I have people who wouldn't be working for me if they couldn't work part-time. As a manager, I feel I'm getting the best end of the bargain. They are getting the schedule they want, and they give me loyalty, good work, and 110 percent in return."

One of the first large companies to find that family friendly policies make good business sense was SC Johnson in Racine, Wisconsin, makers of Johnson Wax and other famous products. In the 1980s it opened a state-of-the-art day care center. This has expanded to include full-day kindergarten, before and afterschool programs, and a summer camp.

Part of this family friendly attitude comes from Helen Johnson-Liepold, vice president of Worldwide Marketing and a fifth-generation member of the company's founding family. She and other top executives make sure that managers are trained to be sensitive to employee family pressures. (Just by calling it "family" pressures, makes the issue equal opportunity and thus eases mothers' pressures.) For example, meetings tend not to be scheduled very early in the morning or late in the afternoon. Parents are allowed to work part-time after the birth of a child, telecommute one or two days a week, and have flexible schedules.

These policies are credited with having the company regularly named to various different 100 Best Corporations to Work For lists, which makes it easy to recruit good people. Furthermore, the company's turnover rate is 5 percent. That is less than half the national average. (Low turnover means low recruiting and training costs.) For these reasons, Helen Johnson-Liepold says that being a family friendly corporation makes good business sense.

Other companies have been jumping on the bandwagon for the same reasons. Abbott Laboratories in Illinois knows that working parents are stressed by finding childcare for school holidays. So, they are launching a new program to provide such care during school holidays in addition to their summer camp program. CIGNA, the insurance giant headquartered in Philadelphia, tries to be a leader in family friendly programs that include telecommuting, job-sharing, on-site childcare, nursing mothers' rooms, on-site health care, and take-home meal services.

Why are companies instituting these policies? Because Mother Power and market forces have made them realize that family friendly policies are good business practices. Companies like Johnson &

Johnson, who sell most of their products to women, wouldn't want the bad publicity that comes from having non–family friendly policies. Other companies like Sears have found that such policies keep employees happy, and happy employees keep customers happy, which translates into higher sales.

Basically, with all the dual career families these days, companies are learning that if they try to force people to work family unfriendly hours, or don't help their employees balance home and work, many of their most talented employees will leave. In tight labor markets, they can't afford such losses. Lisa Benenson says that since the number of workers aged twenty-five to forty-four is expected to drop, simply because of demographic trends, the family friendly policies that the younger generation says it wants will probably continue to grow, even if there is a recession.

Hopefully, they will grow, because no matter how good the child-care or flex time benefits sound, they are rarely available to all employees. In fact, the people earning the least amount of money, those who often need these benefits the most, are the least likely to get them.

However, more and more companies are at least trying to become more family friendly, because they are finding that if they don't, many of their most able employees will go to work for companies that do offer work-life benefits, or they will leave to start their own businesses.

Starting Your Own Business

Millions of mothers decide to work for themselves when employers aren't family friendly. Here's how some women have done that to gain control of their lives and time.

In my mid-twenties, when I was thinking about having a child, I received an offer from a major consulting company to be one of their first female professionals. It was a dream job, one I wanted badly. However, it required extensive travel and very long hours. I knew a number of men who worked there. I also knew the long hours had broken up many of their marriages and cheated their children out of family time.

I realized that I would not be comfortable having children and working like that, but I wanted to have a career. So, I went to graduate school, earning a doctorate in psychology. I figured that if I started my own practice, I could have work I loved, plus be in control of my time. Many women have entered their professions with similar plans, and many women are starting their own businesses for the same reason.

For example, Elizabeth Martin of Santa Fe, New Mexico, started her own public relations business to have flexible hours for her children. By acquiring solid skills and impressive clients, she was able to flow back and forth between having her own small firm and working for large organizations, as the needs of her family and her need for income varied. At different times she had plum jobs on staff for the Children's Television Workshop in New York and the Santa Fe Opera in New Mexico. At other times, in both states, she scaled back and worked for herself.

There has been an explosion of women-owned businesses in the United States in recent years, many started by mothers with motives similar to Elizabeth's and mine. Women now own one third of all the businesses in America. That's eight million enterprises!

If you think these are all little one-woman enterprises, like my psychology practice, think again. Woman-owned businesses employ as many workers as all the Fortune 500 companies combined—that's one fourth of all the workforce. And they contribute 2.3 trillion dollars to our economy. This is a trend that won't abate, since nearly 60 percent of women under age forty say they would like to start a business in the next decade.

Here's an impressive example of a business built by mothers who wanted time off with their kids. Two women who never worked more than three days a week started it—and they just sold it for four million dollars! One co-owner, Joan, a tall, friendly blonde with a casual, down-to-earth manner, agreed to tell me how she created this successful enterprise, as long as I kept her anonymous. The corporation that bought her business demanded secrecy, and, as you can understand, she doesn't want to jeopardize her half of four million dollars. Here's her story with all the facts except her full name and location:

When Joan graduated from a small Catholic woman's college, she had no idea what she wanted to do. "I was an English major and I thought I might like to be in human resources," she remembers, "I went to several employment agencies and they sent me out on interviews. I looked at the people sending me out for jobs and thought, 'I could do a better job than they're doing.' So, I started applying for jobs at employment agencies."

Joan got three job offers: two with salary and bonuses, and one with straight commission. "I took the straight commission," she says. "I was twenty-two and thought I could make more money that way. I guess it showed my entrepreneurial spirit."

After working for a year, Joan was recruited by a larger employment agency that placed temporary workers. She was asked to start a division placing people in permanent jobs, and she made that business successful.

Then, at twenty-eight, Joan gave birth to a son, intending to come back to work part-time. But after she was home with the baby for a while, she realized that even if her boss let her work only three days a week, she would be pestered with work calls the other two. So, Joan decided to open her own employment agency with a friend.

"My friend was in the same business and in the same situation," Joan remembers. "We both had new babies and new houses. Our husbands had jobs that could pay the mortgage, but we had very little money. We each put up a couple thousand dollars to start the business and got a bank loan for another $10,000.

"From the beginning, we realized the business was not going to work unless one of us was there at all times, so we each agreed to work three days a week, overlapping on Wednesdays. Basically it was job-sharing and we planned to have no other employees," she says.

"We went out with a realtor and found a cute space, bought furniture, and put botanical prints on the office walls. We wanted it to look pretty and fun. We opened our doors in January, 1976, and immediately got on the phones, calling companies to get business. Within two weeks we had so much business we had to hire our first employee.

"My partner and I would go out for long lunches on Wednesdays. We solved a lot of business problems—but it was also going out to lunch with a dear friend. There was a feeling of 'Gee whiz, I'm an entrepreneur and this is fun,'" she remembers.

It was also lucrative. Within two years, Joan was earning the same salary she had made when she worked full-time. For more than ten of the twenty-two years she was in business, she made a six-figure income.

What made Joan's business so successful? She attributes much of her success to being a mother. Having a baby and only working three days a week gave her life balance, so she never felt desperate, believing that she was nothing without business success. She explained, "My business is basically sales, and in sales there is nothing that turns people off more than desperation. Desperation makes you push too hard," she explained. "I often competed for business with men who pushed too hard and I won the competition.

"The only reason I started my own business was that I wanted time off to be with my family. I realized there were a lot of other women who felt the same way. As long as we could partner people with job-sharing like my partner and I did, I realized we could get great people who would do a great job without getting burned out," Joan says. "I had this maternal understanding of how moms thought about leaving their children to go to work.

"We hired other mothers who were outgoing and friendly. We all had a lot in common and got along well. For a lot of them, coming to the office was their social life. When they wanted to take a vacation, or take time off for a doctor's appointment or a school play, they worked it out with their job-sharing partner so there was always coverage, just like my partner and I did.

"You can't build a business as big as ours became without being professional, and we were very competitive, very professional, and very demanding of our employees. We had goals for them and there was no 'giving a gal eight tries to get it right.' If they didn't produce, they were asked to leave."

But Joan's employees were very loyal and very motivated because of the friendly, supportive atmosphere in the office. "We paid a little more than the competition and gave performance bonuses. But as long as people got their work done and had coverage, we were not demanding about time or what I call sorrow issues. If someone in an employee's family died, we never said bereavement should only last five days. If you needed ten days, you took ten days. No one ever lost a job because of a family problem. And no one took advantage of this, because we all knew each other and were aware of each others' families."

Joan's agency placed people in permanent jobs, but in the late 1980s she realized "our business was changing and temporary help was the wave of the future. We also wanted to create a business that was saleable, so we could create our retirement in one fell swoop.

"We put a lot of money into opening the temp agency. We hired a consultant, designed new forms, trained staff, [and] got new phones, computers, and a new corporate identity. We went from a staff of twenty-five to a staff of 150, because temps were legally our employees.

"We were no longer a mom and mom operation. It was high-risk, high-reward. That's when the fun went out of the business. With 150 employees, you have workman's comp and sexual harassment suits, because when your temp is working for one of your clients, if something happens, you're responsible.

"There is also a lot of financial risk. I pay a temp a day or two after I confirm the hours worked. Then I bill the company and they might take three to four weeks to pay me. When you have 150 people in the field, that's a lot of float. And sometimes you get stiffed. Once we had a big client who went out of business owing us $50,000."

Less than ten years after the expansion, Joan and her partner went to a business broker who sold their agency to a large corporation. Joan, at age fifty, was able to retire. Her employees felt bereft.

"The corporation who bought us told us and our employees that everything would stay the same. But now they are changing the whole culture and having far fewer part-time people. We made it a big business that was attractive to big business and they are running it that way," she says. It remains to be seen whether the new corporation will be as successful without Joan's Mother Power.

Working At Home

Mothers have always worked at home as a way of contributing economically while caring for their children. In the past, many home-based jobs were dreary or exploitive. These days, the opportunities have never been broader.

When the economy was primarily agricultural, wives shared the labor on the farm. In cities, many immigrants remember their mothers hunched over sewing machines, turning out piece work at home. And, who can forget the mother in the Tennessee Williams play, *The Glass Menagerie*, desperately trying to sell magazine subscriptions over the phone? No wonder women were happy to flock to jobs away from home when equal opportunity began opening doors. Now, the pendulum is swinging back and mothers are in the forefront of rediscovering the benefits of working at home.

Several years ago, Faith Popcorn, probably the best known futurist, spotted a trend she called "cocooning"—making home the center of one's life. Then, three years ago, when she adopted a daughter from China, she began cocooning herself. Feeling torn between home and office, she, like many working mothers, "felt as if [she] was always supposed to be in the other place." So, she says, "I finally gave up this idea of a line between office and personal," and she moved her business out of an office building into her large home.

Similarly, Eileen Fisher who runs a fashion/retail empire bearing her name, wanted less separation between her home and work life. Her operations were much too big to move into her home, but she transplanted them to the suburbs near her house and now works from home frequently so she can carpool her two children and spend time with them.

These women with their own very successful companies are at the top of the work-at-home trend that reaches down throughout all socio-economic stratas. Lynie Arden, who works at home in Oregon, has been tracking the trend since 1985 and reports on the many ways average Americans find home-based jobs.

In 1984, Lynie had three small children to support, but was determined to be a full-time mom. She went looking for work-at-home opportunities and was surprised at the number she found. Having secretarial experience, she chose to type insurance policies at home. She remembers, "My friend said, 'How do I get a job like yours?' and that lead to me start a newsletter on the subject, which lead to a book and it snowballed." By 2001, Lynie had written twelve books on the subject.

Lynie's books list hundreds of companies that hire home-based workers all over the country. When I asked how she found all these sources, she said "I went to a store that sold out-of-town newspapers, and I would buy a huge stack from all over the country. Then I would call the ads. I made friends with people in the Department of Labor and also called industry associations for leads.

"There are work-at-home scams that have been around for decades, but they are pretty easy to spot. Any time an ad asks for money for information about working at home, or charges sign-up fees, watch out. Anything that talks about assembly or envelope stuffing are also often scams," she told me. But the legitimate opportunities have mushroomed.

"When I wrote my first *Work-at-Home Sourcebook* in 1985," she said, "there were about twelve million people who did at least some work from home. The last time I checked the statistics, the Department of Labor estimated that now about forty million people do at least some work from home. This includes people who earn their entire living at home, work part-time at home, or telecommute."

Over four million Americans own their own home-based businesses. While the number of male and female owners is almost equal, Lynie has found that the motivation is different. "Women who work at home are multitaskers and want to take care of their children. Men are more inclined to work at home for freedom, sending their kids to daycare while they work."

Technology has spurred much of the work-at-home growth. For example, several years ago, a woman who worked for a large insurance company in Akron, Ohio, used her knowledge of software programs to start a home-based consulting business so she could spend more time with her daughter. Within seven years it grew into a twenty person operation with over a million dollars in annual sales.

When she started hiring employees, she found a huge pool of talented people—mostly mothers—who wanted to work full-time hours, but do it by telecommuting from home with their kids. She finds that parents who are home and know that their kids are okay can be more relaxed and motivated about their work. As she says, "Being a good mother and a productive worker aren't mutually exclusive. In fact, I think they go hand in hand."

Bringing It Home

These days mothers often feel that everyone wants a piece of their time. With the demands of work, home, and community ever increasing, it has never been more important to establish your priorities.

Yes, it is possible to have a meaningful career, children, and a personal and social life, too. But maybe not all at the same time. Rebecca Matthias, the mother who started the maternity clothes business in the last chapter, found she had to put her social life on hold while her children were young and her business was growing. Other mothers and fathers juggle their finances so that they can work part-time and give themselves some breathing room.

Are you comfortable being a full-time career person, a full-time mom, or something in between? Most research shows that there is no one right choice for mothers and children. It varies because ideally mothers must be happy about their decision to stay home or work outside the home, and there must be a caretaker for the kids (mom, dad, or substitute parent) who truly cares for their well-being.

Unfortunately, many mothers are in circumstances that preclude them being able to control their time and choices, but if you can, take the time you need to make your own personal best decision.

• If you have been working on an extensive home improvement project or a worthy cause that requires long-term effort, and you are feeling burned out, take time off. Recharge your batteries by doing something completely different for a while: work in a different capacity, work for a different cause, or take a sabbatical and smell the roses until you're ready to come back and work again with renewed vigor.

• If you are working for an employer who does not offer the kinds of benefits that help parents juggle work-family responsibilities, clip the 100 Best Companies to Work For list from *Working Mother* magazine and similar lists from other sources. The text accompanying these lists explains whey it saves companies money to institute flex-time, part-time, and job-sharing options. Ask your manager or human resources department to institute such policies for you and others—not as a favor to you, but as a way to improve morale, and retain mothers and fathers who are feeling stressed.

• Explore all the options noted in this chapter: working at home, starting your own business, or going to work for an employer who isn't a workaholic. Just knowing that you have some alternatives can make you feel less trapped. While you are planning a long-term solution to your time squeeze, allow yourself to take some relaxing lunch hours and each evening spend a few minutes relaxing with your kids after work before starting any chores.

chapter fifteen

TO FORM SUPPORTIVE RELATIONSHIPS: REACHING OUT AND CREATING A LIFELINE

*"Before the money came on board, all we had was each other.
Women had to stick together, mother, and protect each other.
That was part of our culture."*
—Willye White, Olympic jumper and coach

Carol Gilligan's seminal book, *In a Different Voice*, showed that women place the highest value on establishing supportive and caring relationships. From the time we are little girls, we develop the ability to create such connections with others. We learn the skills necessary to "tend and befriend" instead of "fight or flight." While a good mother's primary concern is to form a supportive relationship with her child, thank God we also provide the same for each other.

Before giving birth to my Jean Paul, I worked in an office with a friendly group of men and women. I looked forward to going to work each day, not only because I liked my job, but also to see my friends.

In the two weeks between the time I quit my job and gave birth, I was too busy preparing the baby's room to be lonely. After all the hoopla of becoming a new mother died down, I felt terribly alone. The friendships I began making with other mothers felt like a lifeline to me.

When other moms brought their babies over, we talked endlessly about things like colic and toilet training, topics of prime importance to us that would have bored anyone else to death. Since most of us had tight budgets, we formed a baby-sitting co-op so that we could go out and not worry about the cost or quality of childcare. Most important of all, we bolstered each other's confidence to meet the new, frightening demands of motherhood. My husband never seemed to need or want such support from other fathers.

When I look at all the impressive things mothers have accomplished in this book, it is clear that their ability to form supportive relationships allows them to do so much with so little. United together with mutual support, mothers have literally been able to change the world.

One of the early, and still most impressive, examples of Mother Power is Mothers Against Drunk Driving. Starting as a few friends supporting one grieving mother, it has grown into a nationwide movement that made the roads safer for everyone.

Almost twenty years later, a different kind of supportive network made the headlines, when media-savvy mothers began online, supportive, dot.com communities and sold the stock for millions. In every community across the country there are unsung mothers, working to create supportive networks that are the glue of neighborhoods and towns. One of those examples is featured in this chapter, too.

Mothers Against Drunk Driving

In 1980, Candy Lightner's thirteen-year-old daughter Cari was walking home from a church carnival in Fair Oaks, California, when she was killed by a hit-and-run drunk driver. Candy's grief turned to rage when she discovered that the driver was out on bail only two days after another drunk driving incident, and that he had three previous arrests for drunk driving. She quit her real estate job to lobby full-time for changes in the laws regulating driving and drinking. A few friends not only supported her in her grief, they supported her in her cause. Out of that small group grew Mothers Against Drunk Driving (MADD), which has changed America for the better.

It's hard to remember how tolerant people were of drunks on the road before MADD changed our attitudes. As the *New York Times* said, "Drunk driving was common long before Mothers Against Drunk Driving came into existence, but it wasn't until after the group's formation that society began to seriously focus on the problem and take significant steps to curb it."

Thanks largely to MADD, alcohol-related driving deaths in America went from a high of twenty-eight thousand in 1980 to fewer than sixteen thousand currently. MADD accomplished this by building a nationwide network of activists, who successfully lobbied both state legislators to get tough with drunk drivers and federal legislators to change the drinking age from eighteen to twenty-one. They have also forced federal legislation to have national standards for drunk driving blood levels. Equally important, MADD didn't just change laws, they changed how the public feels about drinking and driving.

To illustrate how our perceptions have changed, think of one of Johnny Mercer's famous ballads, "One For My Baby," about a man drinking to ease his pain over the recent break-up with his girlfriend. Just a few decades ago, people empathized when Frank Sinatra sang that tune. These days, instead of feeling sympathetic, most people would be appalled by anyone who behaved as the lyrics describe: the man chatting with the bartender and ordering two more drinks for himself, "one for my baby and one more for the road." Today, thanks to MADD, it is hard to believe that the concept of "one for the road" ever existed.

For years Candy Lightner ran MADD. When she left the organization, after a dispute with the board over finances, it remained strong and vital thanks to the efforts of thousands of mothers all over America.

MADD's six hundred chapters around the country exist not only to monitor and change the laws affecting drinking and driving, but also to support those who have lost loved ones because of drunk drivers. Volunteers will also support the efforts of individuals who want to be sure a particular driver doesn't harm anyone again. They will accompany grieving relatives who want to file charges and attend trials, lending personal support through the grueling process of getting a dangerous driver who harmed a loved one off of the road. Such supportive relationships have been key to MADD's success in fighting the powerful liquor lobby as well as fighting lawyers hired to defend drunk drivers.

Online Support

Traditionally, when mothers need support, they reach for the telephone or go visit a friend. These days, however, another popular way to connect is online.

In 1999, the *Boston Globe* reported surprise when woman.com went public and it's stock valued soared. The same thing happened to ivillage.com. The success of these two online communities, according to the *Globe*, showed "that women, who until recently were secondary cyber-citizens, are becoming an increasingly powerful online economic force. Consequently, websites and Internet providers now include online 'community' pages—often designed with women in mind—as part of their service packages."

The success of these online communities did not come as a surprise to the mothers who created them, knowing that people would flock to a site that provided online support. The sites get millions of hits. However, the fact that millions of dollars were spent in their creation may sink them, just as it has other expensive dot.coms. Here's a story about a mother whose supportive communities through TheHearth.com were online years before her more famous rivals. They have received as many as a million visitors a month, and she started them for less than $100.

Growing up in the small town of Henderson, North Carolina, no one would have guessed that Paula Eisenberg would become one of the first World Wide Web entrepreneurs. "I was the most non-technical kid in town," she claims. However, her Henderson experiences made her intent on providing a safe, supportive home for her children—and a similar place for everyone else online.

Paula had two younger siblings, a sister and a brother Greggie. She told me, "Greggie was a physically normal little boy with the mental capacity of a two-month-old baby. He never learned to talk, and I was embarrassed to bring my friends home because he would urinate on the floor or take his clothes off."

On summer days, when the family was outside, Greggie sometimes wandered away and got lost. The whole neighborhood would help find him. While neighbors offered that kind of caring help, Paula later realized that her family never received the emotional support she thinks they needed. As she recalls, "My father was the kind of person who felt, 'This is your cross and you have to bear it,' and my mother was a very private person who didn't want to be pitied. I don't think she ever talked about her problems to anyone." Paula remembers plenty of good family conversations about history, astronomy, and nature, but no one ever talked about their feelings or problems with Greggie.

Paula married immediately after college and within two years had her first child. "Being a mother made me realize the value of open discussion," she says. "Both my children are the type who need explanation, and we always had good discussions. I liked to hear what they had to say." With her children, Paula developed the skill of drawing people out that made her successful when she started running support forums.

In the 1980s, Paula's husband brought home a computer. At first, she says, "I thought it was an ugly paperweight that was taking up too much room on my dining room table." But, as she taught herself to use it, she discovered the Internet. "We wanted to go on a Caribbean vacation to get scuba diving certification. I not only found a travel site, but a support group for scuba divers. It was my first contact with strangers on the net. They were all so wonderful that it got me hooked. It was another world, and I liked it."

Paula adds, "The whole idea of online support is a very new idea. It started in 1983 when Howard and Martha Lewis, a married couple, started the first online support group on the Internet, before the Web existed. It had to do with sexuality and relationships, and there were libraries of material you could download, plus message boards and live chat rooms.

"I discovered [that site] in 1989 when I was in my late thirties and exploring my own sexual feelings. I was coming out of a period when I only felt like a mommy. I wasn't looking for sexual freedom—I was just tired of restraints on expression. I had been brought up Catholic and felt guilty about everything, and this was a way to talk about anything guilt-free.

"On the forum I was just Paula E., so I could say things I couldn't say in normal conversation. There is an instant intimacy online. It leads people to talk about their lives in a way they wouldn't ordinarily, because they can be as anonymous as they like. That's what facilitates online support groups—people can lay out their soul with others all over the world. It was fascinating to see this happen.

"CompuServe cost $13 an hour in those days, and I didn't realize how much time I was spending online until one month I got a $900 bill! If you wanted to be a leader of one of the Lewis's chat rooms, you could volunteer. If you were accepted, you wouldn't get paid, but you got to be online for free. So, I volunteered.

"My first job for them was to lead live chats in a section called Superior Sex, where people could talk about their sexual relationships.

I was soon promoted to manager where I not only led the chat room, but also helped manage the library, the bulletin board, membership, and discipline problems."

Paula's job was not to give advice. Instead, she tried to get people to share their ideas and experiences in a supportive way. "I would throw out a topic like, 'Ladies, tell me what you like and don't like in bed.' The men loved this too because they could hear what women really thought. Everyone was very interested and very respectful. I kicked them out of the chat room if they were not respectful. You couldn't use gutter language.

"The Web was invented in 1993, but didn't get popular until 1995. Before the Web the Internet was all text—no pictures, no graphics, just typed words on the screen. I started messing around with one of the first Web browsers in 1994 and realized that this was going to be the end of the old CompuServe because the Web with pictures was so easy. You didn't have to know a lot of programming and computer language like you did to use the old CompuServe—and there was no hourly charge, just a flat monthly fee to your Internet service provider.

"It was very exciting to be in on the beginning of the Web—something that was revolutionary. Back then you couldn't take a course in Web design, so I just started looking at the codes on the webpages and learning how to do it…teaching myself the Web computer language, HTML. Howard Lewis didn't want to move to the web, so I decided to do it myself."

She began in 1995 with one forum, Dear Paula. Using a free forum program and doing the design herself, her total start-up cost was $50 for the first month's fee to her Internet service provider. Since hers was one of the first advice/relationship sites listed on Yahoo and other directories, she began getting a million hits a month.

"The response was huge," Paula remembers, " But I didn't like a lot of stuff that was being put on my forum. So, in 1996 I began to require that people register—give their real email address to me. That meant I got far fewer hits, two hundred to three hundred thousand hits a month, but I was able to control what went on my sites and also get banner ad revenue."

By 1997, this one forum had grown into her current website, TheHearth.com, which has eight support forums. Paula has different forums at TheHearth.com. The seven largest, which cover relationships, health, computers, religion, home and garden, family, and technology, get thousands of visitors a month. But the eighth one, called Safe Haven, requires special registration and has only thirty members.

When I asked why she bothers with a forum that has so few people, here's what she said:

"In my Dear Paula forum that deals with relationships, a woman posted a problem about sexual abuse, and a man responded to her saying, 'I'm announcing for the first time that I was raped at camp when I was twelve.' He told a heartbreaking story and said he never got any help to deal with it. Other people began giving lots of support, but after two or three messages, he stopped posting.

"Several people asked why he stopped posting, and he sent me a private email saying, 'Please thank the people for trying to help, but it feels too scary to talk about it to so many people. I wish there was someplace I could just talk to other people who have survived this.' So, I said, 'What if I gave you a place that was really safe?' He said, 'I'd love it.' So, I did."

Paula sounds like a good mother when she describes how she runs her site, "This is like my living room, and people who visit have to abide by my guidelines, because I want it to be a supportive environment. I want people to feel safe so they can say whatever is on their minds without worrying that they are going to be laughed at or made to feel small.

"On my site, you can't attack people personally. You can say, 'I think your ideas are crazy,' but you can't say you're crazy. You can't be insulting or deliberately antagonistic. If people don't follow the rules, I kick them out and block them from coming back in. Sometimes they register under another name and if they behave, that's OK and they can stay.

"I am maternal when I try to keep the peace. When we have the occasional troublemaker who posts provocative messages just to get people riled up, I try to find out why he's doing that. Often, just opening up the discussion about it helps him see that behavior like that won't make him any friends. Usually people like that just slink away, but sometimes they get it and become valuable Hearth members."

For several years, Paula was actively involved in her forums, but now that her personal need for open conversation and support have been met, she has turned much of the control over to carefully chosen volunteer moderators. Paula also considered running TheHearth as a caring business because advertisers once paid good fees to be on her sites. Now, however, as everyone involved in the Internet has learned, it is hard to earn much just from advertising.

Paula is still actively involved in the Internet. She has become a well-paid consultant in corporate Web design and e-commerce. While she is tempted to shut down TheHearth.com, she keeps it alive because she remembers how much she appreciated the online support she received in the early days of the Internet and the Web. She wishes that such support had been available years ago so that she and her mother could have talked about Greggie. So, she continues to provide a supportive electronic living room for others around the world.

Neighborhood Support

The need for online support grows as real life community support declines. Before World War II, most Americans lived their whole lives in the same town, often in the same neighborhood. Now, the average

American moves every five years. Before television and air conditioning, neighbors used to spend summer nights sitting outside on their
front porches or in local parks, greeting each other as they caught the
evening breeze. Most people who grew up in that era miss the sense of
friendliness and support engendered by long-term relationships and
outdoor living, but don't know how to get it back. Here's how Mary
Ann Cricchio brought old-fashioned friendliness and support back to
the Little Italy section of Baltimore.

Seventeen years ago, shortly after pretty, petite Mary Ann graduated
from college, she married Mimmo, a chef, and they started a restaurant
called DaMimmo. Mimmo handles the cooking and the kitchen. Mary
Ann manages everything else.

"While I learned a lot studying business administration in college,"
she told me, "I really learned my business skills by watching my
mother. She was a very strong woman who became a riveter during
World War II, but after my father came back from the war, she was a
housewife. I saw how she organized a home, a husband, and four children—all the lunches, all the activities. So, when I started the restaurant, it didn't seem overwhelming. I have my son and my husband (he's
like my second child) and then I have thirty-five 'children' on staff in
the restaurant who come in every day with their problems.

"Successful management is maternal. Just as my mother listened to
all the problems of the family and tried to make them better, here I
have a restaurant family and I want the family to work. I have barmaids
who are single mothers, others who are students, and men who are the
heads of households. So, I listen to them and try to create schedules
that will work for them. I have to be there when they come in and see
if they've had a hard day or a hard night. I mother all of them. In a
restaurant, everybody [has] to work together and support each other,
just like in a family."

As an owner of one of the eighteen restaurants in the neighborhood,

Mary Ann automatically was granted membership in The Little Italy Restaurant Association. There, her ability to get people to work together in supportive relationships earned the respect of her colleagues. She also created good press and public relations by organizing events like "The Taste of Little Italy," where each restaurant serves its signature dish in an outdoor festival, and the Miss Little Italy contest.

She is rightly proud when she says that in 1998, "I became president of the association, and that was a big step in itself because the president had always been a man. For this neighborhood and for Italian men fifty to seventy years old, it was quite a step to let a woman take over the association." Everyone had confidence in Mary Ann, until her first project as president—replacing a mural—turned into a disaster that set neighborhood residents against the restauranteurs.

The popular mural welcoming people to Little Italy and listing the eighteen local restaurants had to be replaced because it was painted on a building scheduled to be torn down. Mary Ann offered to have a similar mural painted on the side of her restaurant. The association agreed to pay for it, and the artist suggested covering the brick wall with plywood to have a smoother painting surface.

"It's easy to get a permit from City Hall to do a mural," says Mary Ann. But after the artist finished the huge plywood construction, she received a stop-work order because neighbors said she was constructing an illegal billboard, not a mural. A zoning board hearing became "the ugliest event ever in Little Italy, because residents came out against the restauranteurs," she remembers. "Since I live next door to the restaurant, I could sympathize with my neighbors who were afraid that an advertiser might one day take over the billboard, and it wouldn't be conducive with the neighborhood. I left that meeting and felt horrible.

"A month later, we received a notice saying we could not use the big board, but they didn't tell us we had to take it down. At each monthly meeting of the restaurant association, I would say, 'Okay guys, what do you want to do with it?' But they were licking their wounds and left it for months—just a big board hanging over my parking lot. Finally, one of the restaurant owners joked that it looked like a drive-in movie screen, so why not show movies and let people watch in cars in the parking lot."

That remark made Mary Ann remember a visit to relatives in Sicily, where the town of Palermo created big social events by showing outdoor movies in the local town square. She decided that outdoor movies might bring back a sense of community to Little Italy. But how could one woman with a big blank board create a summer movie festival? By creating a supportive network.

She contacted the owner of an independent movie theater, the Senator, who not only agreed to help her hire a projector and projectionist, but also volunteered to provide free popcorn. She convinced a neighbor, John, to allow the movie projector to beam through his bedroom window. Then, she says, "I got No-Neck Pasquale to carry the projector up to John's apartment." She found someone at City Hall who arranged for the street lights to be turned off on movie nights and the streets to be closed if necessary.

After only one month of organizing, on a warm May evening, without telling anyone in the neighborhood, "we tested the projector, and when the movie came on the screen, 130 people came out of their houses, sat down, and watched. We ran Italian films every Friday night for the next twelve weeks, and by the end of the first season we had four thousand people watching Cinema Paradiso. People came in from the suburbs and from as far away as Washington, D.C. When I hand out the popcorn, they tell me, 'This is great! We don't have anything like this. We don't have ethnic neighborhoods where we live.'

"It's great for the neighborhood. The big board that divided the residents and restauranteurs brought the neighborhood back again. It helps the residents because the majority of them are elderly and on a Friday night, they wouldn't have anywhere to go. They would just sit in their houses. But now, two hours before the movie, we have music and they dance in the parking lot in this piazza atmosphere. People come with picnic blankets and the whole family.

"The first year the festival ran for twelve weeks. The next year we expanded to eighteen weeks. It is so popular [that] the festival will go on every summer forever."

The movies bring people back to the neighborhood, not only to eat in the restaurants but to see that Little Italy is a clean, safe, friendly place. As one woman who grew up in Little Italy, but now lives in the suburbs, said, while sitting on a blanket with her kids and watching the local residents greet each other, "The sense of community—that's one thing I miss." Listening to comments like that, Mary Ann knows that by using her maternal skills to build supportive relationships, she didn't just create a movie festival. She helped repair and revive community spirit.

Bringing It Home

The men in our lives never seem to understand why we are on the telephone so much. Most males use the phone merely to check facts with their friends and then end the conversation. Women want more interconnected relationships, and that takes a lot of time, talk, and effort.

We like to check out our decisions about everything from lipstick to life insurance with our friends. We value their supportive advice (or just a good listening ear) when we want to make large or small life decisions.

This trait doesn't mean that we can't make decisions for ourselves. Instead, it means that we value our friends' input and we naturally enjoy a team effort. When we take this approach out of the home and into the office or the world, it can make us successful. It is this cooperative and non-authoritarian approach that makes female doctors and managers preferred over their male counterparts.

Our ability to form supportive relationships is a key aspect of Mother Power. After all, as the great anthropologist Margaret Mead once said, "Never doubt that a small group of thoughtful, committed citizens can change the world. Indeed, it is the only thing that ever has."

• One of the most important functions of a family is to provide support and refuge when the world is knocking a member down. If your family is not working in this manner, hold a family meeting and get everyone brainstorming about how to make the family more supportive. If things don't improve, get family counseling. If the family won't go together, get some counseling for yourself. You might not be able to produce change all by yourself, but you could use a little support if you live in a family that doesn't provide it.

• Remember that as mothers, we cope with stress by using the "tend and befriend" method. So, if you are feeling alone and unsupported, reach out and befriend. When my children were young, I realized that I was spending so much time working and mothering that I didn't belong to any groups of friends anymore. Joining (or starting) a bridge group, book group, sewing group, prayer group, and support group for fellow psychologists, gave me the support I was missing.

• If you have been inspired by the mothers in this book and want to start your own organization, try to make it a team

continued

---

effort. Think of all the people you know and like. Who would be supportive? How could they help? If you get a group together and each person takes on clear responsibilities, you will probably be more effective. All that support will make the task easier and, hopefully, more fun.

chapter sixteen

TO TALK ABOUT OUR PROBLEMS: THE COURAGE TO BE VULNERABLE

"One of the biggest differences between men and women is how they cope with stress. Men become increasingly focused and withdrawn, while women… feel better talking about problems."
—John Gray, *Men Are from Mars, Women Are from Venus*

Parents who teach children to talk openly and constructively about problems give their children power—the power to gather information that can be used for healthy change, and the power that comes from not having to suffer in silent shame. Shame is the antithesis of power, causing people to hide rather than correct their problems.

The ideal parent not only listens to our problems, but, without being dogmatic, offers advice and information that helps us make things better. Because women tend to be more verbal than men, mothers often slip into this role more easily than fathers. If we are lucky, when we grow up, we will have friends who mother us this way, too.

I was fortunate: I could talk to my mother about almost anything. If I had a problem with a friend, a teacher, or a boyfriend, she was there to counsel and console. She listened to my childhood career aspirations (cowgirl, opera singer, clothes designer, writer) and never mocked or teased. Instead, she bought me cowgirl boots the Christmas I was in kindergarten, came to all my school performances, heard me proclaim that I was going to create all my own clothes and never chided when I failed to follow through, read all my published articles accepted by the school paper, and ignored the rejected ones.

My parents were open about the problems they encountered, too. They told me how much my father earned and how they budgeted the money. When his business was doing well, they let me know I could spend more. When his business did poorly, they discussed it in a way that informed without frightening me. Likewise, they told me about their unhappy childhoods due to family alcohol and marital problems. They even told me about my father's drinking problems before he began abstaining. They weren't complaining or blaming; they just wanted me to be aware of those dangers.

In the last few decades, many women have acted like good mothers to our whole society by talking about topics that were previously considered too secret and shameful to admit. For example, I was grateful to have met the prominent sexologist, Dr. Mary Calderone, who pioneered an openness on the one subject that my parents were too shy to discuss: sex and bodies. Likewise, we all owe a debt to the women who have helped make it acceptable to talk about addiction, breast cancer, and domestic violence.

But How Does the Sperm Get to the Egg?

Sex education is still highly controversial. Dedicated mothers and fathers have been on both sides of the battle, honestly trying to do what is right for their children and vehemently disagreeing about what that entails. One side contends that human beings, even small children, have sexual feelings and curiosity, so we must give them all the information and assistance they need to handle those feelings wisely. The other side says that information and access to birth control encourages unwise sexual behavior.

The sex education in my school tried to cut the difference. Each year in elementary school, the teacher would tell us the proper names for body parts and show us movies about sperm, eggs, and babies. Being a curious child, I would always raise my hand and ask, "But how does the sperm get to the egg?" The teacher would blush and avoid answering directly. I didn't get any clear answers at home either.

My husband and I swore we were going to be different with our children, but we didn't know how. When my children were small, I went to a conference on sex education and discovered that we were not alone in our discomfort.

Everyone in the audience presumably had some experience with the topic—we were all mental health and medical professionals, teachers or clergy. The presenter was Dr. Mary Calderone, a tall, elegant, gray-haired woman in her late seventies, the cofounder and executive director of SIECUS, the Sex Information and Education Council of the United States. After a brief talk on the subject of sex education, she opened up the discussion for comments and questions. It soon became clear that the audience was all in the same boat: we could have professional discussions about sex with the adults we counseled, but became confused and embarrassed trying to talk about sex with our kids.

Dr. Calderone was not just open and frank, she was remarkably reassuring when answering our questions. She seemed like the good mother we all needed, letting us know that the subject was perfectly natural and nothing to be uncomfortable about. She was a great role model not only for how to talk about sex without embarrassment or shame, but also where to draw the line between sexual freedom and sexual responsibility.

Mary Calderone grew up with progressive parents (her father was the famous photographer, Edward Steichen). Once, however, when a man exposed himself to her when she was a child, her parents made her feel guilty and ashamed. This incident was the beginning of her desire for more openness of the subject of sexuality.

After an unhappy marriage, she divorced and went to medical school, graduating when she was thirty-five. Two years later, she married a fellow physician and had a long, happy marriage, raising her three daughters from both marriages. In the mid-1950s, she became the medical director for Planned Parenthood, traveling and speaking widely about birth control and family planning. Then in 1964, she cofounded and became executive director of SIECUS. Into her late seventies she was still writing books to help parents talk comfortably about sex with their children.

A man at the conference asked, "What should you do if your child walks in while you are and your wife are making love?" Dr. Calderone said the most important thing is not to yell at the child. Instead, say something like, "Mom and I are having sex, that's private, so please leave and close the door." (I thought that was a great answer, but wondered how anyone could be that composed in such a situation.) Since she believed that both parents and children should respect each other's privacy and not enter a closed bedroom door without knocking, she said parents should later have a calm discussion with the child, reinforcing the concept of privacy to prevent such embarrassing situations.

A woman asked how to handle the day your daughter gets her period. Dr. Calderone suggested that some sort of family celebration should occur, marking this as a happy occasion and milestone of maturity. (Again, I realized I had to work on myself before I could suggest a family dinner or cake in celebration of my daughter's menstruation. Luckily, I had years to mature before that occurred.) Dr. Calderone said menstruation was also a time to reinforce the need to be responsible with your body, now that it was possible to have a child.

Finally, someone asked my old big question, what to say when youngsters ask how the sperm gets to the egg? "Just tell the simple truth," she said, "The father puts his penis in the mother's vagina so his sperm can go from his penis to join her egg." Now, what was the big deal about that? Suddenly, talking about sex with my children seemed simple and nothing to be worried about. Everyone in the audience seemed to feel the same way.

Not everyone in the country would agree. Mary Calderone's contention that children are born sexual with a capacity for sexual pleasure, struck many people as offensive. Equally or more upsetting to many was her belief that children should be allowed to explore their own bodies and masturbate, as long as it was done in private.

Less controversial was her belief that sexuality, like any other natural function, was something that parents had to teach children to use responsibly and appropriately. She set clear guidelines that bodies should not be touched inappropriately or without permission. She also emphasized that sex was a serious matter, and no one should engage in the act without consideration for the self, the partner, and the consequences of the act.

I know that I was always grateful that she acted, in my opinion, like a good maternal role model in the one area that my own mother could not. I was also grateful that I saw her when my children were very young, so I had time to practice her straight forward approach. That helped when my three-year-old daughter loved to run around nude with friends. I could simply be happy that she enjoyed the lovely body God gave her, and calmly explain more appropriate behavior, rather than get upset and make her ashamed. And I was thankful that when my son, in great excitement over his first pubic hair, rushed out of his room to show me, I could do the same.

Mary Calderone died in 1998, a much honored and sometimes vilified person. Her organization, SIECUS, continues to put out helpful material, and her book, *Talking with Your Child about Sex* (written in 1982 when she was seventy-eight and dedicated to her daughters, her grandchildren, and great-grandchildren) still gives much needed good advice to anxious parents.

While our society has become more open about sex, I doubt that Mary Calderone would be happy about how it is done. She would think that all the unprotected and unloving sex in society and in the media was not "appropriate" (to use one of her favorite words). Neither does a friend of mine who teaches a sex education class for parents. So, when a mother in that class asked if it was okay to let her third grade daughter watch *Ally McBeal*, instead of getting upset, my friend referred the mother to SEICUS guidelines on sexuality education for children—information that Mary Calderone had inspired long ago.

The First Lady to Talk about Her Problems

The wives of our presidents are expected to play a maternal role for the nation, so they usually select a non-controversial issue or two to show that they are caring women. Many First Ladies have struggled with painful personal problems, but felt too vulnerable to speak openly about them. Instead, they spoke out about child welfare, White House redecoration, or highway beautification. Even Eleanor Roosevelt, who courageously championed the rights of underprivileged Americans, kept her personal problems private. Betty Ford was the first First Lady to break this code of silence, and we should all be grateful.

In 1974, seven weeks after Gerald Ford took over the Presidency from Richard Nixon, Betty Ford was diagnosed with breast cancer. Instead of hiding her condition, she thought, "If it can happen to me, it can happen to anybody." So, she told the nation about her illness, and how it was detected through a routine check-up.

Today, it is hard to imagine how much courage it took to reveal her radical mastectomy. In those days, women simply did not talk about their bodies in public. Betty Ford took a chance on being strongly criticized. Instead, the public felt profound respect for Betty's openness. More important, her revelations encouraged public health officials to roll out campaigns to boost breast cancer awareness. Cancer researchers refer to the subsequent "Betty Ford Phenomenon": so many women rushed out to get mammograms that the breast cancer rate surged because of early detection.

In many countries around the world, women are still dying of breast cancer because they are too ashamed or uninformed to get proper check-ups. Luckily, thanks to Betty Ford's example, many women are speaking out and setting a good example for them. One example is Lisa Rey, wife of the United States ambassador to Poland under Bill Clinton.

Diagnosed with breast cancer shortly before moving to Poland, Lisa realized that a strong code of silence still prevailed in her new country. She gave a groundbreaking interview about her disease to the leading women's magazine in Poland, and is credited with starting a Betty Ford Phenomenon there. "I realized how many women were dying because they were too embarrassed to have their breasts examined or too embarrassed to mention a lump in their breasts," she told me. "I wanted to help them." Since returning to Washington, Lisa continues to help fight breast cancer in Poland by raising money and sharing American public relations techniques on the subject.

Since Betty Ford announced that she had breast cancer, many breast cancer advocacy and support groups have sprung up and joined the National Breast Cancer Coalition, a lobbying group. The fact that so many women have become open about their medical problems, and that there has been such effective lobbying, forced Congress in 1993 to pass a law requiring gender equality in medical research.

Perhaps the most impressive public relations campaign for breast cancer was undertaken by Evelyn Lauder, a cosmetics executive. In the early 1990s, she realized that AIDS activists had done a phenomenal job of increasing awareness of that disease, but there was less awareness of the more widespread disease of breast cancer. Having had breast cancer herself, and wanting to help other women avoid the problem, she says, "I figured I was good at selling makeup, so I should be good at selling this cause." She has raised more than $30 million for innovative research and treatment, plus has raised awareness through the sale of pink ribbons.

As we all know, Betty Ford's role as the most open First Lady was not confined to cancer. Several years after her mastectomy, in the aftermath of her husband's stressful, unsuccessful Presidential campaign, Betty's dependence on alcohol and prescription drugs got out of control. Since an alcoholic will often ignore concerns expressed by individuals, Betty's twenty-year-old daughter, Susan, arranged a family intervention where Betty was confronted by her husband and children, who, together, convinced her to face her problems and immediately go into treatment for their sake as well as hers.

Once again, Betty could have easily kept her addictions secret. Celebrities have been doing that for years, and the whole culture of addiction treatment encouraged anonymity. Instead, Betty Ford went public with the fact that her addictions had required her to spend a month in a rehabilitation center. Again, her openness inspired millions of people to face their own similar problems. In 1982 she cofounded the Betty Ford Center for treatment in California and remains an active advocate, trying to make sure that health insurance programs cover alcohol and drug treatment.

Her daughter Susan, now a mother of two in New Mexico, is on the board of the Betty Ford Center and speaks around the country in support of breast cancer research. "People come up to me and say, 'Your mother has made such a difference,'" she says. "I just want to keep the ball rolling, but I will never fill my mother's shoes." She, like I, is not ashamed of the fact that her parent had an addiction problem. Instead, she is proud of having a parent who bravely admitted the problem and conquered it.

It Happens to "Nice" People

Several decades ago, perhaps the only personal problem more secret than alcoholism was family violence. So, in 1999, when *People* magazine had their 25th anniversary issue, they wrote about Charlotte Fedders in their "Profiles in Courage" section, because "she brought wife-beating among the upper crust out of the closet."

You may not remember Charlotte Fedder's name or even her story, which was splashed around the headlines in the mid-1980s, but she played a big role in changing the way the public, the media, and the helping professions treat domestic violence. And since one poll showed that 46 percent of Americans personally know someone who has been physically beaten by a spouse, she very well may have helped someone you know. Here's her story:

Charlotte was a shy, blonde nursing student when she met her husband, John, a tall, articulate law student in 1965, in the cafeteria at Catholic University. They married and seemed to build an ideal life: a beautiful house in the Washington, D.C. suburbs, membership in a prestigious country club, five handsome sons, and John's important job in the Reagan Administration as the chief of enforcement for the Securities and Exchange Commission. Even with all this, Charlotte's life was far from happy.

Soon after they married, the first time Charlotte disagreed with John and refused to back down, he hit her in the ear, breaking her eardrum. When she was pregnant with her first child, he hit her repeatedly in the stomach, saying he didn't care if he killed her and the baby. This kind of abuse would flair up at various times over their years together. She received a black eye, a wrenched back, and was almost thrown over a banister. Furthermore, John enforced dogmatic household rules for Charlotte and the boys. The house had to be spotless, there could be no laughing at the dinner table, and if the boys broke the rules, they would get hit with a fraternity paddle. Why did she stay?

To a large degree, society, the media, and even mental health professionals accepted the myth that such things did not happen to "nice" people in "nice" families. So, Charlotte blamed herself for not pleasing her husband. When she went to have her broken eardrum checked, she was ashamed, sure that the doctor would blame her if he found out her husband hit her.

When Charlotte did find the courage to confide the truth, her fears were realized. A priest told her to give her husband time and "just love him." A doctor told her that both she and her husband were immature. The police were so unhelpful when she went to the station house with a black eye that she left "feeling like a crybaby."

Over the years, through activities with her children, she began to develop some strength and self-esteem. She reports that the first time she began to have an identity as Charlotte, rather than just Mrs. Fedders, is when she agreed to coach her son's elementary school soccer team. That experience made her realize, "I can do something." She joined a reading group, went on the board of her childrens' school, and started reading anything she could find on domestic violence.

Finally, in 1983, after a beating, she went to a neighbor's house and told what was happening. Like many women in abusive situations, she was not willing to make changes for her own sake, but decided her children deserved better. This lead to a separation, but basically the reasons were hushed up.

In 1984, listening to Ronald Reagan's State of the Union message where he promised a drive against "horrible crimes like sexual abuse and family violence," she wrote a letter detailing her experience. While she never mailed the letter, a copy she gave her sister ended up at *The Wall Street Journal*, which broke the story. It caused a sensation, as did Charlotte's testimony at her divorce trial in 1985, and her testimony before Congress in 1986 and 1987 when Reagan tried to cut funding for domestic violence and victim's assistance programs.

She was flooded with mail from other women, thanking her and telling their own grueling stories. While most of the women were as anonymous as she had once been, many of the women had well-known names.

When the story first broke, John quickly retired from the SEC, but fought hard to retain control over Charlotte and the family finances. She had to declare bankruptcy and work several jobs, including an early morning paper route, to support herself and her sons. After the publicity over her 1987 life story, *Shattered Dreams*, died down, she drifted back into the quiet life she always preferred. These days, when she gives an occasional interview, she says that she is poorer, but happier than ever. More important, she says she is proud that she finally had the courage to take her children out of a violent home.

Under old English law, there was the "rule of thumb": husbands could only beat their wives with sticks smaller than the width of their thumbs. While psychologists never would say that it was right to beat a woman, until recently many believed that most victims in some way "asked for it." Then, after Charlotte Fedders spoke out and so many other women followed her example, my profession learned the truth: *any* woman can get caught in the trap of domestic violence. We learned that abusers often start out being very charming. They often seem very interested in every aspect of their lovers' lives. Usually it is a slow transformation from interest to absolute control, from charm to critical destruction of self-esteem, from giving everything to denying the wife anything—job, money, friends—that could give her the independence to leave.

While many victims of domestic violence still feel the abuse is their fault, at least these days, thanks to Charlotte Fedders and other brave women who not only spoke out, but moved out, at least they know they are not alone.

Bringing It Home

Admitting that you have a problem and talking about it are not signs of weakness. In fact, it takes more strength and courage to admit a problem than to defensively cover it up. This openness can be healthy, not only in the home, but in the workplace. (Managers hate when an employee tries to cover up a problem until it is too far gone to correct.)

Some people equate talking about problems with complaining. Actually, they are polar opposites. Complaining is just moaning and groaning, without any thought of how to change the situation. Constructive talking about a problem (whether it is a problem in your personal life, family life, workplace, or society) lays out the issues. This is the first step to correcting the situation. Once a problem is out in the open, you can begin to generate possible solutions.

> • Select a friend or family member whom you admire—someone who is both discreet and effective—and make a date to talk together. (If there is no one you can trust, make an appointment with a professional or go to a self-help group meeting.) Take a few notes about your problem to help you overcome your discomfort when you begin to confide. Ask for assistance to brainstorm possible solutions or sources of help. Then take at least one small step to understand the issues and make things better.
>
> • If you form or join a group of people with similar problems, at first it just feels good to know that you are not the only one suffering with this issue. Eventually, you may be able to solve the problem collectively. Groups of mothers have pooled their money to help each other start businesses together or one at a time.

I read about a group of single mothers who each learned a home-improvement skill: basic carpentry, painting, and roofing. Then they helped each other fix up their dilapidated homes. Even more impressive, Holly Curtis, the director of Peace at Home, a group in Boston that combats domestic violence, told me that the first woman's refuge was started in England by a group of women who began sharing stories about how they were being battered.

• If you let talking become hating, you will lose your effectiveness. For example, I was extremely proud of the way my daughter, Nicole, ran "Take Back the Night," a speak-out against rape on her college campus. She was careful not to let the evening become a male-bashing event. She knew that men suffer from rape as well as women: as victims as well as by grieving when it happens to someone they love. Furthermore, if men did not come and listen, how would they spread the word and help control the problem of date rape on campus? So, by reaching out and including men on the planning committee, she created an event that was more than just talk.

chapter seventeen

TO KNOW WHY SOMETHING HAPPENED: KNOWLEDGE TO MAKE THINGS BETTER

"Holy Mother Earth, the trees and all nature are witnesses of your thoughts and deeds."

—Native American (Winnebago) prayer

If I had to guess the five most common words in a mother's vocabulary, I would list: please, no, yes, stop, and why. I include "why" because we are always asking questions like, Why did you hit your brother? Why did you spill your milk? Why didn't you do your homework? or, Why did you come in so late last night?

Even though we know the answers to such questions are rarely enlightening, we still feel compelled to ask in hope of learning the cause of the problem and how to correct it. Mothers have taken this need to know why something happened and used it with greater success beyond the home.

For example, while the scientific community and major environmental groups are predominantly run by men, groups of noisy, persistent grassroots mothers have forced them to change the way they operate. Accusing environmentalists of caring more about whales and rain forests than poor kids with asthma and cancer, mothers are insisting that more focus be placed on toxins in our poorest neighborhoods. Likewise, they have forced scientists to no longer dismiss "cancer clusters" (areas with unnaturally high levels of cancer) as mere statistical flukes. You will meet some of the mothers who are at the forefront of the movement to investigate the effects of toxic industrial waste and clean it up.

The next two mothers researched other things that are making people sick. Mary Pipher discovered a widespread phenomena poisoning our children when she wondered why strong, assertive little girls began losing self-confidence in junior high school and becoming sexual before they were ready, developing eating disorders and turning to drugs and alcohol. Looking at the media aimed at adolescents, she found the answer: we are living in a "girl-poisoning" society.

Jessie O'Neill grew up wealthy and wondered why the rich aren't happy. Her research has shown that too much focus on money causes Affluenza, a condition that poisons relationships, ambition, and self-worth. Even if you aren't rich, affluenza could be affecting your family.

Why Are Our Children Getting Sick?

Most people who read *A Civil Action* are intrigued by the flamboyant lawyer, Jan Schlichtmann, who risks all, trying to prove that corporate toxic waste caused high levels of leukemia in Woburn, Massachusetts. However, I think the real hero of the story is Anne Anderson, the mother who vowed to find out why her child and many others were getting sick—and forced Schlichtmann to do something about it.

In 1979, when Anne read in the *Boston Globe* that some Woburn wells contained high levels of industrial solvents, she realized that the drinking water might be poisoning residents. In a grassroots effort that has become standard procedure for other mothers around the country, she tried to find all the people in the community with leukemia like her son. Mapping them, she discovered a "cancer cluster," in the area served by contaminated wells. With this data in hand, she led her community in a crusade.

She contacted her senator, Ted Kennedy. She contacted the *Boston Globe* and held a news conference. She spoke briefly, but made headlines by saying that "We fear for our children." More important, she got Jan Schlichtmann's firm to agree to take the case against two industrial polluters in town. Then, when Schlichtmann kept dragging his feet and failed to begin the suit, she shamed him into being more aggressive: he was pontificating on a radio talk show when she telephoned and asked on air why he was ignoring her calls.

She is a great example of Mother Power, because she consistently took the high road. While the lawsuit asked for damages, she honestly said she wasn't in this endeavor for the money. She didn't want "blood money," as she called it. She just wanted the polluters to say they were sorry and clean up the mess. Then, during the trial, she wanted to be strong, and feared crying on the witness stand. But Schlichtmann knew that the honest tears of a grieving mother could sway a jury.

Anne Anderson helped make "cancer clusters" a publicly accepted concept. But it took many other committed mothers to force scientists to seriously study the problem. One of the most vocal of those mothers, Lois Gibbs, emerged as a community spokeswoman during the Love Canal scandals.

Lois was a twenty-seven-year-old mother, who repeatedly had to take her young son and daughter to the doctor for liver problems, asthma, and an unusual blood disorder. Then she discovered why her kids and others in the neighborhood were sick: her housing development had been built on a toxic waste dump.

In the 1940s and '50s, Hooker Chemical Company (later taken over by Occidental Chemical) had poured 21,800 tons of dangerous chemicals into a large trench in Love Canal, not far from Niagra Falls. Lois's house was one of the modestly priced homes later constructed on the site. The toxic chemicals started leaking into the environment, and, in 1978, New York State officials declared a health emergency.

While officials and Occidental began fighting over what to do about the problem, Lois began leading protests, insisting that the government buy Love Canal houses and move the residents out. The young house-wife who previously had lead a quiet life at home, suddenly became a vocal and persistent political activist. She organized her neighbors to picket at legislators' homes, hand out leaflets at black tie state dinners, and surround the governor with a ring of preschool children to gain attention for the cause. Within a year, the government agreed to buy Love Canal homes and clear the area.

Lois moved with her two children to Falls Church, Virginia. Her children's health problems went away after the move, but she decided to form the Citizen's Clearinghouse for Hazardous Wastes to help the three thousand people who called the Love Canal volunteer office with toxic waste problems in their area, too. As she said shortly after founding her organization, "When someone calls me up, says they have a sick kid, and blames it on a chemical dump, I'll do anything to help."

By the early 1990s, Lois was scolding environmentalists for caring about whales, while neglecting pollution problems in poor neighbor-hoods at home. She wanted Earth Day not just to encourage recycling, but to focus on public health problems in American ghettos and rural backwaters—the places that suffer the most, but have little political clout or money to fight for a clean-up. As she put it, "When you say 'environmentalist,' the image you get is of some person eating yogurt or bean spouts," said Lois. "We folks at the grassroots level are gener-ally blue-collar people who smoke cigarettes, drink Budweiser, and like to eat at McDonald's"—and the ones with kids living on top of toxic dump sites or with sludge incinerators in their backyards. Her words stung, and now environmentalists, while retaining lofty worldwide goals, are putting more effort into toxic waste at home.

The scientific community was a harder nut to crack. Many believed, like Dr. Bruce N. Ames, director of the National Institute of Environmental Health Sciences Center at the University of California at Berkeley, that, "There are so many types of cancer and birth defects that just by chance alone you'd expect any one of them to be high in any one little town," and claimed that there "is no convincing evidence that synthetic chemicals in the atmosphere are an important cause of cancer in humans."

"Bull," said mothers around the country who were tracking cancer clusters in their communities from California to the East Coast. For example, in 1998, the same year that Dr. Ames dismissed such thinking, Linda Gillick, whose son has a rare form of cancer, organized a local movement to demand an investigation of why cancer rates for children were so abnormally high in her town in New Jersey. With motherly common sense, she said, "When you have something that is grossly abnormal, you need to find out the indicator that is different from somewhere else. What do we have that's different? That's the key."

"Logical as it may sound," reported the *New York Times*, "Mrs. Gillick's assumption represents a challenge to science's traditional approach to cancer clusters." But, so many groups of mothers and others are demanding that science address their concerns, millions of dollars are now being directed to investigate cancer clusters. "This is pushing science to a new era—of eco-genetic epidemiology...where molecular biomarkers of disease and geographical variations are examined together," said a spokeswoman for the Environmental Protection Agency.

Here's a translation of what that spokeswoman said: now, all across America, health officials are using new techniques to see if they have overlooked chemicals in the air, water, and soil where there are cancer clusters. States like Hawaii, Illinois, California, New York, and New Jersey have undertaken statewide cancer mapping studies, because groups of mothers have forced them to do so.

As of now, no one knows whether the mothers or the scientists are right. But at least the mothers have been instrumental in forcing experts to examine why so many of their kids and neighbors are getting sick.

Why Are Our Daughters Acting Crazy?

There are many forms of environmental toxins. Mary Pipher, a psychologist in Lincoln, Nebraska, found that the air waves are full of them.

Most female psychologists take a motherly interest in their patients. Mary Pipher of Lincoln, Nebraska, is no exception. After being a practicing psychologist for twenty years, Mary became alarmed in the early 1990s that something terrible was happening to adolescent girls. In her bestselling book, *Reviving Ophelia*, she wrote, "many girls come into therapy with serious, even life-threatening problems, such as anorexia or the desire to physically hurt or kill themselves. Others have problems less dangerous, but still more puzzling such as school refusal, underachievement, moodiness, or constant discord with their parents. Many are the victims of sexual violence." The strongest and most assertive generation of preadolescent girls was cracking up on the shoals of adolescence.

Like other mothers, Pipher noticed that most preadolescent girls are curious about the world, outspoken, involved in many interests, and generally fun to be with. Then, during early adolescence, something dreadful seems to happen: girls give up their interests and joy in life. They become sullen, moody, and often dangerously depressed. She wondered why this was happening to her adolescent patients. Her curiosity was personal as well as professional, since her own outgoing daughter was changing into one of those moody adolescents, too.

Adolescents have always been moody. Their parents have rarely understood them. But Pipher's research found something much more dangerous was going on these days. "I am saying that girls are having more trouble now than they had thirty years ago, when I was a girl, and more trouble than even ten years ago. Something new is happening," she asserted.

"Adolescence has always been hard, but it's harder now because of cultural changes in the last decade. The protected place in space and time that we once called childhood has grown shorter. There is an African saying, 'It takes a village to raise a child.' Most girls no longer have a village."

Instead of a village, she discovered, "They are coming of age in a more dangerous, sexualized, and media-saturated culture. They face incredible pressures to be beautiful and sophisticated, which in junior high means using chemicals and being sexual."

Pipher was saying the same thing that my colleagues who work with adolescents were telling me: girls are pressured to begin experimenting with drugs and alcohol and perform oral sex on boys as early as junior high. I had dismissed my colleagues' reports as completely out of the mainstream. But when I read *Reviving Ophelia*, I realized I was wrong. After all, Pipher works in the heartland. If it is happening in Nebraska, as well as suburban New York, I realized it is happening everywhere, as Pipher contends. How can that be?

Mary says that we live in a "girl-poisoning culture." She writes, "The more I looked around, the more I listened to today's music, watched television and movies, and looked at sexist advertising, the more convinced I became that we are on the wrong path with our daughters."

I felt sick when I read this book. I went in my daughter's room and looked at her "teen magazines"—some of which I had actually bought her. The models were anorexic and I couldn't find one article about achievement. The whole emphasis was on "improving" your looks, attracting boys, and being sexual.

I paid for MTV and HBO for my kids, but rarely watched myself. Now I turned in and was disgusted by what I had allowed into my home. Passing through the den when the kids were watching, I had noticed that many of the videos and movies were sexual and violent. I thought kids dismissed this stuff as mere fantasy. Now I asked myself, how could I, as a psychologist, have been so stupid and naive?

From the time I was in graduate school, I read studies showing that what children watch on television or movie screens affects their thinking and behavior. Why would I not realize that, faced with a daily barrage of sex, violence, and anorexic models/actresses, this generation of children would be damaged? Why did I allow all that dangerous trash in my home?

Like most parents, I felt overwhelmed by the sheer volume of bad influences. They are everywhere and growing. As a recent article in the *New York Times* noted, "Family viewing was a notion promoted in the mid-1970s...Shows for youngsters dominated until the early 1990s. Then NBC, positioning itself as the network for hip, young adults, saw no competition before nine o'clock. The network infiltrated family viewing time with *Mad About You*, a sexy, sophisticated comedy, followed next year with the coy frankness of *Friends*." Coy frankness? Everybody sleeps with everybody, and that's portrayed as perfectly okay.

These days, girls are not just pressured to be too sexual, too young—they are pressured to be too skinny, too. Everybody knows that it is common for models and actresses to be anorexic. So what?

Pipher found the anorexic ideal presented by models and actresses presents not just a physically unhealthy ideal, but a soul-killing one, too. Here's how Pipher explained why, "They epitomize our cultural definitions of feminine: thin, passive, weak, and eager to please." Our strong, assertive preadolescents are suddenly faced with a terrible choice: if you want to be beautiful and popular, stop being strong and stop being yourself. Like Ophelia in *Hamlet*, our girls are encouraged to give up everything to try to please, and to try to attract love. When they are rejected, like Ophelia, they feel like dying. But if they are accepted, a large part of themselves—the strong, independent part—dies too.

But, if you think too-skinny models, "coy frankness," soft porn movies, and the sexual/violent/drug-related lyrics of songs isn't bad enough, then you not have you seen the current video games. As the major consumers of video games, boys are exposed to even more destructive training than girls. As the *Monitor*, a publication of the American Psychological Association, reported in November 2000, "Video games teach kids how to be violent, reward them for that violence, and demonstrate that violence has no negative consequences. This generation of children is being schooled in the art of violence by a private tutor, while parents remain unaware of the problem." No wonder that so many young men are in trouble with the law, and that date rape statistics are climbing.

When my daughter, Nicole, and I drove around looking at colleges in her junior year of high school, we listened to the audio tape of *Reviving Ophelia*. "Oh my God," my daughter said, "this describes exactly what happened to me and my friends!" All those bright little girls who liked being smart, thought their bodies were just fine, laughed at silly, innocent things, and enjoyed being athletic and musical, suddenly gave up most of their joy in junior high. That's when the media aimed at adolescents starts telling them that their bodies should be thinner than normal, their faces should be prettier than they are, they should be more sexual than they are ready to be, and they should have fun with alcohol and drugs.

What are parents to do? Here are some of the things Mary Pipher suggests:

• Create a home that offers "girls affection and structure. Set firm guidelines and communicate high hopes...Remember that rules in the absence of loving relationships are not worth much."

• Listen to your daughters "who need as much parent time as toddlers. It's good to ask questions that encourage daughters to think clearly for themselves. When possible, congratulate your daughters on their maturity, insight, or good judgement."

• "When teenagers temporarily lose their heads, which most do, they need an adult there to help them recover. When daughters have problems, it's important not to panic. Panicky parents make things worse."

Pipher also advises, if possible, to not make raising daughters a do-it-yourself project. Fathers play a much more important role with their adolescent daughters than many suspect. Pipher found that too many girls have distant relationships with their fathers. She also found that "Supportive fathers had daughters with high self-esteem and a sense of well-being. These girls were more apt to like men, to feel confident in relationships with the opposite sex, and to predict their own future happiness. They described fathers as fun, deeply involved, and companionable." On the other hand, "Rigid fathers limit their daughters' dreams and destroy their self-confidence...Sexist fathers teach their daughters to relinquish power and control to men."

Mary Pipher gives us guidelines to use at home, but her research also challenges us as parents to try to clean up the societal forces that are poisoning our kids. We have to pressure our schools to be more challenging and enforce rules against drugs, drinking, and sexual harassment—for the sake of our girls as well as our boys. We have to pressure our government representatives to crack down on the media, which is poisoning our children.

For example, a recent Federal Trade Commission hearing found that the music industry's marketing plans specifically targeted children, regardless of the labels warning of songs' explicit content. (Anyone who listens to Eminem—nominated for a 2000 Grammy for the best album of the year—knows the industry lies when it says it is policing itself.) Same with movies. In a "big" concession after the FTC hearings, Disney said it would no longer have children under seventeen participate in focus groups for its R rated films. The fact that Disney, of all companies, is making R rated films is just one more example of why our daughters live in a girl (and boy) poisoning culture—and why our adolescents are acting so crazy.

Why Aren't the Rich Happy?

Mary Pipher asked why girls weren't happy. Jessie O'Neill asked the same about the rich. Both found answers that have profound implications for our society.

Jessie O'Neill's grandfather was president of General Motors, so she grew up with so much money that she never needed to work. One day, when Jessie was pushing her daughter on a swing set, the little girl looked at the Bloody Mary in her mother's hand and asked, "Do you have to drink?" That innocent question not only made Jessie join Alcoholics Anonymous, but it led her to question why so many people who have "everything," also have alcohol, drug, and self-esteem problems.

Jessie went back to school, earning a masters in psychology and counseling, and began studying the culture of affluence. She found that many of us, not just the very wealthy, are afflicted by what she calls Affluenza—a relationship with money that makes us sick. But first, here's what she discovered about the very rich:

Very rich families usually have a Founding Father, a workaholic, devoted to earning a fortune. Often self-absorbed, he typically marries a beauty, who is self-absorbed, too. The Founding Father is too busy with work to have much to do with the kids. His wife is too busy being social and beautiful to have much to do with the children, either. The youngsters, raised by servants, have everything that money can buy, but don't have what every child needs: parental love and attention, good values, and the ability to handle frustration.

Such "poor little rich kids" often grow up to be alcoholics, who beget children with addiction problems, too. As Jessie wrote in her book, *The Golden Ghetto*, "I believed with all my heart that something outside myself could make me happy. That, after all, is the overriding message of an affluent culture: money, possessions, the right friends, and the right experiences" make people content. But since that never brings true self-esteem and inner peace, she, like many others, blindly turned to alcohol, drugs, and food to fill the void.

Such problems became much more widespread, thanks to a phenomenon that grew in the 1980s and '90s: workaholism. Now it isn't just men intent on becoming Founding Fathers, who work and neglect their families. These days, there are plenty of female workaholics, too.

You can find Affluenza in every country of the world, and it has spread through every level of society. As Jessie wrote, "It is as much about the factory worker who wastes his potential for happiness fantasizing about being rich, as it is about the wealthy person whose life is devoid of meaningful relationships and filled with nothing but work and the accumulation of money. It encompasses the middle-class couple who both work two jobs, and whose children spend the majority of their waking hours in the care of strangers—not because they need the money to survive, but because they believe that the accumulation of more material possessions will bring them happiness and fulfillment."

Workaholics, like all addicts, avoid true feelings. So do people with other forms of Affluenza: those who spend too much time accumulating or hoarding things and money. They think another dress, or car, or house, or raise, or win at the poker table will make them happy. Of course, it never does.

The cure for Affluenza is not a quick fix. It is never as simple as forcing a rich person to give away money, a trust-fund slacker to get a job, or a workaholic to spend more time with the kids.

The cure, as Jessie found in her therapy practice with the rich, involves finding your real self and developing a healthy relationship with money. The goal is to genuinely recognize that security and self-worth are not based on money. Instead, real security, she writes, comes when people identify their actual feelings and stop running away from childhood fears and shame. Once they stop relating feelings of inferiority and superiority to money, they can begin to behave in ways that nurture and expand their true selves. Equally important, they can begin to make genuine, loving connections to others.

For Affluenza victims, as for all of us, developing true security and self-worth usually involves finding a way to make a contribution to society. It means learning to give both money and affection in positive ways. As she says, "When we give from our hearts, the feeling of joy is clear."

Most of all, she wants our children to no longer be influenced by Affluenza. We can do that by giving children our time and good values, not just money and things. She writes, "If you believe that your parents cared so little for you that they didn't bother to spend time with you, how as an adult could you ever believe that anyone could ever really love you? Showered with toys, lessons, and the trappings of social status, rather than with time and love...how does one become an adult who can create realistic, healthy emotional and physical boundaries in one's relationships with others or oneself. Love, after all, is about nurturance, time spent talking, playing, touching, laughing, and crying together."

Love is also about teaching values and responsibilities. No matter how wealthy you may be, she says it is "important to give children age-appropriate responsibility within the household. This will help them feel valued, integral, and necessary to the family. Their self-esteem and self-worth will grow accordingly. Parents also need to allow their children to feel the consequences of their behavior. Don't buy their way out of mistakes. Being held accountable for one's actions is an important step toward learning what the acceptable boundaries are within our society." And she counsels, "Say no to some material requests to teach them to tolerate frustration and delay gratification."

Affluenza is all around us. We all know kids (and adults) who are bored, even though they have a lot of toys. Every time we go to a restaurant, we see parents who cannot say no to their kids and teach them to tolerate frustrations, kids who are allowed to be noisy and spoil the evening for other diners. And we all know kids who are practically raising themselves because their parents don't understand that love is more important than money and status.

"Rich or poor," she writes, "it is a challenge to all human beings to create a satisfying and worthwhile life. In that sense, we are all alike." We are also all alike in that we have to create a sense of self-esteem that isn't based on money, and a way to value others that is based on who they really are, not just on how much they are worth. By doing that for ourselves and our children, all of us can begin to make the world free from Affluenza.

As Jessie O'Neill wrote in the dedication to *The Golden Ghetto*, "But most of all, this book is for my daughters, Rebecca and Maggie, in the hopes that by beginning to break the bonds of dysfunction, we can offer them a world in which the measure of a person's worth and the barometer of a person's happiness is not equated with the bottom line on his or her balance sheet." Her book gives all of us that challenge and the tools we need to meet it.

Bringing It Home

One of the ways to tell a good mother is that she asks "Why?" not to blame, but to determine accountability. We must hold our children accountable for their naughty deeds and even for their mistakes, not to make them feel bad about themselves, but to teach them how to do things better, and to teach them that their actions have consequences. The same thing is true in society.

We must join the battle against corporations that are poisoning our society, whether through toxic waste or toxic media. We must hold them accountable for their actions. We must support legislators and citizens groups that are trying to force a clean-up. And we can make sure that our own attitudes don't encourage the toxic spread of Affluenza.

The forces that pollute our air and our airwaves are very powerful, but so is Mother Power. If enough of us insist on a clean-up, we can make it happen not only in our homes, but in society as a whole.

However, if you aren't ready to join one of these grassroots crusades, at least take a long car trip with your daughter and listen to the audio version of *Reviving Ophelia*.

• Assertion training stresses that you have the right to ask any-thing—but the other person has the right to tell or not. Is there someplace where you would like to assert your right to ask questions? Is there a family secret that has been kept from you too long? You have a right to ask what really happened and why. If you are not told, you have a right to investigate further.

• Are you upset about an issue? You don't have to have "proper credentials" to research it. Aspire to be an amateur expert and

continued

---

begin to read up and ask questions about any topic that interests you. If someone asks why you want to know, simply say, "I'm doing research on the subject." That usually opens more doors than the equally true, "I'm just curious."

As a young psychologist, I was asked to treat several children who had been harmed by harsh conditions in foster care. I was curious about why babies were allowed to spend years in such impermanence when there were so many people who wanted to adopt. Initially, I never intended to use this research for anything except my own understanding.

• Once you have some information, you may wish to put it to good use. For example, last year, Ikea wanted to build a huge store in a largely residential area about a mile from my home. It would have clogged the small roads for miles around and would not have been good for either Ikea or the neighborhoods that surround the intended site. In a David versus Goliath effort, so many homeowners turned up so much effective evidence as to why the project would not be good for either the sponsoring municipality nor the company, that the project was canceled.

On another personal note, the research I did on foster care and adoption eventually made me want to write about the issue. I turned it into an article for the *New York Times* magazine and that lead to a book.

chapter eighteen

TO FIND A WAY TO STOP GRIEVING: TURNING PAIN INTO ACTION AND PURPOSE

When you are dead, your mother will mourn
you till the day she dies.

—**Arab Proverb**

As a psychologist, I learned that men and women grieve in different ways. While both feel deeply, men usually are able to put aside their pain more easily than women. Most mothers are still grieving long after fathers have decided "we need to stop thinking about this and go on with our lives." I have seen couples torn apart by this difference when dealing with the death or disability of a child. It almost happened to me.

My husband pushed away his worries about our son's health by burying himself in work. My worries about Jean Paul were a constant part of my life. I tried to use them in constructive ways, searching for effective treatments that could save his life, and inventing ways to keep his spirits up.

Knowing the odds were against him, I began secretly grieving long before he died. Remembering him as a smiling, curly haired little boy broke my heart. I often felt a stab of pain thinking of the smart, sweet young man he had become—a tall, skinny fellow who gave lots of hugs;

a man who loved his work, his fiancée, and the idea of becoming a daddy; the person I could always call if I needed the answer to a question or a laugh.

I understood why European peasant women in mourning wore black for the rest of their lives. I even understood how Indian women could throw themselves on a funeral pyre. I also understood how inappropriate it was for me to think this way, because I needed to be strong. I had to help my son fight his disease. My daughter needed my strength and optimism. I had a practice full of patients who depended on me.

My husband never let himself think that Jean Paul might die. I looked equally untroubled as I divided my time between my practice and my family. Only my closest friends saw me weeping. And no one knew that I was teetering on the edge of a deep depression.

Most friends thought I was a pillar of strength. My patients, who are supposed to be shielded from problems in their therapist's private life, didn't suspect my son was ill, but noticed a softening in my manner. As one said, "What's going on, Dr. Plumez? You seem so much nicer." I simply smiled that enigmatic smile psychologists sometimes use.

I did feel a deeper compassion as I tried to help my patients with their pain. But, I couldn't imagine finding a way to stop my own pain and live a productive life if Jean Paul died.

When I saw the Mothers of the Plaza de Mayo, it felt like I had been thrown a lifeline. Here were women who stayed strong after dealing with much more than I had to bear. (After all, the death of a child is one thing, but having your child disappear and then be tortured to death by your government is quite another.) The Mothers taught me that there is life after death, but I knew their way of surviving was not mine. I could never become a revolutionary.

As I searched for more role models, I found that they all—the Mothers in Buenos Aires, like mothers who survive grief everywhere—have three things in common. They find appropriate ways to express their feelings.

They find ways to turn their pain into action. And they find ways of giving their life, and the fate they have been dealt, positive meaning.

I prayed that a miracle would save Jean Paul. When the doctors told us he was going to die, I prayed for a different kind of miracle: that I could feel the joy of sharing his life, more than the pain of losing him. I also prayed that I would be capable of sharing what I learned about how other mothers overcome grief.

Writing this book has been my therapy, my way to cope with grief and mourning. This chapter presents mothers who have found other constructive ways to deal with death in their family. While undirected grief saps energy, grief turned into meaningful action becomes Mother Power.

Finding a Way to Express the Feelings

"My two children were killed in an accident on the first day of spring," a Michigan mom, Patricia Loder, told me. "A motorcycle crashed into the car they were sitting on, and my son was dead at the scene. He was five. My daughter died a few hours later. She was eight.

"I didn't think that anyone could hurt as bad as I did and survive. A friend recommended The Compassionate Friends (a self-help group for bereaved parents and siblings). I didn't want to go. I didn't think that talking about it would help, but my husband insisted we go.

"At one of those meetings a mom talked about how there was a video tape that never shut off in her head—a video tape of the day her child died. I thought, 'My goodness, somebody else has the same thing happening to them.' I started to listen. It was a slow process of realizing that I was not alone. Another person shared my grief. That began the healing process."

Patricia Loder, like many people who attend meetings at The Compassionate Friends (TCF), initially listened to others' stories and then slowly began to talk about her own. Eventually, she felt strong enough to begin to comfort newcomers. Later, she and her husband volunteered to write newsletters for TCF, and recently she became their executive director.

In fact, all the paid executive directors of The Compassionate Friends in the United States have been mothers. When I asked why, Patricia commented, "Mothers have nurturing instincts, although we're not used to thinking about how valuable our maternal strengths are and how we use them."

Patricia says that mothers play a key role throughout the organization because, "we reach out, and we are in tune with our feelings. That doesn't mean that some men aren't into feelings—there is a mix at our meetings. But men often think they have to be macho, and women break down the barriers, allowing others to cry and comfort each other.

"It is a very maternal situation. That's very helpful for men who come. We've had men who walk away saying, 'I grew up in a society that said I wasn't supposed to cry, but this is the worst possible thing that could happen to me, and it's okay if I cry.' The mothers here show them that."

TCF started by chance in 1968 in Coventry, England, when two sets of parents met under tragic circumstances in the local hospital. One family was losing a son to cancer, the other's child was fatally injured in an accident. After both boys died, the two couples began meeting. As one later recalled, "Together, amidst free-flowing tears, the four of us were able for the first time to speak openly of our children, without feelings of guilt...together, we were able to accept, for the first time, the words used by many well-meaning friends, but rejected almost universally by parents who have lost a beloved child—'I understand.' We *did* understand, all four of us, and in the immensity of our grief we all suffered together."

A local minister noticed that the two couples were helping each other in ways neither he nor anyone else could, so he asked if they would meet with other bereaved parents. Those informal meetings grew into The Compassionate Friends. In 1971, a *Time* magazine article about this British group inspired an American couple to found the first chapter in the United States. Now, TCF has grown into the largest self-help bereavement group. They are in twenty-three countries around the world, and have almost six hundred groups in the United States alone.

Patricia emphasizes that there is no right or wrong way to grieve. Everybody's grief is different. However, she knows that talking about your loss with understanding people can be an important part of the process. That's why TCF is so valuable, because as she explains, sooner or later, "Your friends and family think you're dwelling on it, but you need to talk about it and talk about it until it sinks in. Our organization allows people to talk with others who truly understand their feelings. We've all been there, and when someone truly understands your feelings, it's very healing."

That healing is especially needed by people who feel pain when the rest of the world is celebrating. Holidays are hard for all bereaved parents, but they are especially hard for people like former TCF Executive Director Diana Cunningham whose son, Jimmy, was killed in a car accident on New Year's Eve. Many others in her Compassionate Friends group in Riverside, California, "felt resentment when wished a 'Happy New Year.' How could they ever be happy again when their son or daughter or brother or sister or grandchild had died? I heard time and time again 'Thank goodness the holidays are over!'"

Diana decided to give a thank-goodness-it's-over open house at the end of the holiday season. Everyone brought something to eat and a story of some "really dumb thing that had been said to him or her during the holiday season." That party became a popular tradition.

Whether sharing the pain of the holidays, or general feelings of loss, many people find comfort through being with those in similar circumstances. But TCF offers more than just mutual commiseration. "The secret of TCF's success is simple," as its website explains. "As seasoned grievers reach out to newly bereaved, energy that has been directed inward begins to flow outward and both are helped to heal. That healing then allows the bereaved to begin to refocus their lives away from the tragedy: to more fully appreciate happy memories from the past, and to begin to make some positive plans for the future." Grief begins to turn into action.

Turning Grief into Action

The next mother found a more public way to talk about her grief and turn it into action. I almost missed the opportunity to meet her, but friends convinced me to do my civic duty.

"Oh, give me a break," I thought when friends insisted that I come to a fund-raiser for Congresswoman Carolyn McCarthy. "She doesn't represent my district," I told them, "She doesn't even represent yours!" But they persisted, saying that citizens have to support honest politicians who battle well-funded special interests. In theory, I agreed, but I have to admit that I went to the fund-raiser only because I knew the food would be good—a well-known restauranteur was throwing the party.

I found more than good food. I found inspiration. That's because, whether you agree with Carolyn's politics or not, it's always inspiring to meet an honest, caring politician. It was also inspiring to meet someone who has transcended grief in such a positive and unexpected way.

When Carolyn was young, no one would have predicted that she would someday make *Ladies' Home Journal's* list of 100 Most Important Women or the *Congressional Quarterly's* 50 Most Effective Legislators. In fact, when she graduated from high school in 1962, she had no idea what she wanted to do with her life.

Soon after graduation, however, a tragedy gave her life direction.

Her boyfriend was badly injured in a car accident, and she helped the nurses care for him. When he died, she decided to become a nurse herself. Three years later at age twenty, she had earned a Licensed Practical Nurse degree and was working with intensive care patients, when she met her husband, Dennis McCarthy.

Carolyn says that she and Dennis lived a quiet life in a middle-class suburban neighborhood on New York's Long Island. She continued nursing and loved being a homemaker, raising her only child, Kevin. Perhaps the most extraordinary thing about her life was the close relationship she had with her husband. "We were best friends who did everything together," she said. "There was nothing we didn't talk about."

Then on December 7, 1993, a mentally ill man wielding an assault weapon sprayed a Long Island commuter train with bullets. He killed Dennis and five other people. Kevin and eighteen others were wounded. Kevin was paralyzed and for weeks couldn't speak. When he finally began speaking, the only word he would say was, "Why?" While helping to nurse him, Carolyn promised that she would do everything she could to keep another family from experiencing such pain.

The gun control movement is full of people like Carolyn: parents, partners, and friends who have lost people they loved. Like them, Carolyn turned grief into action by speaking to community groups and lobbying Congress to ban assault weapons. She was relieved and gratified when Congress passed such a ban.

Then the unthinkable happened. The gun control lobby pushed for a repeal of the ban against assault weapons, and her own congressman, republican Dan Frisa, voted to repeal the ban against nineteen different kinds of assault weapons, including the one that had been used against her family. She was outraged.

A life-long Republican, she went to party officials and asked them not to back Frisa's bid for reelection. When they refused, she decided to switch parties and run as a Democrat against him. Since her district is heavily Republican and hadn't elected a Democrat for years, no one thought she had a chance. But in a campaign fueled by her own righteous indignation, plus a lot of Mother Power, she won in 1996 with 57 percent of the vote.

She came to Congress as an avenging mother. Being new to politics, Carolyn says, "I thought I could get things done in one term in Congress, but I was wrong." Seeking reelection in 1998, she explained in her campaign literature why she wanted a second term, "Unfortunately, there are some out-of-touch members of Congress who have resolved to oppose any and all efforts to make our streets, schools, and homes safer. Consider, for example, my efforts to simply require that a safety lock be sold with every handgun in the United States. When the House considered juvenile crime legislation last year, the Congressional leadership would not even allow us to debate this initiative to keep guns safely stored, out of the hands of kids, and out of our schools. While the majority of Americans believe we need more effective national gun legislation, Congress has been stalled by the influence of the gun lobby."

Kevin continued to improve with Carolyn's help and his own strong will. By 1998, he had almost completely recovered the use of his limbs and was planning to be married. But the memory of what happened to him and Dennis continued to inspire Carolyn. Even though the gun lobby targeted her as one of the representatives they most wanted to defeat, she won reelection on a platform full of Mommy Issues.

By the time I met her, when she was running for a third term in 2000, she said that ending gun violence involved far more than gun control. Unlike many politicians who see committee work as a bother—especially work on committees that don't earn headlines or big special interest dollars—Carolyn loved her work on the House Education and Workforce Committee. Through it, she quickly realized that better education and job opportunities were key to ending violence in our society. She had also come to realize that creating needed reforms was a long-term battle.

When I talked to Carolyn, she told me she was dealing with a different kind of grief. A life-long Catholic, she was hurt and troubled that priests in her district were preaching against her, because she is pro-choice. "I meet with them and tell them 'I am on your side of the issues in everything else,'" she told me. "'I work constantly to help the poor and families. I support a higher minimum wage, better education, and health care reform—everything you care about.' But I can't win them over." However, this new grief did not stop her. Nor did it keep her from being reelected.

Finding Meaning and Purpose in the Loss

Not everyone can turn their tragedy into something as extraordinary as a run for Congress, but everyone who grieves has to find a way to make peace with their loss. Fortunately, there are almost as many different ways to find meaning and purpose as there are grieving mothers. Here are three women who each found her own way.

Over the ages, women have turned to religion when tragedy strikes. These days, however, it is also possible for them to join the growing number of women who are becoming clergy and bringing Mother Power to religion. The Reverend Fairfax Fair of Houston, Texas, is one who did just that.

Three years after Fairfax married Bart Fair, her college sweetheart, they discovered two things: Fairfax was going to have a baby and Bart had an incurable form of cancer. While battling the cancer, Fairfax had to come to terms with the fact that after losing Bart, she would have to support her son Walker as a single mother. "I began writing away for information about law school, medical school, and business school," she told me, "But I couldn't even read the catalogs. The only thing that interested me was religion.

"I can't say I was 'very religious' before Bart's illness. I grew up in the First Presbyterian Church in Warren, Arkansas. My father was an officer of the church, but women weren't allowed to be even that in those days. That is one reason why it was so difficult to accept that God was calling me to go to seminary."

While Fairfax hadn't always gone to church on a regular basis, she had always had a deep faith in God. Once, as a child when a tornado swirled through her town, she lay down on the floor and recited the Lord's prayer. With the tornado of Bart's illness swirling around her, she held on to her faith in God again.

"I didn't tell anyone that I wanted to go to seminary until two months after Bart died, because I didn't want anyone thinking this was just a grief reaction," she told me. While her grief had drawn her to religion, there were many other reasons why she wanted to be a minister. She had appreciated the many ways that people from her church had reached out and supported her while Bart was sick. She wanted her life work to involve being a similar source of support for other people.

A year after Bart died, Fairfax entered Union Seminary in Richmond, Virginia, and eventually became a Presbyterian minister. Like most new clergy, she found a job as an assistant in a large church, where her duties including being a spiritual parent to the youth group. By the time I met her, she had her own church in Houston where her maternal strength was used in many ways.

"The church I was called to lead, St. Luke's, had a very loyal, active congregation," she said, "but it was an aging population. The church rolls were shrinking as congregants died, and no one thought we could bring in new members. But I didn't want to be a minister who presided over the death of a church."

Mothers are good at growing things, and Fairfax put her energy into growing her church, but as any clergy member knows, this is no easy task. Like a mother who encourages her children make new friends,

Fairfax encouraged her vestry to make visitors feel especially welcome. To make sure that visitors came, she went out of her way to meet and greet people who lived in the neighborhood.

Even though I was only going to be in Houston for a few months while my son was getting medical treatment, Fairfax reached out to me in her friendly way. While conducting services, she smiled like a proud mother at her congregation, and included me in her warm outreach. She shared some of the story of her loss to make me know I was not alone in my trouble, and offered to help me and my family in any way she could. It is this kind of warm, maternal caring that makes her a fine minister, and it helped get her over her own grief.

While prayer and all the existing medical help could not save her husband, faith helped Fairfax through the ordeal. That same faith and her maternal strengths are keeping her church alive.

Another common form of resolving grief caused by an illness is to promote medical knowledge or research. For example, a friend of mine whose child has diabetes, became an active fund-raiser for the Juvenile Diabetes Foundation. But, when a child is affected by a rare problem, there often is no fund-raising group and little medical knowledge. Here are two mothers who had to create their own.

On Valentine's Day in 1997, Jill Kelly gave birth to a son, Hunter. She and her husband, Buffalo Bills football star Jim Kelly, were thrilled to have a brother for their three-year-old daughter, Erin. Quickly, however, they realized something was wrong with the baby.

Initially, Hunter's symptoms seemed like colic, but much worse. By three months, he was having seizures and couldn't swallow. The diagnosis was disastrous: infantile Krabbe's, a rare, fatal disease caused by the lack of an enzyme that helps protect brain cells. Medical intervention could make Hunter comfortable, but there was no cure.

Jim retired from the Buffalo Bills just before Hunter was born. His new job as a football commentator with NBC required him to travel extensively. At first Jill didn't understand how he could leave the family and his sick baby. Hunter's physician explained that fathers and mothers often react differently when a child is dying. While they both love the child, mothers have a greater capacity to be there with the suffering every day. Luckily, Jill's mother took a leave of absence from her job to lend emotional support.

Just having maternal support was not enough. "When your child is dying, you try to figure out why," Jill said. " I prayed to know how we could make Hunter's life count. I told Jim, 'Maybe we can help other children by raising money for research.'"

The Kellys created a foundation, Hunter's Hope, with $500,000 of their own money to research how to replace the enzyme for Krabbe's disease. Such knowledge might also help cure other degenerative diseases like Tay-Sachs.

The interviews Jill gives about Hunter's disease and the fund-raising appearances she makes raise awareness of the disease and bring in funds for the foundation. She also hopes Hunter's story will help other parents value their children. As she said in an interview with *McCall's* magazine, "We hope that parents everywhere will heed Hunter's message: love and appreciate your kids. If they do, then what a remarkable purpose our son will have served."

Judi Clark, a divorced single mother in the suburbs of Detroit, has a similar goal. "I'm trying as hard as I can to make some purpose out of my daughter's death," she said, "She can't die without a purpose, or I'd go out of my mind." While Judy doesn't have the Kelly's wealth or fame to publicize the problem that killed her daughter, her crusade will probably save as many lives.

The story of how her daughter, Samantha, died is the stuff of every mother's nightmare. On a Friday night in January, 1999, fifteen-year-old Samantha told Judi she was going to the movies with a couple friends. Instead, the three girls went to a party where GHB, a date-rape drug, was secretly mixed into their Mountain Dew, and Samantha, unaware, ingested the drug.

GHB can be made in any kitchen using recipes found on the Internet. Even though ingredients include paint remover, furniture polish remover, or drain cleaners, GHB is odorless, colorless, and tasteless. GHB usually produces a mild euphoria and then memory loss. It can also cause unconsciousness, respiratory failure, and death.

Samantha passed out after sipping her drink. Judi, who had fallen asleep on the sofa awaiting Samantha's return, was awakened by a phone call in the middle of the night. Rushing to the hospital, she found her daughter dead of respiratory failure.

Judi took six months off from her job as a construction worker to study GHB and seek to control it. Here is some of what she found: law enforcement officials knew GHB was a growing problem, but didn't keep accurate statistics because it is not illegal in every state. However, they knew it was involved in at least fifty-five hundred cases of abuse since 1990 and had caused at least forty-nine deaths. It was a favorite drug of sexual predators, but it was also popular among teenagers because it caused euphoria and had a false reputation for building muscles. Kits for making it were being sold on the Internet.

Judy began a letter-writing campaign to politicians, asking them to help stop the spread of GHB. Two Michigan Republicans, Representative Fred Upton and Senator Spencer Abraham agreed to sponsor bills that added GHB to the federal government's list of most-controlled substances, a list that includes heroin and LSD. Now that it is on that list, the Drug Enforcement Administration will take a more active role in tracking and fighting GHB.

The men who drugged Samantha were convicted of involuntary manslaughter and poisoning in one of the first criminal cases in the nation involving GHB. Even though this case and Judi's crusade made headlines, overdoses have become more frequent since Samantha's death. Judi comes home from work and continues her crusade against GHB at night, finding a purpose in Samantha's death and her own grief: trying to save other kids from GHB.

Bringing It Home

Tragedy and loss provoke existential crises where we ask, "What's the meaning of life?" Mired in grief, it is all too easy to think that life is meaningless, but we must work through that stage to reclaim our lives.

Friends may offer their own spiritual beliefs or coping suggestions, but if they try to force them upon us, they make matters worse. That's because each of us must struggle to find our own meaning in life. Sooner or later we have to decide what we want our life to stand for. These can be the most important decisions we ever make.

All the women in this book found different ways to contribute to society, and thereby, make their lives meaningful. You may decide that you want to take one of these paths, or you may come up with a completely different solution to your existential issues. Perhaps, for now, raising your children is enough. Later, you may need to find meaning outside your home. Regardless of how you choose to make your life meaningful and work through grief, you have a deep, innate supply of Mother Power to help you cope with whatever life throws at you.

• How can you begin to express your feelings? If you join a group like Compassionate Friends, you don't have to talk if you don't want to. Just sitting there and listening to others express similar emotions can begin the process of healing. You may prefer to express yourself by writing about your grief in a private journal or putting together a photo album of the person you lost.

continued

• How can you begin to turn your grief into action? If you join a self-help group, initially you will be the one who is supported and comforted. Eventually, you will be able to use your grief to comfort others. That action helps the other person and you as well. There are many other ways to take action, as you have seen in this book.

• How can you find meaning and purpose in your loss? A terrible loss seems to make people either more religious or less. If you are one of the lucky ones who finds spiritual meaning through grief, bless you. If you have the opposite reaction, you will have to look for another way to turn what you feel into something other than depression. As you have read, some mothers do this by fighting disease, hunger, guns, war, or dictators. Some even do it by writing books. Keep searching for your way to turn pain into Mother Power.

BECOMING OUR OWN HEROES

"We are surrounded by strong, courageous, accomplished women. Any one of them could be a hero. A hero could be you."
—Nike ad

By now I hope you are convinced that you, like all the women in this book, have a large supply of Mother Power ready to use whenever you choose. On the other hand, I realize that you may be thinking, "If mothers have so much power, why do I feel so powerless?" If you're asking that question, you are not alone.

Being a good parent—mother or father—is often a thankless, grueling job. The rewards for all our hard work may not be seen for years. When we give, it isn't always noticed. When we are fair, we frequently get a complaint instead of a compliment. That's why parents often feel much more competent when dealing with the outside world than with their own children.

Lisa Belkin recently wrote about this in her weekly *New York Times* column that deals with work and family. She described a week-long course in negotiating skills for high-powered executives. Corporations pay top dollar to send key managers for this training. When the course trainer asks executives in his class why they want to learn negotiating skills, you would expect them to say that they need to be tough when dealing with unions or when trying to open foreign markets. Not so. Instead, these powerful men and women sheepishly admit that they need the training to deal with their kids, saying things like "My daughter won't clean her room," or, "My son doesn't respect his curfew," or, "My toddler won't eat vegetables."

Similarly, when Meryl Streep was recently honored at a leadership conference, she spoke about the confidence-sapping aspect of motherhood. She said, "I go home and ask very nicely if everyone would please scrape, dump, and load their dishes into the dishwasher before they go upstairs! I am a voice crying out in the wilderness. I am a virtual leader [the powerful roles she plays outside the family] and an actual mother, a very specific schizophrenia I'm sure I share with many."

Being in such worthy company, I will reveal that I, like every other parent, have had that power-draining feeling when dealing with my kids. A few years ago I received the Distinguished Psychologist award from five hundred colleagues in my county psychological association. Only one week later, when my son and daughter were being obstinate, I got so frustrated that I literally began jumping up and down and yelling.

I am known to be even-tempered. As a psychologist, I have been trained to keep my cool in the most difficult situations. People pay good money to get my advice about serious matters. And yet my two children made me act like a five-year-old. All I could think was, "If any of my colleagues saw me now, they would yank that award off my office wall and throw it away."

So, paradoxically, if we are to feel confident in our Mother Power, we should flex that power outside the home as well as in it. In fact, if we are to feel confident about any sort of power, it is often the outside world that will affirm it more than our families, because motherhood can drain self-confidence.

As a psychologist, I have noticed a very disturbing phenomenon: how quickly mothers can lose self-confidence and verve. Moms who work outside the home are often so overwhelmed by their guilt or their at-home chores that they begin to lose their sense of selves. Devoting even a small amount of time to a Mother Power project, especially one they share with their children, can add spark to their lives. That project, however, should not be just one more chore or burden—it has to be something they sincerely care about and enjoy.

For example, I know a busy physician in New York who collects toys, clothes, and school supplies for orphans in her native country, Haiti. She has turned this into a family project with her daughter and husband. It makes her feel good to share her success with the neediest back home.

Similarly, Evelyn Jackson, the teacher you met in chapter 7, felt her whole life got a boost when she took a creative approach to the problems she encountered at her school. Instead of feeling overwhelmed by a difficult job, long commute, and family responsibilities, she exudes excitement when she talks about her award-winning project, The People's Court.

Loss of confidence can be an even greater problem among women who become full-time moms. I have worked with many women who quit successful careers to stay home with their children and within months became afraid to use the telephone for fear that they had nothing of interest to say to adults.

In such situations, it is easy to become overly involved with our children, projecting our own aspirations and needs for achievement and approval onto them. That's a doubly dangerous situation. It stunts the mother's growth and puts too much pressure on the kids.

It's also easy to fall prey to the fashion or decorating magazine message that appearance is far more important than substance. Of course, it's nice to have a home that is attractive and comfortable. Of course, shopping for clothes is fun. But if it becomes our life focus, if our talents and need for achievement are only directed inside the home and toward ourselves and our children, it is easy to become competitive instead of cooperative with the rest of the world. That never leads to happiness.

Just as many mothers who have careers say that children give their life balance, full-time mothers who invest some time in Mother Power projects find that this gives their parenting balance. Working for a rewarding Mother Power project can boost our sense of self-esteem when the kids are giving us a hard time. It can give us a healthy break so that we want to come back home and throw ourselves into the most important and challenging job—parenting.

Before investing time in a Mother Power project, there is a hurdle many of us have to overcome: we may admire Mother Power heroes, but not believe we can be like them. We tend to see them as different from us, see them as better and stronger people. We know our own fears and weaknesses all too well, so it is hard to believe that anyone as flawed as we are can accomplish that much.

So, before most of us can use our Mother Power, we have to look at the attitudes and fears that sap our power. For example, you might be thinking:

The women in the book are special, but I'm just ordinary. When mothers were starting the peace process in Northern Ireland, practically every woman who volunteered came in saying, "I'm only an ordinary housewife." Many found talents they never knew existed, like giving stirring public speeches to encourage others to join the cause. Many others simply added their voice and bodies to the throngs marching for peace. But every voice and body is important when trying to accomplish a goal.

By profiling only leaders and heroes, I may have given the false impression that Mother Power is only for those who want to start a project or be the leader of an important movement. Not so. Every movement needs people who want to stay out of the spotlight and simply work for the cause.

I don't have the time or money to do much. So, just do a little. Every little bit counts and sometimes a small effort takes on a larger life of it's own. Remember Iris Sanchez, the woman you met in chapter 3 who was feeling particularly grateful on Thanksgiving and made thirty turkey sandwiches for homeless people? Gradually her efforts became larger as she started a food pantry through her church, which has grown into an ever-expanding operation. But, if her efforts had never gone beyond those thirty turkey sandwiches, that would have been okay, too. A little something is better than nothing.

I'm too shy. Many of the women in this book started out shy. Once they found something they felt passionate about, they gained self-confidence. Others remain shy, but feel so strongly about their causes that they use Mother Power in spite of being self-conscious. Here's how shy people can find the courage to tap into Mother Power: they volunteer or start projects with a friend.

For example, Evelyn Jackson got the courage to start her People's Court project only because she realized how much "her kids" needed help. Asking some of her best friends on the faculty to help with the initial planning gave her the support and confidence she needed to overcome her innate shyness. Today, Evelyn remains somewhat shy even after the success of The People's Court and winning a Teacher of the Year award. She is successful in spite of it.

I've been through a terrible tragedy and can hardly get through the day, much less help anybody else. In the aftermath of tragedy, depression and shock may sap your energy. Just getting out of bed in the morning feels like a major accomplishment. If this is how you're feeling, you probably need to get support for yourself, rather than give it to others. That support is available through therapists and counselors, and also through support groups formed by people going through the same kind of grief you are experiencing. After getting the support you need, you can complete your recovery by helping others and turn grief into healing action.

As you have read in this book, many people find that by taking action in the midst of a personal tragedy, they convert grief into Mother Power and accomplish their goals.

In the wake of the World Trade Center disaster, New York City firemen were lauded as heroes. Bravely rushing into the burning buildings, 343 died when the towers collapsed. Two months later, when Mayor Giuliani suspended the painstaking search for bodies in favor of a more speedy site clean-up, the remains of many firefighters, along with thousands of others, had not yet been recovered from the tons of rubble.

Groups of firemen held angry protests. Their two powerful unions tried to enforce the firefighters' code: never leave the scene of a fire until every brother and civilian is found. But, the mayor wouldn't budge. Suddenly, however, when a young mother organized a group of firefighters' widows and relatives, the mayor backed down. He agreed to continue searching for the remains of her husband and others, and to let her group consult on redevelopment plans to ensure that the site be treated as a sacred burial ground. In the words of the *New York Times*, "As the widows of Sept. 11 unite, grief finds a powerful political force."

I'd like to use my Mother Power, but I don't know where to use it. This is the fun part. Let your mind freely explore possibilities without being self-critical. Then think about what your town, state, country, or the world needs. Next, think about causes you care about.. Don't be motivated by guilt or by what you think you *should* do. Instead, begin to write down what you would *like* to do.

Imagine, for example, that someone gave you a million dollars to donate to any cause or charity. Where would you donate the money? Perhaps you would like to give your time and effort where you would donate that million dollars. If you could wave a magic wand and create a business or a non-profit organization that would provide a service you and others need—what would it be? Check the Internet or ask the reference librarian to see if such a business or organization exists. If so, why not help it. If not, consider starting one.

I believe the world needs more Mother Power, but , for a variety of reasons, I'm not ready to use mine now. Is there anything I can do that takes hardly any time or effort? Definitely. Support Mother Power when you see it. Donate to politicians who are fighting for Mommy Issues. Write your newspaper and favorite magazines to let them know you want more stories about women doing admirable things. Write teen magazines and tell them you will not subscribe for your daughter unless they begin stressing girls' achievements as much as beauty and sex. Give a copy of *Mother Power* to a friend who needs a boost in self-esteem or an outlet for her skills. Know that your own Mother Power is there to use whenever you are ready. Then you might become a hero, too.

Anyone Can Become a Hero

The biggest surprise I found through my research is that anyone who taps into Mother Power can be a hero. Most of the women you have read about in this book are ordinary women who did extraordinary things using Mother Power. Few started with the desire to be a hero. Instead, they started with a desire to change something—part of their lives or part of the world.

Often no one would have predicted their success, given that most lacked what the world thinks is necessary to become a hero: super strength or intelligence, large amounts of money, influence, training, or talent. In fact, in many cases their only strength was Mother Power—and they didn't even know what it was! After several years of research, I know that every good mother has the potential to be a hero, because every good mother has Mother Power.

Mother Power can be used at any stage of life. Mothers in their twenties and grandmothers in their seventies are using it. It is never too late to begin. Mother Power can age beautifully, because, as novelist Dorothy Sayers wrote, "Time and trouble will tame an advanced young woman, but an advanced old woman is uncontrollable by any earthly force."

Heroes and Leaders Are Made, Not Born

The women in this book became heroes and leaders as they set about accomplishing their goals. Sometimes that goal was huge: stopping a war, ending gun violence, cleaning up New York City. More often their goals were small in the beginning—they just wanted to help someone in need, stand up to an unfair situation, or be creative. Sometimes they were simply trying to alleviate the pain they felt after a tragedy. Each small step gave them more confidence and built determination to accomplish more.

Burnout Is the enemy

Many of the goals mothers have and the Mother Power battles they fight against disease, poverty, injustice, or violence are long-term efforts. Many such battles are made against well-entrenched, well-funded special interests. After working for years with no major success, it is hard not to lose faith and energy. Only those who know how to recharge their batteries (by taking time-off, switching tactics, and maintaining a balanced lifestyle) can sustain a long fight. That's why it is so important for new people with fresh supplies of Mother Power to join existing causes.

Mother Power Is Just Beginning to Be Felt

Even though women have been exerting their Mother Power for a long time, and the movement is growing stronger all the time, the major impact is yet to come. In the last thirty years, the Civil Rights and woman's liberation movements helped all of us recognize our rights and find our voices. Mothers are the last large group to exercise those rights and make their concerns heard. All around the world, more and more mothers are beginning to speak and demand that society become fairer, kinder, and more humane. The more of us who add our voices to the throng, the better the world will be.

Once you start looking and listening for Mother Power, you will hear those voices everywhere. However, it is under-reported in the media. Pick up women's magazines and hidden among all the articles about clothes, makeup, and food, you will probably find a hero profiled. In newspapers, if you scan past the war, crime, and stock quotes, you'll discover the occasional story about an inspiring mother, too. After thumbing through all the insipid articles about celebrities in general interest magazines, you will probably find one doing something maternal and worthwhile. If the media ever discovers that people like inspiration as much as trivia, you will see a lot more Mother Power stories.

Closer to home, I bet you will realize that some of your friends and acquaintances are using Mother Power. I was surprised that I knew so many people using it.

For the last few decades, women have been made to feel that they must choose between being professional and being maternal. What a relief to discover that we don't have to be split in two anymore. As I interviewed mothers for this book, all of them were pleased when I asked how their maternal skills had contributed to their success. It feels great to come out of the closet and admit—or proclaim!—that our maternal skills are extraordinarily useful outside the home. It is energizing to realize that just by being who we are, we have Mother Power.

While the use of Mother Power is growing, it is still the greatest untapped natural resource in the world, because most mothers don't even know it exists. However, since caring mothers and fathers make up a huge portion of the population—probably the majority—if most of us use just a tiny bit of our Mother Power, the world can't help but change for the better.

Mother Power can make the world a kinder, fairer, and more humane place. Mother Power can give your life greater meaning, purpose, and energy. See for yourself how good it feels to use some of it. And let me know how it works out.

NOTE TO READERS

If you know a good Mother Power story, please send it to me through my website, motherpower.net. I want to collect these stories to make a sequel, and also research Father Power, too.

I have donated my whole advance, and pledge to donate at least half the royalties from these books to Mother Power projects.

Mother Power discussion questions can be accessed at www.source-books.com.

SOURCES

Interviews and conversations with the following people gave me ideas, quotes, and insights used in *Mother Power*: Hebe Bonafini, Ebel Petroni, Marie Claire Brook, Lt. Michael Foote, Mary Mudd Quinn, Joan McGovern, Ann Colorado, Iris Sanchez, Maurice Weaver, Kathy Staudt, Mary Stein, Shannon Carter, Deborah Frank, Wilhelmina Holladay, Lisa Carlson, Evelyn Jackson, Maureen Kanka, Jo Luck, Daryl Roth, Migs Woodside, Karel Amaranth, Barbara Tremitiere, Marlene Fanta Shyer, Angela Cheves, Shannon Murray, Barbara Hohlt, Barbara Kilpatrick, John Lukens, Lisa Benenson, Lynnie Arden, Elizabeth Martin, Paula Eisenberg, Mary Ann Cricchio, Lisa Rey, Carolyn McCarthy, Fairfax Fair, Pat Loder, Laura Katz, Holly Curtis, Ed Madera, Pamela Schafer, Rita Freedman, Marge Schlenoff, Sharon Golub, Suzanne Reiffel, Gloria Kahn, Georgia Hooper-Peek, Jamie Greene, Ona Robinson, Annie Mahr, Melany Gray, Suzanne Carpenter, Susan Amlicke, Sandy Constabile, Rosita Fichtel, Susan Vieser, Dorothy Rainier, Judy Silberstein, Mary Stein, Lois Steinberg, Janet Lan, Rita Marlow, and Anne Herman.

In addition, I used the following written material as sources:

Introduction

Eisenberg, Anne. "Female M.D.s More Open with Options, Patients Say." *The New York Times* (17 August 1999): F8.

Kass, Sharon. "Employees Perceive Women as Better Managers than Men, Finds Five Year Study." *American Psychological Association Monitor* (September 1999): 6.

Murphy, Mary. "How Women Took Over the News." *TV Guide* (9 October 1999): 16–23.

Roberts, Cokie. *We Are Our Mother's Daughters*. New York: Wm. Morrow, 1998.

Smith, Dinitia. "Into the Deeply Private Mind of a Poet." *International Herald Tribune* (11-12 September 1999): 20.

Taylor, Shelley et al. "Behavioral Responses to Stress in Females: Tend-and-Befriend, Not Fight or-Flight." *Psychological Review* 107, no.3 (2000): 411-429.

Chapter 1: Fearlessly Protective

Bohlen, Celestine. "Mothers Help Sons Outwit Draft Board in Wartime Russia." *The New York Times* (30 January 2000): A1, A10.

Eng, Lily. "President Salutes 2 Local Drug Warriors." *Los Angeles Times* (3 March 1990): A1.

Gentleman, Amanda. "Russian Mothers Worry for Sons in Chechnya." *The Globe and Mail* (11 October 1999): A10.

Hill, Albert Fay. *The North Avenue Irregulars*. New York: Cowles, 1968.

International Peace Bureau. "Committee of Soldiers' Mothers of Russia." <http://ipb.org/women/russia2.htm>.

"Itar-Tass Asian News-in-Brief." *ITAR/TASS News Agency Newswire*, 25 August 1999.

Matloff, Judith. "Russia's Powerhouses of Dissent: Mothers." *The Christian Science Monitor* (24 February 2000): 1.

"*North Avenue Irregulars* Editorial Review." *Amazon.com.*
<http://www.amazon.com/exec/
obidos/ASIN/076400557X/qid=944093.../102-2451970-
238883>.

"Russians Rush to Help Freezing Troops Withdrawn from
Chechnya." *ITAR/TASS News Agency Newswire*, 29 December
1996.

Chapter 2: Peacemakers

Ben Dor, Rachel. "The Cry which Became a Movement." *Look to
Horizon: Women and Mothers for Peace.*
<http://4mothers.org.il/peilut/crying.htm>.

Crossette, Barbara. "Women Seek Louder Voice as World
Peacemakers." *The New York Times* (28 May 2000): Y4.

Engle, Dawn, and Evan Suvanjieff. "An Interview with Betty
Williams." <http://theodore-sturgeon.mit.edu:8001/
peacejam/betty/interview.html>.

Holzworth, Christine. "Parent Power at the Mall." *AARP Bulletin*
(September 2000): 19.

Nocon, Shelly. "Betty Williams Strives for Peace: Nobel Peace
Laureate Worked for Peace in Violent Northern Ireland." *The
Cavalier Daily* (21 September 1998): 1.

"Profile." *Peace People.*
<http://www.peacepeople.com/profile/history.html>.

Shachar, Eran. "The Home Front Goes on the Offensive."
HaKibbutz, 3 April 1997.
<http://4mothers.org.il/peilut/front.htm>.

Sontag, Deborah. "Israel Honors Mothers of Lebanon Withdrawal."
The New York Times (3 June 2000): A3.

Watson, Rhoda. *Along the Road to Peace: Fifteen Years with the Peace People*. Belfast: Community of Peace People, 1991.

Chapter 3: Giving

Burkitt, Janet. "Boy's Gift in Death Spurs Organ Donors Worldwide." *The Seattle Times*, (10 March 2000):E6.

Fields-Meyer, Thomas et al. "Perfect Stranger." *People* (8 November 1999): 93-94.

Hoffman, Jan. "Blessed are the Needy, for Iris Is on the Job." *The New York Times* (24 November 2001): B2.

Leary, Kevin. "All Italy Mourns Slain Bodega Boy." *The San Francisco Chronicle* (4 October 1994): A15.

"Nicholas Green." *People* (15 March 1999):75-76.

Safran, Claire. "My Son's Heart Beats On." *McCall's* (August 1998): 49-52.

Yellin, Emily. "A Teacher's Gift? Why, Most Certainly." *The New York Times* (18 December 1994): A12.

Chapter 4: Emotional

Bellows, Melina Gerosa. "Rosie's Kids." *Ladies' Home Journal* (20 November 2000): 142-146, 184.

Blalock, Heidi. "Boston Medical Center's Grow Clinic Director Battles on for Hungry Children." *Collection Magazine* (Spring 2000): 4-5.

Eisenberg, Anne. "Female M.D.s More Open with Options, Patients Say." *The New York Times* (17 August 1999): F8.

Murphy, Mary. "How Women Took Over The News." *TV Guide* (9 October 1999): 16-23.

Powell, Joanna. "Invisible Moms." *Working Mother* (July/August 2000): 50-56.

Reed, J.D. et al. "Katie's New Life." *People* (27 November 2000): 154-161.

Chapter 5: Creative

Lubow, Arthur. "An Author of a Certain Age." *The New York Times* (15 August 1999): 30-33.

Lyall, Sarah. "A Rights Advocate Who's Also Britain's First Lady." *The New York Times* (7 September 2000): A3.

Magona, Sindewe. *To My Children's Children.* New York: Interlink Books, 1994.

Miller, Marjorie. "Blair Says He'll Deliver On Promise to Help with Baby." *Los Angeles Times* (10 April 2000): A1.

Peri, Camille. "Why It's Time for Mothers Who Think." *Salon* 16 June 1997. <http://www.salon.com/mothers/mamafesto.html>.

Rehak, Melanie. "Lullabye Diva." *The New York Times Magazine* (29 August 1999): 16.

Slatalla, Michelle. "Inventor Fills Girls' Desire for Their Own Gadgets." *The New York Times* (30 September 1999): G7.

Smith, Dinitia. "Into the Deeply Private Mind of a Poet." *International Herald Tribune* (11-12 September 1999): 20.

Verkaik, Robert. "Cherie Delivers Paternity Leave Hint to Her Husband." *The Independent* (21 March 2000): 1.

Walter, Natasha. "How The Silent Doll at Tony Blair's Side Emerged As The Acceptable Face of Modern Feminism." *The Independent* (25 March 2000): 9.

Chapter 6: Fair

Baker, Beth. "Fighting For Funeral Rights." *AARP Bulletin* (November 1999): 18-20.

Gonzalez, David. "In Panama's New Dawn, Woman Takes Over." *The New York Times* (2 September 1999): A12.

Krauss, Clifford. "A Revolution Peru's Rebels Didn't Intend." *The New York Times* (29 August 1999): A1.

Milulski, Barbara et al. *Nine and Counting.* New York: Wm. Morrow, 2000.

Mundans, Seth. "Indonesia Selects Opposition Leader for Vice Presidency." *The New York Times* (22 October1999): A1, A10.

Mydans, Seth. "In Debris of Economic Crash: Thailand's Faith in Authority." *The New York Times* (10 August 1999): A1.

Neuharth, Al. "Can Panama's Lady President Pull It Off?" *USA Today* (17 September 1999): 11A.

"Nita Lowey." *Glamour* (December 1998): 133.

Schmidt, Julie. "Daughter of Indonesia's Founding Father Now Vice President." *USA Today* (22 October 1999): 16A.

Chapter 7: Teach Right from Wrong

Hanley, Robert. "Parents Get Satisfaction from Ruling." *The New York Times* (24 February 1998): B6.

Laurence, Charles. " The Murder That Led to Megan's Law." *The Daily Telegraph* (30 January 1997): 17.

Martin, Hugo. "Victim's Mother Begins Campaign." *Los Angeles Times* (1 August 1998): B1.

Terry, Don. "Mother Rages Against Indifference." *The New York Times* (24 August 1998): A10.

Zamichow, Nora. "Spokesman for Slain Girl's Mother Quits." *The Los Angeles Times* (18 September 1998): B1.

Chapter 8: Nurture

"The Bellwether Prize for Fiction: Defining a Literature of Social Change." *The Bellwether Prize Web Site.* <http:// www.bellwether-prize.org/change.html>.

Denitto, Emily. "Daryl Roth Walks Tall in NY Theater World." *Crain's New York Business* (15 May 2000): 8-9.

Hale, Lorraine, and Constance Johnson. *Thirty Years to the Day.* New York: Hale House, 1999.

Kingsolver, Barbara. Interview by Diane Rehm. *Diane Rehm Show.* WAMU, 5 November 1998.

Lambert, Bruce. "Clara Hale, 87, Who Aided Addicts' Babies, Dies." *The New York Times* (20 December 1992): 50L.

Pristin, Terry. "Facing Scrutiny, President of Hale House Will Resign." *The New York Times* (8 May 2001): B3.

Pristin, Terry. "Hale House's Fund-Raising Is Prompting More Questions." *The New York Times* (18 May 2001): A1.

Chapter 9: Comfort Those in Distress

Coles, Robert. *Children of Crisis.* New York: Little, Brown and Company, 1964.

Coles, Robert. *The Story of Ruby Bridges.* New York: Scholastic, 1995.

Evans, Sherrell. "Harassed Child Fights Back." *The Atlanta Constitution* (17 December 1995): 1G.

Greenhouse, Linda. "Court Is Asked Not to Extend Harassment Law in School." *The New York Times* 13 Dec. 1999: 13.

Kelly, Dennis. "81% of Teens Report Sexual Harassment." *USA Today* (2 April 1993): 1A.

Rankin, Bill. "Can Kids Sexually Harass?" *The Atlanta Constitution* (30 September 1998): 1A.

Sommers, Christina. "The Preteen Sexual Harasser." *The New York Times* (9 January 1999):15A.

Chapter 10: See the Good in Our Children

Blume, Judy. "Judy Answers Your Questions About Writing." *Judy Blume's Official Web Site*. <http://www.judyblume.com/ans-writing1.html>.

Blume, Judy. "Judy Blume's Books." *Judy Blume's Official Web Site*. <http://judyblume.com/margaret.html> and <http://judyblume.com/blubber.html>.

Blume, Judy. "Judy Blume Talks about Censorship." *Judy Blume's Official Web Site*. <http://www.judyblume.com/censors.html>.

Bono, Chastity, and Billie Fitzpatrick. *Family Outing*. New York: Little, Brown and Company, 1998.

Bono, Chastity, and Billie Fitzpatrick. "The Family Secret that Rocked Cher's World." *McCall's* (October 1998): 46–51.

Lipson, Eden Ross. "The Dark Underbelly of Writing for Children." *The New York Times* (8 July 2000): B7, B9.

Peterson, Linda. "Sometimes Angels Don't Wear Halos." *McCall's* (March 1999): 68-70.

"PLFAG's Rich Past Provides Solid Foundation for Future." *Parents, Families and Friends of Lesbians and Gays*. <http://www.pflag.org/history.html>.

Plumez, Jacqueline Hornor. *Successful Adoption*. New York: Harmony Books, 1987.

Weinraub, Bernard. "New Potter Book is Casting a Spell." *The New York Times* (3 July 2000): A1, A10.

Chapter 11: Ask for Help

Hanover, Donna. "Don't Mess with Bette!" *Good Housekeeping* (March 1996): 82-86.

Hanson, Cynthia. "Acts of Courage." *Ladies' Home Journal* (November 1998): 40, 44.

Hellman, Peter. "Public Works: Divine Intervention." *House & Garden* (March 1997): 41-43.

Mahmoody, Betty, and Arnold Dunchock. *For the Love of a Child.* New York: St. Martin's Press, 1992.

Mahmoody, Betty, and William Hoffer. *Not Without My Daughter.* New York: St. Martin's Press, 1987.

Mandell, Jonathan. "Always Divine, Now Garbage Had Made Her a Saint." *The New York Times* (17 November 1999): 10.

Martin, Douglas. "Experiment in Green." *The New York Times* (9 July 1995): 26.

Chapter 12: Nag

"A Brief History of La Leche League International." *La Leche League International* February 13, 2001. <http://www.lalecheleague.org/LLLIhistory.html>.

Holditch, W. Kenneth. Introduction to *The Neon Bible*, by John Kennedy Toole. New York: Grove Press, 1989.

Kakutani, Michiko. "A Novelist's Story of Love, Pain and (Neon) Signs of Life." *The New York Times* (12 May 1989): C29.

Lipsyte, Robert. "A Sports Sisterhood, Measured in Olympiads." *The New York Times* (17 October 1999): A1, A28.

Milulski, Barbara et al. *Nine and Counting.* New York: Wm. Morrow, 2000.

Percy, Walker. Foreword to *A Confederacy of Dunces,* by John Kennedy Toole. New Orleans: Louisiana State University Press, 1980.

Sipchen, Bob. "Dead Men Do Tell Tales." *Los Angeles Times* (13 March 1989): View 1.

Stuart, Reginald. "Pulitzer Novel's Publication Is Tale In Itself." *The New York Times* (15 April 1980): A14.

Chapter 13: Do It Ourselves

Alvord, Valerie. "Major Child-Support Group Evolves from One Woman's Pain, Frustration; ACES' Legislative Agenda: Make IRS Collection Agency." *The San Diego Union–Tribune* (11 April 1999): A-1.

Cross, Sue. "Child Support Activist Is Terror of the Courtrooms." *Los Angeles Times* (24 February 1985): 2.

Dugger, Celia. "Women Still Segregated, but Now at Grad School." *The New York Times* (14 August 1999): A4.

"History of ACES." *Association for Children for Enforcement of Support.* <www.childsupport-aces.org/history.html>.

Lukens, Kathleen. *Song of David.* Nanuet, NY: Venture Press, 1989.

Matthias, Rebecca. *MothersWork.* New York: Currency, 1999.

Thomas, Robert. "Kathleen Lukens, 67, a Mother Foremost, Dies." *The New York Times* (18 October 1998): 47.

Willlis, Cary B. "Woman Made Waves to Improve Collection of Child Support." *The Courier-Journal* (3 April 1996): 4B.

Chapter 14: To Take Time Out

Arenson, Karen. "Millicent McIntosh, 102, Dies: Taught Barnard Women to Balance Careers and Family." *The New York Times* (5 January 2001): A16.

Ellner, Rachel. "Faith Popcorn's Manhattan Cocoon Is A Buzzing Hive With 28 Workers." *House of Business* (July/August 2000): 12-13.

Hickey, Mary. "How Women Have Changed the Workplace." *Ladies' Home Journal* (April 1999): 60-68.

Olsen, Elizabeth. "The Champions of Productivity." *The International Herald Tribune* (7 September 1999): 1.

Roberts, Cokie. *We Are Our Mother's Daughters.* New York: Wm. Morrow, 1998.

Rosenberg, Merri. "A Designer Who Lives Like her Clients." *The New York Times* (10 September 2000): WE8.

U.S. Bureau of the Census. *Statistical Abstract of the United States, 2000.* Washington, D.C., 2000.

Chapter 15: To Form Supportive Relationships

Belluck, Pam. "'Rages' Maybe Aren't All they're Cracked Up to Be." *The New York Times* (1 August 1999): 3WK.

"Candy Lightner: A Grieving Mother Who Helped America Get MADD." *People* (15 March 1999): 110.

Clines, Frances X. "A Cinematic Paradiso in a Bit of Old Baltimore." *The New York Times* (11 August 1999): A1.

Eisenberg, Anne. "Female M.D.s More Open with Opinions, Patients Say." *The New York Times* (17 August 1999): F8.

Kass, Sharon. "Employees Perceive Women as Better Managers than Men, Finds Five-Year Study." *American Psychological Association Monitor* (September 1999): 6.

Lipsyte, Robert. "A Sports Sisterhood, Measured in Olympiads." *The New York Times* (17 October 1999): A1, A28.

Matthews, Jay. "One California Mother's MADD Drive to Bar Highways to Drunken Killers." *The Washington Post* (16 June 1984): A2.

McFadden, Robert. "Mothers Against Drunk Driving Strips Founder of 2 Major Posts." *The New York Times* (4 October 1985): A16.

Rosenberg, Beth. "Web For Women." *Boston Globe* (21 October 1999): C4.

"Victims." *Mothers Against Drunk Driving Online.* <http://www.madd.org/victims/default.shtml>.

Chapter 16: To Talk about Our Problems

"Betty Ford, America's First Lady of Candor." *People* (15 March 1999): 169.

"Betty Ford and Susan Ford Bales, Health Care Advocates." *People* (7 March 1994): 229.

Calderone, Mary, and James Ramey. *Talking With Your Child About Sex.* New York: Ballantine Books, 1982.

Cassata, Donna. "Former Wife of Ex-SEC Official Tells Her Story in Book." *Los Angeles Times* (15 May 1988): 2.

"Charlotte Fedders." *People* (15 March 1999): 114.

Evans, Sandra. "Battered Wife Seeks to Shield Others." *The Washington Post* (30 April 1987): C6.

Girard, Keith. "Fedders Divorce Granted on Grounds of Cruelty." *The Washington Post* (15 October 1985): B1.

Hargrove, Thomas, and Guido Stempel. "Domestic Abuse Cloud of Silence Coming to End." *The Plain Dealer* (9 February 1995): 2A.

McGrory, Mary. "A Shattering Ruling." *The Washington Post* (20 October 1987): A2.

Naughton, Jim. "Charlotte Fedders, After the Dream." *The Washington Post* (1 November 1987): D1.

Nemy, Enid. "Evelyn Lauder: From Pink Lipstick to Pink Ribbons." *The New York Times* (2 February 1995): C1.

Perlmutter, Ellen. "A Battle of the Sexes." *Pittsburgh Post-Gazette* (30 September 1997): G1.

Peterson, Karen. "Charlotte Fedders Now 'Reveling in Recovery.'" *USA Today* (16 December 1997): 9D.

Saperstein, Saundra. "Wife's Cries for Help Unheeded." *The Washington Post* (19 April 1986): C3.

Chapter 17: To Know Why Something Happened

Clay, Rebecca. "The FTC Calls on Psychologists' Expertise." *Monitor on Psychology* (November 2000): 48-49.

Harr, Jonathan. *A Civil Action.* New York: Vintage Books, 1995.

Loth, Renee. "Bringing Earth Day back down to Earth." *The Boston Globe* (21 April 1991): A33.

O'Neill, Jessie. *The Golden Ghetto.* Center City, MN: Hazelden, 1997.

Pipher, Mary. *Reviving Ophelia.* New York: Ballantine Books, 1995.

Powers, Scott. "Dioxin Pioneer Seeks New Dumps to Battle." *The Columbus Dispatch* (25 January 1996): 9C.

Sachs, Susan. "Public Clamor Puts Focus on 'Clusters' in Cancer Research." *The New York Times* (21 September 1998): A1, B5.

Salamon, Julie. "Sex at 8: The Partridges Don't Live Here Anymore." *The New York Times* (10 December 2000): WK6.

Shabecoff, Philip. "High Levels of Dioxin Found at Niagra Falls." *The New York Times* (5 June 1986): A25.

Shribman, David. "A Woman Transformed by a Cause." *The New York Times* (30 October 1981): A20.

Chapter 18: To Find a Way to Stop Grieving

Bradsher, Keith. "3 Guilty of Manslaughter in Slipping Drug to Girl." *The New York Times* (15 March 2000): A14.

Bradsher, Keith. "Daughter's Death Prompts Fight on 'Date Rape' Drug." *The New York Times* (16 October 1999): A8.

Compassionate Friends. *The History of the Compassionate Friends, 1968-1997*, 1997.

Cunningham, Diana. "From the Exec's Desk." *We Need Not Walk Alone*. The Compassionate Friends: 21, no. 4 (Holiday 1988).

"Grief Support after the Death of a Child." *The Compassionate Friends*. <http://www.compassionatefriends.org>.

Kelly, Jill. "How Our Son Will Live On." Compiled by Barbara Bartocci. *McCall's* (May 1998): 58-62.

Rader, Dotson. "I Didn't Have Time for Anger." *Parade Magazine* (7 October 1997): 11.

Conclusion

Belkin, Lisa. "Home, Office and Vegetables." *The New York Times* (2 February 2000): G1.

Berry, Dan. "As Sept. 11 Widows Unite, Grief Finds Political Voice." *The New York Times* 25 November 2001: A1, B7.

Streep, Meryl. "Leading, Acting and Choosing." *The New York Times* (17 November 1999): G1.

ABOUT THE AUTHOR

Jacqueline Hornor Plumez, Ph.D. is a psychologist, career counselor, and freelance journalist who writes about relationships, psychology, careers, and travel. She is the author of *Divorcing A Corporation: How To Know When—And If—A Job Change Is Right For You* and *Successful Adoption: A Guide to Finding a Child and Raising a Family*. She practices psychotherapy and career counseling in Larchmont, New York. In 1990 her 500 fellow psychologists in Westchester County voted her their Distinguished Psychologist, and they gave her their Distinguished Service Award in 1993. She received a B.S. in business administration from Bucknell University and a Ph.D. in psychology from Columbia University.